Contents

SECTION II SCHOOL AND COMMUNITY FOCUS

From Trauma to Resiliency

From Trauma to Resiliency integrates research and practice of trauma-informed care, reviewing the neuroscience of trauma and highlighting relationship-based interventions for diverse populations that have faced multiple traumas. Chapters explore the experiences of oppressed groups that include survivors of abuse, war, poverty, Indigenous youth, Middle Eastern refugee mothers, individuals who identify as sexual and/or gender minorities (SGM), and children and youth involved in child welfare, foster care, and juvenile justice systems. In each chapter, contributors provide strengths-based, trauma-informed strategies that can be used in clinical settings, school-based programs, and in urban communities where food insecurity, limited access to health services, and community violence are prevalent. Professionals and students in counseling, social work, psychology, child welfare, education, and other programs will come away from the book with culturally affirming, trauma-informed interventions and models of care that promote well-being and resilience.

Shulamit Natan Ritblatt, PhD, Professor Emerita in the Department of Child and Family Development at San Diego State University.

Audrey Hokoda, PhD, Senate Distinguished Professor in the Department of Child and Family Development at San Diego State University.

"Starting with the focus on families and importance of attachment-based practices, this book takes an expansive perspective on trauma and resiliency, presenting research and clinical application, as well as recommendations for professionals in a wide variety of sectors, including education, child welfare, juvenile justice, and public health. Identifying the intergenerational, culturally focused, community-based work that systems must embrace, this book will be a guide to many family-serving professionals for years to come."

Julie Beem, *executive director, Attachment & Trauma Network, Inc.*

"This highly informative book integrates research and practice and provides specific examples of applied interventions and prevention programs addressing traumas."

Bahira Trask, PhD, *professor and chair, Department of Human Development and Family Studies, University of Delaware*

"Providing a broad system perspective on trauma related to individuals, families, schools, and communities through leaders in the field, this book highlights cutting-edge trauma-responsive practices and provides insights on transforming systems to better support cultures of care, hope and healing."

Dana R. Brown, *ACEs science statewide facilitator, Learn4Life, and organizational liaison, PACEs Connection*

"The lessons presented in this book will serve as an invaluable resource for all scholars and practitioners that treat and work with vulnerable individuals, families, communities, and schools. This couldn't be a more timely book."

Katia Paz Goldfarb, PhD, *associate provost for Hispanic Initiatives and International Programs and professor of family science and human development, Montclair State University*

"Many of us have been waiting for this book for years. Diverse populations are often unseen in the research and in the practice literature. Yet, oppression, social injustice, poverty, and lack of privilege negatively impacts these communities' access to high-quality and culturally affirming trauma-informed care. Complex trauma requires effective integrated-systems treatment, and so the authors have used a transdisciplinary approach. This text is a must for practitioners who want to hold a truly trauma-informed lens."

Barbara Stroud, PhD, *infant mental health specialist, founder and past president, California Association for Infant Mental Health*

From Trauma to Resiliency

Trauma-Informed Practices for Working with Children, Families, Schools, and Communities

Edited by
Shulamit Natan Ritblatt
and Audrey Hokoda

Routledge
Taylor & Francis Group

NEW YORK AND LONDON

Cover image: Photo by Teresa Grame

First published 2023
by Routledge
605 Third Avenue, New York, NY 10158

and by Routledge
4 Park Square, Milton Park, Abingdon, Oxon, OX14 4RN
Routledge is an imprint of the Taylor & Francis Group, an informa business

Library of Congress Cataloging-in-Publication Data
Names: Ritblatt, Shulamit Natan, editor. | Hokoda, Audrey, editor.
Title: From trauma to resiliency: trauma-informed practices for working with children, families, schools, and communities/ edited by Shulamit Natan Ritblatt and Audrey Hokoda.
Description: New York, NY: Routledge, 2023. |
Includes bibliographical references and index.
Identifiers: LCCN 2022010581 (print) |
LCCN 2022010582 (ebook) | ISBN 9780367482633 (hardback) |
ISBN 9780367482626 (paperback) | ISBN 9781003046295 (ebook)
Subjects: LCSH: Family social work. | Social work with children. |
Social service. | Psychic trauma. | Resilience (Personality trait)
Classification: LCC HV697 .F756 2023 (print) |
LCC HV697 (ebook) | DDC 362.82–dc23/eng/20220331
LC record available at https://lccn.loc.gov/2022010581
LC ebook record available at https://lccn.loc.gov/2022010582

ISBN: 978-0-367-48263-3 (hbk)
ISBN: 978-0-367-48262-6 (pbk)
ISBN: 978-1-003-04629-5 (ebk)

DOI: 10.4324/9781003046295

Typeset in Adobe Garamond Pro
by Deanta Global Publishing Services, Chennai, India

We dedicate this book:

to our families and all who survived and prevailed;
to strength, resiliency, and hope.

Figures and Tables

Figures

Tables

Preface

Shulamit Natan Ritblatt and Audrey Hokoda

Throughout our careers, we have worked with marginalized communities, children, and families who have experienced traumas of loss, poverty, abuse, divorce, bullying, and social injustice. As professors at San Diego State University, we have taught our students, utilizing "learning by doing" pedagogy, helping them to apply their theoretical knowledge when working with at-risk communities. Our years of work in the field have brought us to the realization that early experiences of trauma impact the developmental trajectory and well-being of the individual, and that early prevention and intervention matters.

Our belief in the power of early prevention and intervention has become our life conviction and professional mission. We have worked throughout the years to help transform systems of care and education, to enhance the knowledge and parenting skills of families with children struggling to cope and face their adversities, and to train professionals to work with traumatized populations utilizing trauma-informed practices. Writing and editing a book about trauma has required a constant examination of self in the inner internal mirror. Looking carefully at our own personal families' histories and reflecting, we realized that our interest and work in this area has very early familial roots. Our experiences include many of the traumas highlighted in the book: Loss of parents at a young age, food insecurity, poverty, violence, physical and sexual abuse, being refugees, and historical trauma due to persecutions and internment. These intergenerational experiences with traumas inspired us professionally and personally and led to our desire to address trauma by creating and implementing trauma-informed programs within diverse communities.

It takes a village to make a difference. We have followed the work of leading professionals in the field, Drs. Vincent Felitti, Allan Schore, Dan Siegel, Alicia Lieberman, Bruce Perry, and many others. We joined committees and organizations, such as the San Diego Trauma-Informed Guide Team (SDTIGT), the Early Childhood Mental Health Leaders' Collaborative (ECMH-LC), the California Association for Infant Mental Health (CalAIMH), and the California Campaign to Counter Childhood Adversity (4CA), to advocate for relationship-based programs and policies. Our colleagues and co-authors are similarly dedicated to making a difference and pushing for systemic changes that recognize the impact of trauma on individuals accessing services. This timely book is a collective effort of professionals sharing their work and provides an opportunity to learn about the work that is done with trauma-experienced communities, families and individuals, and its transformative impact.

We would like to thank our co-authors who worked collaboratively and diligently to write while trying to work virtually providing services and support to families, children, students, and professionals during the pandemic. We appreciate their trust in us and their willingness to share their extensive knowledge and applied work experience, particularly when their plates were full to the brim. We would also like to take a moment to acknowledge our families' patience and help. Special thanks to our husbands, David and Chris, who have been there for us, encouraging, loving, and supporting.

Our hope is that this book will help you, the reader, learn about the work in the field so you can gain insight and wisdom about different methods of interventions, about the need to be flexible and open to tailor the intervention to the specific family (precision medicine), as one size does not fit all. We hope that we all remember, as professionals in the field, that working with individuals, families, and communities experiencing trauma requires self-awareness, humility, and self-care. Let's all remember that trauma can be experienced by each one of us and we all need someone to lean on.

Ritblatt and Hokoda

About the Editors

Shulamit Natan Ritblatt, Professor Emerita of Child & Family Development at San Diego State University, received her PhD in child and family development from Florida State University. Prior to coming to the United States, she worked as a clinical child psychologist in Israel after completion of her master's in clinical child psychology in Tel Aviv University. Her focus has been preparing students and professionals to work in the field with children and their families, focusing on and emphasizing the importance of the socio-emotional base in early development and learning. She served as department chair and director for the Center for Family, School, and Community Engagement. Ritblatt is an expert in early childhood social-emotional development with the focus on early childhood mental health and learning readiness. Her work focuses on prevention and early intervention, utilizing relational, reflective, and trauma-informed practices to support healthy development of children and their families and enhance family engagement in education.

Audrey Hokoda is a Professor in the Child and Family Development Department at San Diego State University. She received her BS in psychobiology from the University of California, Los Angeles, and her doctorate in clinical psychology at the University of Illinois, Urbana-Champaign. As Principal/Co-Principal Investigator on over 20 studies/community projects focused on youth violence prevention programs, she has worked with many partners (e.g., school districts, government, social service agencies) in San Diego County and Mexico to develop and implement evidence-based prevention programs addressing bullying, teen relationship violence, domestic violence, and trauma. In 2018–2019, she was the recipient of the SDSU Senate Excellence in Teaching Award making her a Senate Distinguished Professor.

Contributors

Introduction: *Understanding trauma and the importance of relationship-based practices to promote resiliency* by Ritblatt, S. N. and Hokoda A

Shulamit Natan Ritblatt, PhD

Ritblatt, Professor Emerita, an expert in early childhood social-emotional development focusing on mental health, prevention, and early intervention, utilizing relational, reflective, and trauma-informed practices.

Audrey Hokoda, PhD

Hokoda, SDSU Senate Distinguished Professor, Principal/Co-Principal Investigator on over 20 evidence-based prevention studies/community projects addressing bullying, teen relationship violence, domestic violence, and trauma in San Diego County and Mexico.

Chapter 1: *Working with Low-Income Depressed Mothers and Their Infants* by Newton, R. P.

Ruth P. Newton

Newton is a clinical psychologist endorsed by the California Center for Infant-Family and Early Childhood Mental Health as an Infant-Family and Early Childhood Mental Health Specialist and Reflective Practice and Facilitator Ill/Mentor.

Chapter 2: *A Biological Imperative to Thrive: Supporting Military Families with Young Children* by Flowers, K. A., Hilt, D. K., and Hokoda, A.

Kim A. Flowers, LCSW, IF-ECMH RPF-M.

Flowers, Sr. Director of Family Support Services for Head Start, Early Head Start, and Services to Pregnant Women programs. Endorsed as a Reflective Practice Facilitator Mentor. She has over 30 years of providing clinical services in home-visitation, education, military, and community mental health settings, and has supported the professional development of early childhood professionals at Alliant International and SDSU Universities.

Donna K. Hilt, MS

Hilt holds an MS in child development, a graduate certificate in Early Childhood Social Emotional Behavior Intervention Specialist (EC-SEBRIS) and a BA in social work from SDSU. Over 25 years of experience in family support services with military families and communities.

Audrey Hokoda, PhD

Hokoda, SDSU Senate Distinguished Professor, Principal/Co-Principal Investigator on over 20 evidence-based prevention studies/community projects addressing bullying, teen relationship violence, domestic violence, and trauma in San Diego County and Mexico.

Chapter 3: *Prevalent but hidden: Sexual abuse, its impact and the healing process for children and parents* by Ritblatt, S. N., and Cruz, M.

Shulamit N. Ritblatt, PhD

Ritblatt, Professor Emerita, an expert in early childhood social-emotional development focusing on mental health, prevention and early intervention; utilizing relational, reflective, and trauma-informed practices.

Miranda Cruz

An early childhood educator with a Site Supervisor's Permit, trainer and supervisor for over 23 years. Certified Peer Specialist. A survivor and founder of a peer-run, non-profit: 7 Graces for Sexual Abuse Survivors.

Chapter 4: *Developing Child Resiliency through Art Intervention: A Strengths Perspective* by Grame, T.

Teresa Grame, LCSW, ATR-BC, RPT-S, PhD candidate: Developing Child

Grame, a board-certified art therapist, applies the arts in her work with families impacted by trauma. In addition, she facilitates art experiences with providers to promote well-being.

Chapter 5: *Utilizing Trauma-Informed Practices Working with Refugee Women to Address War Trauma and Enhance Parenting Skills* by Ritblatt, S. N., and Hokoda, A.

Shulamit N. Ritblatt, PhD

Ritblatt, Professor Emerita, an expert in early childhood social-emotional development focusing on mental health, prevention, and early intervention; utilizing relational, reflective, and trauma-informed practices.

Audrey Hokoda, PhD

Hokoda, SDSU Senate Distinguished Professor, Principal/Co-Principal Investigator on over 20 evidence-based prevention studies/community projects addressing bullying, teen relationship violence, domestic violence, and trauma in San Diego County and Mexico.

Chapter 6: *Creciendo Juntos (Growing Together): Building Leadership in Latino Parents in a Trauma-Informed Elementary School* by Hokoda, A., Rodriguez, M., Ritblatt, S. N., Schiele, S., and Ingraham, C. L.

Audrey Hokoda, PhD

Hokoda, SDSU Senate Distinguished Professor, Principal/Co-Principal Investigator on over 20 evidence-based prevention studies/community projects addressing bullying, teen relationship violence, domestic violence, and trauma in San Diego County and Mexico.

Maria del Carmen Rodriguez, MS

Rodriguez, Lecturer at SDSU. Holds an MS in child development and a graduate certificate in Early Childhood Social Emotional Behavior Intervention Specialist (EC-SEBRIS). Has extensive experience working in impoverished communities with primarily Latino immigrant families and children.

Shulamit N. Ritblatt, PhD

Ritblatt, Professor Emerita, an expert in early childhood social-emotional development focusing on mental health, prevention, and early intervention; utilizing relational, reflective, and trauma-informed practices.

Shannon Schiele

Schiele is a faculty member in the Family Studies Department at Southwestern Community College. Previously, she was a lecturer at San Diego State University in the Child and Family Development Department where she earned a master's degree in child development.

Colette L. Ingraham, PhD, NCSP

Ingraham, Professor, Department of Counseling and School Psychology at SDSU. Nationally board certified in school psychology, she is internationally known for her research on multicultural consultation and her leadership in school psychology. She is interested in ways to promote the learning and development of all students, through consultation, prevention, intervention, and systemic change.

Chapter 7: *Pride and Shame: Working with Gender and Sexual Variance* by Kent, N. M.

Nicole M. Kent, MFT, PhD

Kent (she/her) is a therapist and teaches at SDSU. She has over 20 years of experience running a group for SGM youth, and is a clinical supervisor at the North County LGBT resource center.

Chapter 8: *Promoting Wellness with Native American Youth: Culturally Informed Resilience Practices to Reduce the Effects of Trauma* by Robinson-Zañartu, C., Huynh, A., and Kinlicheene, B.

Carol Robinson-Zañartu, PhD

Robinson-Zañartu, Professor Emerita. She taught school psychology for some 30 years and served as department chair for 16 of those. She has been awarded over $15 million in federal grants to prepare school psychologists and collaborators to serve diverse populations, 9 of which has focused on issues of Native and Indigenous youth.

Ann Huynh, MS, EdS

Huynh, a school psychologist with LA Unified School District. Ann graduated from SDSU with an MS in counseling with an emphasis in school psychology and an EdS in school psychology. She was a scholar on the Native American/Indigenous Scholars and Collaborators Project (NAISCP), a graduate assistant for Trauma Leaders Consortium (TLC), and a recipient of the Gertrude Bell scholarship.

Bryanna Kinlicheene, MS (she/her)

Kinlicheene, a third-year Diné scholar in the NASP-Approved School Psychology Program, studying and learning on Kumeyaay Land at SDSU. Currently, she is a part of the Native American and Indigenous Scholars Collaborative (SHPA) and works with Native and Indigenous youth at Campo Elementary.

Chapter 9: *Centering the Community's Voice and Needs in Gang Prevention and Intervention Through a Trauma-Informed Lens* by Nuñez Estrada, J., Hernandez, E., and Sandoval Hernandez, J.

Joey Nuñez Estrada Jr., PhD

Estrada Jr., Associate Professor, Director of the School Counseling Program in the Department of Counseling and School Psychology at San Diego State University. His scholarship focuses on working with socially just community organizations and school environments by challenging systemic inequities and eradicating school and community barriers to student success, specifically for carceral system-impacted youth and families.

Edwin Hernandez, PhD

Hernandez, Assistant Professor, Counseling Program, College of Education, California State University, San Bernardino (CSUSB). His scholarship focuses on the policies and practices that promote or hinder the educational experiences, opportunities, and success for racially minoritized youth who have been pushed out of traditional schools and consequently enrolled at high-need and under-served schools, such as continuation high schools.

Jesus Sandoval Hernandez

Hernandez, a former gang member, became a pastor in City Heights in 2003 and was appointed as the executive director of the City's Commission on Gang Prevention and Intervention. He works with gang members and families utilizing the wraparound approach.

Chapter 10: *Children Experiencing Loss and Deprivation of Parental Care* by Ritblatt, S. N., Hokoda, A., Behana, N., Wojtach, B., Walsh, C., and Gonzalez, C.

Shulamit N. Ritblatt, PhD

Ritblatt, Professor Emerita, an expert in early childhood social-emotional development focusing on mental health, prevention, and early intervention; utilizing relational, reflective, and trauma-informed practices.

Audrey Hokoda, PhD

Hokoda, SDSU Senate Distinguished Professor, Principal/Co-Principal Investigator on over 20 evidence-based prevention studies/community projects addressing bullying, teen relationship violence, domestic violence, and trauma in San Diego County and Mexico.

Nory Behana, MS

Behana, an experienced Lecturer and Director of Foster, Adoptive, and Kinship Care Education with an eventual annual million-dollar grant from the California Community Colleges Chancellor's Office to provide education to Resource Families in San Diego County.

Barbara Wojtach, LCSW

Wojtach has worked in child welfare for over 25 years. She a lecturer at SDSU, a full-time Program Manager in Resource Parent Education at Grossmont College, and a Licensed Clinical Social Worker.

Christopher Walsh, LMFT

Walsh, Clinical Director. Licensed Marriage and Family Therapist with over 25 years' experience in the field of mental health serving as an administrator, consultant, educator, and provider of psychotherapy (specialized in integrative psychotherapy).

Christina Gonzalez, MS

Gonzalez, MS from SDSU. Educator and advocate for families and children with special needs. She spent a few years in a small orphanage in Mexico implementing trauma-informed care.

Chapter 11: *Healing around the Table: A Trauma-Informed Approach to Community Nutrition Education* by Bhagwan, M. and Markworth, A.

Monica Bhagwan, MA

Bhagwan has 15 years of experience implementing community food programs. She has a BA from Vassar College, and MA in Food Studies from NYU, and receives continuing education on trauma.

Adrienne Markworth, MA

Markworth, Founder and ED of Leah's Pantry, the national leader in trauma-informed nutrition. She holds a Bachelor's from the University of Virginia and a Master's from the University of San Francisco.

Chapter 12: *Trauma-Informed System Change in Child Welfare* by Walsh, C. R., and Bernstein, M.

Cambria Rose Walsh, LCSW

Walsh, LCSW, was the project director of the Center for Trauma-Informed Policies, Practices, and Programs at Rady Children's Hospital. She currently provides support to organizations around creating trauma-informed systems.

Melissa Bernstein, PhD

Bernstein directs the Advancing California's Trauma-Informed Systems (ACTS) and Trauma-Informed Licensing Team (TILT) Initiatives. Her research centers around supporting systems in planning for, implementing, and sustaining evidence-based, trauma-informed change.

Introduction

Understanding Trauma and the Importance of Relationship-Based Practices to Promote Resiliency

Shulamit N. Ritblatt and Audrey Hokoda

Often, we tend to think about trauma as an event that might happen to some of us. However, events such as natural disasters, economic downfalls, and pandemics have exemplified the universality of encountering trauma and the need to remember that trauma can affect individuals, families, relationships, organizations, and systems everywhere. Hence, trauma has no boundaries and limits in regard to gender, age, race, ethnicity, socioeconomic status, or geography. And yet we also know that, in the face of trauma, individuals exhibit strengths, adaptation, growth, and resilience (Cicchetti & Garmezy, 1993; Laney, 1996). Based on their own individual traits of personality and temperament, the timing and duration of the traumatic experiences, and one's support network and cultural value system provided by family and community, one can heal and thrive despite facing terrible adversities (Tummala-Narra, 2007). This is an ecological perspective that considers not only the individual's capital but also the family and community resources that influence how one adapts in the face of trauma (Harvey, 2007; Tummala-Narra, 2007; Ungar, 2013).

This book integrates research and practice, highlighting relationship-based interventions for diverse populations who have faced various forms of chronic adversities. Chapters explore the experiences of oppressed groups that include survivors of abuse, war, and poverty, Indigenous youth living on reservations, Middle Eastern refugee mothers with young children, individuals who identify

DOI: 10.4324/9781003046295-1

1

as LGBTQIA, and children and youth involved in child welfare, foster care, and juvenile justice systems. In each chapter, contributors provide strengths-based, trauma-informed strategies that can be used in clinical settings, school-based programs, and in urban communities where food insecurity, limited access to health services, and community violence is prevalent. The chapters underscore the universality of trauma, and professionals and students in counseling, social work, psychology, child welfare, education, and other fields will be introduced to innovative, culturally affirming interventions and models of care that promote well-being and resilience.

Background Research on Trauma and Resiliency

The book is important because trauma is prevalent; about 45% of school-aged children have experienced trauma and adverse childhood experiences—ACEs (Sacks & Murphey, 2018). Exposure to trauma in childhood and its effects on the brain development and the well-being of individuals are well documented in the literature (Corbin, 2007; Felitti et al., 1998; Perry, 2001; Saxe et al., 2006; Schore, 2001; van der Kolk, 2014). Negative long-lasting effects include physical illnesses (e.g., pain, gastrointestinal disorders, cardiovascular disease) and mental health problems such as depression, Post-Traumatic Stress Disorder (PTSD), and risky behaviors such as drug and alcohol use, sexual promiscuity, and anti-social behaviors (Abajobir et al., 2017; Flores-Torres et al., 2020; Kleber, 2019; Linden & Arnold, 2021; Sowder et al., 2018).

SAMHSA defines

> Individual trauma results from an event, series of events, or set of circumstances that is experienced by an individual as physically or emotionally harmful or life threatening and that has lasting adverse effects on the individual's functioning and mental, physical, social, emotional, or spiritual well-being.
>
> *(SAMHSA, 2014a)*

Each trauma includes three major components: **Event**, **Experience**, and **Effect**. Traumas start with a triggering **event** which occurs either once (single-episode trauma/acute trauma) or repeatedly. Kira and colleagues (2012) offered a developmental-based taxonomy of trauma that includes individual types (e.g., attachment trauma), single (e.g., car accidents) and complex traumas (e.g., repetitive ongoing), and cross-generational traumas that transmit through family or collectively (historical and social structural). The continuous **experience** of an **event** over time (complex trauma) puts the individual at higher risk for long-term lasting **effects** on physical and mental health. Individuals react to triggering events differently as we attach a "meaning" to the event and this in return determines our perception of the event as traumatic or not. People might go through the same event and experience it differently based on their past experiences, resources, cultural beliefs, and support.

This book highlights the experiences of diverse individuals and families who have experienced attachment-related, complex, and cross-generational traumas. The chapters present their journeys of resilience and recovery, influenced by their personal strengths, the meaning they attach to their experiences, and their families. In order to develop culturally responsive programs that best serve diverse families facing traumas, we must learn about these journeys, their strengths, and the meaning they attach to their experiences. We must understand research on the neuroscience of trauma and principles of trauma-informed care that inform how we can best create safety and engage families in interventions that promote their well-being. This background information, presented in more detail in many of the chapters, is briefly presented next.

The Neuroscience of Trauma

Chronic exposure to trauma can cause neurobiological disruptions that primarily affect the areas of the hypothalamic–pituitary–adrenal axis that are responsible for emotion and behavior regulation (Schore, 2009). When one is stressed, the amygdala of the limbic system, processes the sensations determining whether the cues signal a threat to survival. Appraisals of threats are met with a release of stress hormones (e.g., cortisol) that activate heightened fear and threat responses. After the initial fear and threat responses in the limbic and brainstem regions are activated, the higher-order responses of the prefrontal cortex begin as one interprets the cues of the situation, assesses the level of danger, and problem-solves ways to respond. However, when individuals are exposed to chronic traumas and are repeatedly experiencing this heightened fear and threat state, this can cause disruptions in the connections between the prefrontal cortex and the limbic areas of the brain. This results in an individual responding to stressors with the more primitive subcortical responses of fear and hyperarousal without being able to access the prefrontal cortex that helps cognitively process their experiences, regulate their arousal and fear, and self-soothe (Perry, 2009; Schore, 2001; van der Kolk, 2014).

Other neurological theories also explain the trauma on emotional regulation and executive functioning skills. For example, McLaughlin and colleagues (McLaughlin & Sheridan, 2016; Sheridan & McLaughlin, 2014, 2016; Sheridan et al., 2017) propose that the effects of trauma are based on two principles: Threat and deprivation. Experiencing a high degree of threat can lead to fear and mistrust and therefore can result in emotional reactivity, whereas deprivation experiences lead to dramatic changes in cortical volume and thickness that result in poor executive and cognitive functioning (Sheridan et al., 2012; McLaughlin et al., 2014).

Importance of Attachment and Early Childhood

The timing of the trauma is critical. When children experience adverse trauma in their early years, there can be negative lasting effects in brain development (Corbin, 2007; Schore, 2001). Because the brain is rapidly growing with neural circuits being formed during early childhood, their brains are more malleable, and trauma during this sensitive period of development can alter both the structure and function of the brain (Schore, 1994; Siegel, 1999). However, closely attuned parenting or caregiving provides safety and helps the child process the threat and regulate their fear and stress responses (Fonagy et al., 2002; Slade, 2002).

Caregivers who provide quick and consistent responses in the face of traumas help a child form higher levels of stress tolerance. Children exposed to chronic trauma without the co-regulatory help of attuned parenting may develop a low threshold for stress tolerance and may respond to even minor stressors with heightened fear and threat responses. Without caregiver help to manage the intense fear and sensations of threat, a young child's immature neurobiological regulatory system can be overloaded, altering the brain structure in response to threats (Perry, 2009).

Resiliency and Intergenerational Effects of Trauma on Families and Communities

A potential outcome of traumatic experiences is Post-Traumatic Growth (PTG) (Joseph, 2009; Tedeschi, & Calhoun, 1996; Xiaoli et al., 2019). When individuals experience traumas, their core beliefs that anchor them and their sense of trust in the world and the people in it, their assumptive world, might be crushed. Rebuilding it requires cognitive effort which involves deliberate reflection rather than intrusive rumination. The deliberate repetitive recalling of the events and reflecting on them while managing the emotional distress helps to develop clarity and comprehension as well as produce a narrative with meaning and purpose (Triplett et al., 2012). Factors contributing to the development of post-traumatic growth include social support, optimism, positive reevaluation of the situation, cognitive reflective capacity, agreeable personality traits, and spirituality (Henson et al., 2021).

The way parents respond to traumatic, stressful events affect them and their children's well-being. Their inner strengths in coping with traumas and stressors can serve as a buffer to negative outcomes in their children. The Center for the Study of Social Policy (CSSP, n.d.) has developed a Protective Factors framework that is based on protective conditions that mitigate risk and adversity as well as promotive factors that enhance and support well-being. These protective factors that support building positive outcomes and resiliency are: (1) parental resilience, (2) social connections, (3) knowledge of parenting and child development, (4) concrete support in times of need, and (5) social and emotional competence of children (https://cssp.org/resource/about-strengthening-families-and-the-protective-factors-framework/).

Mothers' own trauma and attachment history has a major impact on the child's attachment and mental well-being. Painful memories of past unresolved trauma by the parent can interfere with the ability of the parent to provide sensitive care and emotional attunement to the child and can hinder the formation of secure attachment in the child. Evidence for intergenerational transmission of trauma and insecure attachment has been established (Iyengar et al., 2019). When mothers can recall memories of loving moments with their own caregivers (Angel memories), they can regain internal strengths from these memories to provide positive parenting interactions to their children. These Angel memories were found to serve as a protective factor in the transmission of past traumas to their offspring (Lieberman et al., 2005; Narayan et al., 2017; 2019).

Trauma-Informed Practices and Interventions

Trauma-informed practices have been successful in reducing trauma symptoms in survivors. According to SAMHSA (2014a), trauma-informed care is a strength-based approach that focuses on relationship building and supports family self-determination utilizing six principles: Safety, trustworthiness and transparency, peer support, collaboration and mutuality, empowerment, and cultural, historical, and gender sensitivity. The trauma-related behaviors and symptoms are considered adaptive coping strategies. The four "Rs" describe the processes included in this approach: **Realization**, the understanding of trauma and its effects; **Recognition** of the signs of trauma, utilizing screenings and assessments; **Response** integrates the understanding of a person-specific trauma and tailoring appropriate treatments accordingly; and **Resist re-traumatization** of clients by avoiding the use of triggering memories or interventions that can re-traumatize and interfere with the recovery process.

Research on the neuroscience of trauma has informed clinical strategies and interventions for survivors of ACEs (Hambrick et al., 2019b; Navalta et al., 2018; Perry & Hambrick, 2008; van der Kolk, 2014). Perry and colleagues have developed the Neurosequential Model of Therapeutics (NMT) which emphasizes the critical role of positive relationships with adults who are attuned to the physiological and mental states of a traumatized survivor. This model encourages the selection of an appropriate intervention that meets the needs of the child and the family and targets the specific areas of the brain which have been affected by the trauma and adverse experience. This model calls for a better understanding of the type of experiences and their timing to provide "precision medicine" and improve intervention's outcomes (Perry, 2009; Hambrick et al., 2019a). The major benefit of this approach is in its neurodevelopmental perspective and the tailoring of the intervention to meet the specific needs and level of functioning of the individual.

Another feature of trauma-informed interventions influenced by research on the neuroscience of trauma (e.g., Perry, 2009; Porges, 2004; van der Kolk, 2014) is the use of expressive right-brain activities (e.g., arts, music, painting/drawing, dance, movement, yoga, drama, role-play) with survivors (Baker et al., 2018; Malchiodi, 2020; B McFerran et al., 2020). Because trauma survivors have difficulty accessing the cortex (Broca's area) that governs language, they can benefit from interventions that are not traditional talk-based therapies but rather focus on regulating sub-cortical brain stem activity (Faulkner, 2017; Perry & Dobson, 2013; van der Kolk, 2014). Repetitive motor, rhythmic activities (e.g., yoga, dancing, meditative breathing) and rhythmic balancing exercises can help one remain in a calm emotional state, be able to access higher-order thinking, and restore neural circuits between subcortical and cortex that have been compromised by trauma (Perry, 2009; van der Kolk, 2014).

Building an environment where survivors feel safe to reflect on their past traumatic experiences and their strengths are goals of trauma-informed interventions. Use of cultural brokers who understand and share the group's values, traditions, and communication styles (Jezewski, 1990) can help participants feel emotionally connected and more engaged, helping them feel safe and supported (Lin et al., 2018). Reflective practices are also successful in trauma-informed interventions. Reflective practices can help participants recall memories and express emotions in a safe place, and this can help build healing and growth by giving survivors a better understanding of their experiences and their strengths (Triplett et al., 2012). Using the reflective process can also promote mutual collaboration and supports participants' sense of control as service providers can continually modify and tailor the course of interventions as participants reflect and share their preferences and concerns (Butler et al., 2011).

Policies and Trauma-Informed Systems

Organizations that implement trauma-informed programs need a strong commitment from administration to make system-wide policy changes to ensure high-quality services for clients and support for their service providers. The National

Child Traumatic Stress Network (NCTSN, 2012, 2016) describes characteristics of trauma-informed systems in which there is collaboration across disciplines (e.g., education, criminal justice, child welfare) to provide evidence-based services for children and families affected by trauma.

Agencies implementing trauma-informed policies educate all clients and service providers on traumatic stress and infuse trauma-informed principles into their organizational practices and policies. Providers are taught to recognize the high prevalence of traumas among the population and utilize trauma-informed practices (Cutuli et al., 2019). Universal screenings for trauma histories and symptoms guide intervention services. Trained staff who are knowledgeable in using screening tools and who follow-up on positive trauma indicators with referrals to in-depth assessments and interventions are critical to trauma-informed systems of care.

Organizations and systems that serve trauma survivors must recognize the emotional stress and potential secondary trauma experienced by their providers and create a workplace environment that minimizes secondary traumatic stress and is attentive to the well-being of their staff (Kerig, 2019). Trauma-informed self-care (TISC) is a restorative practice that serves as a safeguard, and there are benefits for staff members who have engaged in self-care practices (Salloum et al., 2015). The use of reflective supervision is another important practice to support staff in a trauma-informed system of care. Supervision for trauma-informed practice requires a safe space to build trust with the providers through a collaborative empowering process (Berger & Quiros, 2014). Practicing mindfulness was found to be an effective strategy to reduce prejudice and bias, to increase self-awareness, and to support openness, sensitivity, and attunement to the clients' needs (Clark et al., 2019). Attending to the mental well-being and self-care needs of the therapists and service providers is critical to the provision of relational quality interventions and it is obligatory to staff well-being, retention, and morale (Clark et al., 2019; Menschner & Maul, 2016).

Trauma-informed systems of care have a sociocultural understanding of trauma and understand the impact of structural inequity and the unique needs of diverse communities that face traumas related to race, culture, gender, and marginalization. The perceived meaning of traumatic events, help-seeking, and coping strategies are affected by the family, culture, and history; hence, providers need to gain an understanding of culturally specific beliefs and ideas (SAMHSA, 2014b).

Organization of the Book

Integrating research and practice, this book highlights relationship-based interventions that build on the resilience of diverse populations that have faced multiple traumas. Organized into two sections, the first section has a focus on child and family interventions and the second section is focused on school and community programs. As we examine trauma and resilience using an ecological framework, there is overlap in these sections as there are macro-level cultural, historical, and socio-political factors influencing survivors, as well as their families and communities.

Section I: Child and Family Focus

The first section comprises seven chapters and describes psycho-educational and clinical interventions focused on individual and family. The strengths-based trauma-informed programs are largely influenced by research on the neuroscience of trauma and attachment theory and focus on strengthening family protective factors for building resiliency.

Newton (Chapter 1) focuses on maternal depression in pregnancy and the postpartum year and its effects on infant development. Synthesizing research on attachment and neurobiology of trauma, she describes parent–infant dyadic interventions utilizing attunement and synchrony, and proposes several clinical and policy recommendations for addressing the needs of pregnant women and postpartum mothers and their babies. Flowers, Hilt, and Hokoda (Chapter 2) also describe programs guided by attachment theory and research on infant and early childhood mental health while focused on the challenges (e.g., deployment, worry of danger) facing military families. They present trauma-informed prevention and intervention strategies that professionals across disciplines can use to serve this important population and help them overcome barriers to accessing services.

The next two chapters, guided by attachment theory and knowledge that traditional therapies which rely on verbal and cognitive skills may not be effective with individuals exposed to chronic trauma, highlight the use of expressive arts in promoting resiliency. Ritblatt and Cruz (Chapter 3) present a pilot intervention targeting parents of children who have experienced sexual abuse. Utilizing trauma-informed practices, the psycho-educational program focuses on safety, providing a space for parents to build relationships, and to receive and give peer support. The program uses a peer-mentorship model and right-brain expressive activities (e.g., art, music) to encourage reflection, self-care, and healing. Grame (Chapter 4) presents trauma recovery art therapy interventions for children and their families grounded in evidence-based principles of trauma-informed practice. She presents a variety of art materials and techniques, and describes a framework for building on the resilience of trauma survivors through the process of creating and exploring artwork.

The last three chapters in this first section focus on culturally affirmative programs targeting individuals and families whose traumas and stressors include war, migration, poverty, and systemic bigotry and oppression. Ritblatt and Hokoda (Chapter 5) describe the experiences of Middle Eastern refugee women who have experienced multiple traumas and are now adapting to living in the US. A ten-session psycho-educational program is described that focused on safety and trusting relationships and was led by a cultural broker who embraced their shared family and cultural traditions. During the group sessions, women engaged in expressive art and reflective practice activities to explore the effects of traumas on their relationships and their parenting, and the narrative of survival that they want to share with their children.

Hokoda, Rodriguez, Ritblatt, Schiele, and Ingraham (Chapter 6) highlight a school-based parent leadership program, *Creciendo Juntos* (Growing Together), for primarily Spanish-speaking Latino parents in a high-need urban community. Culturally responsive trauma-informed strategies and school–community partnerships are described which helped build a sense of community at the school where parents felt empowered to help their children and families by leading workshops on trauma and becoming activists beyond their local community.

Kent (Chapter 7) describes the experiences of people who identify as sexual and/or gender minorities (SGM) who are at higher risk of abuse, family alienation, homelessness, and mental health problems. She discusses the pervasive and systematic biases that have created obstacles for equity in providing care addressing medical, mental health, educational, and security needs, and offers resilience-building, trauma-informed approaches of care.

Section II: School and Community Focus

The second section of the book has five chapters and describes programs that focus on school and community and highlights systems-level, trauma-informed policies for professionals across disciplines. The chapters highlight the need for organizations to make system-wide policy changes that includes cross-disciplinary collaboration and training protocols for addressing inequities affecting traumatized communities. The call for culturally informed and affirmative practices that support awareness, healing, and resilience-building are shared across the chapters.

The notion of the provider (healer) going through a parallel reflective process that enhances compassion toward others and supports self-growth is highlighted.

Robinson-Zañartu, Huynh, and Kinlicheene (Chapter 8) discuss the effects of historical and intergenerational trauma on Native American youth and describe a school-based program that builds their cultural identity and resilience. Honoring Indigenous knowledge and values, they propose an innovative culturally grounded model of resilience that focuses on healing, identity awareness, and reflection in both the youth and the school psychologists and counselors working with them.

Estrada, Hernandez, and Hernandez (Chapter 9) focus on the needs of young people impacted by gangs and gang violence. They present a theoretical framework for understanding gang culture and the system-induced traumas that contribute to gang involvement. They also describe community-based, healing-centered approaches that can be used by professionals across disciplines to address the needs of gang-involved youth and their families.

Ritblatt, Hokoda, Behana, Wojtach, Walsh, and Gonzalez (Chapter 10) describe the multiple traumas affecting children who have lost parental care and review arrangements of care (e.g., orphanages, foster care) that best meet their needs. The chapter highlights the importance of high-quality relationships and caregiver education on ways to provide safety and promote resilience, and describes trauma-informed programs that may help these vulnerable children heal and thrive.

Bhagwan and Markworth (Chapter 11) describe nutrition and food security initiatives that incorporate the understanding of trauma and adversity and its relation to food, lifestyle habits, and nutritional health. They provide a systems framework for public health programming and messaging addressing nutrition and food insecurity that is compassionate, non-stigmatizing, and trauma-informed, and they present a program, *Around the Table*, that can serve as a guide for how to infuse trauma-informed principles into other food and nutrition interventions.

In our last chapter (Chapter 12), Walsh and Bernstein describe two training programs that create organizational trauma-informed change for the Child Welfare System. Incorporating essential elements developed by the National Child Traumatic Stress Network, the first program focuses on training the workforce on trauma-informed practices, and the second program focuses on strategies to implement trauma-informed change at an organizational level. The authors review challenges and lessons learned from implementing the programs and provide recommendations for new initiatives incorporating trauma-informed changes to their systems.

Conclusion

This book presents a collection of trauma-informed programs that are tailored to the needs of diverse groups of people who have faced adversities. The chapters describe evidence-based practices that are guided by the neuroscience of trauma, the importance of relationships, and trauma-informed principles that emphasize the safety and strengths of survivors. Family and community interventions are presented that promote family protective factors and address the unique needs of families impacted by historical and structural inequities related to race and gender.

Several of the chapters discuss trauma-informed, system-level policies that involve collaborations across disciplines and that provide continuity of care for families facing adversities. Examples of organizations implementing policies to promote self-care, specialized training, and reflective supervision to support the well-being of their service providers are highlighted.

Our goal for the book is to provide the opportunity for students and professionals from across disciplines to learn about trauma-informed practices and impactful stories of resilience from individuals who have faced adversities. We hope readers will be motivated to learn more about trauma-informed practices and be inspired to make a difference and push for compassionate policies that recognize the impact of trauma on individuals, families, and communities.

References

Abajobir, A. A., Kisely, S., Maravilla, J. G., Williams, G., & Najman, J. M. (2017). Gender differences in the association between childhood sexual abuse and risky sexual behaviours: A systematic review and meta-analysis. *Child Abuse and Neglect, 63,* 249–260.

Baker, F. A., Metcalf, O., Varker, T., & O'Donnell, M. (2018). A systematic review of the efficacy of creative arts therapies in the treatment of adults with PTSD. *Psychological Trauma: Theory, Research, Practice, and Policy, 10*(6), 643–651. https://doi.org/10.1037/tra0000353

Berger, R., & Quiros, L. (2014). Supervision for trauma-informed practice. *Traumatology, 20*(4), 296–301.

Butler, L. D., Critelli, F. M., & Rinfrette, E. S. (2011). Trauma-informed care and mental health. *Directions in Psychiatry, 31,* 197–210.

Center for the Study of Social Policy (CSSP). (n.d.). About strengthening families™ and the protective factors framework. Retrieved from https://cssp.org/wp-content/uploads/2018/11/About-Strengthening-Families.pdf

Cicchetti, D., & Garmezy, N. (1993). Prospects and promises in the study of resilience. *Development and Psychopathology, 5*(4), 497–502.

Clark, R., Gehl, M., Heffron, M. C., Kerr, M., Soliman, S., Shahmoon-Shanok, R., & Thomas, K. (2019). Mindfulness practices to enhance diversity-informed reflective supervision and leadership. *Zero to Three.*

Corbin, J. R. (2007). Reactive attachment disorder: A biopsychosocial disturbance of attachment. *Child and Adolescent Social Work Journal, 24*(6), 539–552. https://doi.org/10.1007/s10560-007-0105-x

Cutuli, J. J., Alderfer, M. A., & Marsac, M. L. (2019). Introduction to the special issue: Trauma-informed care for children and families. *Psychological Services, 16*(1), 1–6.

Faulkner, S. (2017). Rhythm2Recovery: A model of practice combining rhythmic music with cognitive reflection for social and emotional health within trauma recovery. *Australian and New Zealand Journal of Family Therapy, 38*(4), 627–636. https://doi.org/10.1002/anzf.1268

Felitti, V. J., Anda, R. F., Nordenberg, D., Williamson, D. F., Spitz, A. M., Edwards, V., … Marks, J. S. (1998). Relationship of childhood abuse and household dysfunction to many of the leading causes of death in adults. *American Journal of Preventive Medicine, 14*(4), 245–258. https://doi.org/10.1016/s0749-3797(98)00017-8

Flores-Torres, M. H., Comerford, E., Singnorello, L., Grodstein, F., Lopez-Ridaura, R., de Castro, F., ... Lajous, M. (2020). Impact of adverse childhood experiences on cardiovascular disease risk factors in adulthood among Mexican women. *Child Abuse and Neglect, 99*, 104175.

Fonagy, P., Gergely, G., Jurist, E. L., & Target, M. (2002). *Affect regulation, mentalization, and the development of the self.* New York: Other Press.

Hambrick, E. P., Brawner, T. W., & Perry, B. D. (2019a). Timing of early-life stress and the development of brain-related capacities. *Frontiers in Behavioral Neuroscience, 13*, Article 183.

Hambrick, E. P., Brawner, T. W., Perry, B. D., Brandt, K., Hofmeister, C., & Collins, J. O. (2019b). Beyond the ACE score: Examining relationships between timing of developmental adversity, relational health and developmental outcomes in children. *Archives of Psychiatric Nursing, 33*(3), 238–247.

Harvey, M. R. (2007). Toward an ecological understanding of resilience in trauma survivors: Implications for theory, research, and practice. In M. R. Harvey & P. Tummula-Narra (Eds.), *Sources and expressions of resiliency in trauma survivors: Ecological theory, multi-cultural practice* (pp. 9–32). Binghamton, NY: Haworth.

Henson, C., Truchot, D., & Canevello, A. (2021). What promotes post traumatic growth? A systematic review. *European Journal of Trauma and Dissociation, 5*(4), 100195.

Iyengar, U., Purva Rajhans, P., Fonagy, P., Strathearn, L., & Kim, S. (2019). Unresolved trauma and reorganization in mothers: Attachment and neuroscience. *Perspectives Frontiers in Psychology, 10*, 110. https://doi.org/10.3389/fpsyg.2019.00110

Jezewski, M. A. (1990, August). Culture brokering in migrant farm worker health care. *Western Journal of Nursing Research, 12*(4), 497–513.

Joseph, S. (2009). Growth following adversity: Positive psychological perspectives on posttraumatic stress. *Psychological Topics, 18*(2), 335–343.

Kerig, P. K. (2019). Enhancing resilience among providers of trauma-informed care: A curriculum for protection against secondary traumatic stress among non-mental health professionals. *Journal of Aggression, Maltreatment and Trauma, 28*(5), 613–630. https://doi.org/10.1080/10926771.2018.1468373

Kira, I. A., Somers, C., Lewandowski, L., & Chiodo, L. (2012). Attachment disruptions, IQ, and PTSD in African American adolescents: A traumatology perspective. *Journal of Aggression, Maltreatment and Trauma, 21*(6), 665–690.

Kleber, J. R. (2019). Trauma and public mental health: A focused review. *Frontiers in Psychiatry, 10*, 451.

Laney, M. D. (1996). Multiple personality disorder: Resilience and creativity in the preservation of the self. *Psychoanalysis and Psychotherapy, 13*(1), 35–49.

Lieberman, A. F., Padrón, E., Van Horn, P., & Harris, W. W. (2005). Angels in the nursery: The intergenerational transmission of benevolent parental influences. *Infant Mental Health Journal, 26*(6), 504–520. https://doi.org/10.1002/imhj.20071

Lin, C.-H., Chiang, P. P., Lux, E. A., & Lin, H. F. (2018). Immigrant social worker practice: An ecological perspective on strengths and challenges. *Children and Youth Services Review, 87*(C), 103–113.

Linden, M., & Arnold, P. C. (2021). Embitterment and posttraumatic embitterment disorder (PTED): An old, frequent, and still underrecognized problem. *Psychotherapy and Psychosomatics, 90*(2), 73–80.

Malchiodi, C. A. (2020). *Trauma and expressive arts therapy: Brain, body, and imagination in the healing process.* New York: The Guilford Press.

McFerran, K. S., Lai, C. H. I., Wei-Han Chang, W. H., Acquaro, D., Chin, T. C., Stokes, H., & Crooke, D. H. A. (2020). Music, rhythm and trauma: A critical interpretive synthesis of research literature. *Frontiers in Psychology, 11.* https://doi.org/10.3389/fpsyg.2020.00324

McLaughlin, K. A., & Sheridan, M. A. (2016). Beyond cumulative risk: A dimensional approach to childhood adversity. *Current Directions in Psychological Science, 25*(4), 239–245. https://doi.org/10.1177/0963721416655883

McLaughlin, K. A., Sheridan, M. A., Winter, W., Fox, N. A., Zeanah, C. H., & Nelson, C. A. (2014). Widespread reductions in cortical thickness following severe early-life deprivation: A neurodevelopmental pathway to attention-deficit/hyperactivity disorder. *Biological Psychiatry, 15*(8), 629–638. https://doi.org/10.1016/j.biopsych.2013.08.016

Menschner, C., & Maul, A. (2016). *Brief: Strategies for encouraging staff wellness in Trauma-informed organizations.* Center for health Care Strategies. Robert Wood Johnson Foundation.

Narayan, A. J., Ghosh Ippen, C., Harris, W. W., & Lieberman, A. F. (2017). Assessing angels in the nursery: A pilot study of childhood memories of benevolent caregiving as protective influences. *Infant Mental Health Journal, 38*(4), 461–474. https://doi.org/10.1002/imhj.21653

Narayan, A. J., Ghosh Ippen, C., Harris, W. W., & Lieberman, A. F. (2019). Protective factors that buffer against intergenerational transmission of trauma from mothers to young children: A replication study of angels in the nursery. *Development and Psychopathology, 31*, 173–187.

Navalta, C. P., McGee, L., & Underwood, J. (2018). Adverse childhood experiences, brain development, and mental health: A call for neurocounseling. *Neurocounseling, 40*(3), 266–278.

The National Child Traumatic Stress Network (NCTSN). (2016). Creating trauma informed systems. Retrieved from https://www.nctsn.org/trauma-informed-care/creating-trauma-informed-systems

The National Child Traumatic Stress Network NCTSN Core Curriculum on Childhood Trauma Task Force. (2012). *The 12 core concepts: Concepts for understanding traumatic stress responses in children and families.* Core Curriculum on Childhood Trauma. Los Angeles, CA and Durham, NC: UCLA-Duke University National Center for Child Traumatic Stress. Retrieved from https://www.nctsn.org/sites/default/files/resources//the_12_core_concepts_for_understanding_traumatic_stress_responses_in_children_and_families.pdf

Perry, B. D. (2001). The neurodevelopmental impact of violence in childhood. In D. Schetky & E. Benedek (Eds.), *Textbook of child and adolescent forensic psychiatry* (pp. 221–238). Washington, DC: American Psychiatric Press.

Perry, B. D. (2009). Examining child maltreatment through a neurodevelopmental lens: Clinical applications of the Neurosequential model of therapeutics. *Journal of Loss and Trauma, 14*(4), 240–255. https://doi.org/10.1080/15325020903004350

Perry, B. D., & Dobson, C. L. (2013). The neurosequential model of therapeutics. In J. D. Ford & C. A. Courtois (Eds.), *Treating complex traumatic stress disorders in children and adolescents: Scientific foundations and therapeutic models* (pp. 249–260). New York: The Guilford Press.

Perry, B. D., & Hambrick, E. P. (2008, Fall). The neurosequential model of therapeutics. *Reclaiming Children and Youth, 17*(3), 38–43.

Porges, S. (2004). Neuroception: A subconscious system for detecting threats and safety. *Zero to Three, 24*, 19–24.

Sacks, V., & Murphey, D. (2018). *The prevalence of adverse childhood experiences, nationally, by state, and by race/ethnicity* (Research Brief No. 2018-03). (2018, February). Retrieved from Child Trends website: https://www.childtrends.org/publications/prevalence-adverse-childhood-experiences-nationally-state-race-ethnicity

Salloum, A., Kondart, D. C., Johnco, C., & Olson, K. R. (2015). The role of self-care on compassion satisfaction, burnout and secondary trauma among child welfare workers. *Children and Youth Services Review, 49*, 54–61.

Saxe, G. N., Ellis, B. H., & Kaplow, J. B. (2006). *Collaborative treatment of traumatized children and teens: The trauma systems therapy approach.* New York: Guilford Press.

Schore, A. N. (1994). *Affect regulation and the origin of the self: The neurobiology of emotional development.* Hillsdale, NJ: Erlbaum.

Schore, A. N. (2001). The effects of early relational trauma on right brain development, affect regulation, and infant mental health. *Infant Mental Health Journal, 22*(1/2), 201–269.

Schore, A. N. (2009). Relational trauma and the developing right brain: An interface of psychoanalytic self psychology and neuroscience. *Annals of the New York Academy of Sciences, 1159*(1), 189–203.

Sheridan, A. M., Peverill, M., Finn, S. A., & McLaughlin, A. K. (2017). Dimensions of childhood adversity have distinct associations with neural systems underlying executive functioning. *Development and Psychopathology, 29*(5), 1777–1794.

Sheridan, M. A., Fox, N. A., Zeanah, C. H., McLaughlin, K. A., & Nelson, A., III (2012). Variation in neural development as a result of exposure to institutionalization early in childhood. *Proceedings of the National Academy of Sciences, 109*(32), 12927–12932. https://doi.org/10.1073/pnas.1200041109

Sheridan, M. A., & McLaughlin, K. A. (2014). Dimensions of early experience and neural development: Deprivation and threat. *Trends in Cognitive Sciences, 18*(11), 580–585.

Sheridan, M. A., & McLaughlin, K. A. (2016). Neurobiological models of the impact of adversity on education. *Current Opinion in Behavioral Sciences, 10*, 108–113. https://doi.org/10.1016/j.cobeha.2016.05.013

Siegel, D. (1999). *The developing mind.* New York: Guilford.

Slade, A. (2002). Keeping the baby in mind: A critical factor in perinatal mental health. *Zero to Three, 22*, 10–16.

Sowder, K. L., Knight, L. A., & Fishalow, J. (2018). Trauma exposure and health: A review of outcomes and pathways. *Journal of Aggression, Maltreatment and Trauma, 27*(10), 1041–1059. https://doi.org/10.1080/10926771.2017.1422841

Substance Abuse and Mental Health Services Administration (SAMHSA). (2014a). *SAMHSA's concept of trauma and guidance for a trauma-informed approach.* HHS Publication No. (SMA) 14-4884. Rockville, MD: Substance Abuse and Mental Health Services Administration.

Substance Abuse and Mental Health Services Administration (SAMHSA). (2014b). *Trauma-informed care in behavioral health services. Treatment improvement protocol (TIP) series 57.* HHS Publication No. (SMA) 13-4801. Rockville, MD: Substance Abuse and Mental Health Services Administration.

Substance Abuse and Mental Health Services Administration (SAMHSA). (2018, May 9). Serious mental illness and trauma: A literature review and issue brief. Retrieved from https://www.samhsa.gov/sites/default/files/programs_campaigns/childrens _mental_health/samhsa-smi-and-trauma-lit-review-and-issue-brief.docx

Tedeschi, R., & Calhoun, L. (1996). The posttraumatic growth inventory: Measuring the positive legacy of trauma. *Journal of Traumatic Stress, 9*(3), 455–471.

Triplett, K. N., Tedeschi, R. G., Cann, A., Calhoun, G. L., & Reeve, C. L. (2012). Posttraumatic growth, meaning in life, and life satisfaction in response to trauma. *Psychological Trauma: Theory, Research, Practice, and Policy, 4*(4), 400–410.

Tummala-Narra, P. (2007). Conceptualizing trauma and resilience across diverse contexts: A multicultural perspective. *Journal of Aggression, Maltreatment and Trauma, 14*(1–2), 33–53.

Ungar, M. (2013). Resilience, trauma, context, and culture. *Trauma, Violence, and Abuse, 14*(3), 255–266. https://doi.org/10.1177/15248380/3487805

van der Kolk, B. (2014). *The body keeps the score: Mind, brain and body in the transformation of trauma.* London: Allen Lane.

Xiaoli, W., Kaminga, A. C., Wenjie, D., Deng Jing, D., Wang Zhipeng, W., Xiongfeng, P., & Aizhong, L. (2019). The prevalence of moderate-to-high posttraumatic growth: A systematic review and meta-analysis. *Journal of Affective Disorders, 243*, 408–415.

CHILD AND FAMILY FOCUS

I

Chapter 1

Working with Low-Income Depressed Mothers and Their Infants

Ruth P. Newton

> *The precursor of the mirror is the mother's face.*
>
> —*Donald Winnicott (by permission of The Marsh Agency
> Ltd., on behalf of The Winnicott Trust CIO 1174533)*

Introduction

*Lucretia, a 36-year-old Hispanic mother, was referred with postpartum
depression that began after she had her fourth child. At the time of
referral, she endorsed moderate depression with suicidality on the PHQ-
9. At intake, her risk assessment indicated that she had current suicidal
thoughts without a plan and one previous suicide attempt with pills
when she was 25. Lucretia had both depression and anxiety during
pregnancy and was tearful at intake, stating she doesn't feel supported
by her husband, his family, and her own mother. She stated, "I'm not
worth anything. My husband makes me feel like I'm an imbecile, and
my mother-in-law says I don't know how to parent because I messed*

DOI: 10.4324/9781003046295-3

up my 9-year-old." Due to financial difficulties, Lucretia lives with her husband, their infant, their 3 older children ages 9, 13, and 14, and her husband's parents. Her fourth child is a seven-month-old boy named Miguel; the baby was not planned.[1]

Postpartum depression (PPD) has been found to be between 10 and 20% in the general population (O'Hara & McCabe, 2013); however, age, low income, ethnicity, single parenting, and quality of social support have been found to interact with these rates, with depression in pregnancy increasing the likelihood of a PPD (Robertson et al., 2004). Rates of PPD in a Hispanic population have been found to be higher with 33% of Hispanic mothers reporting depression at five months postpartum (Gress Smith et al., 2012).

Lifetime histories of mood disorders, childhood trauma, psychiatric disorders, anxiety, adverse life events, family histories of psychiatric disorders, and lower socioeconomic status have all been found to increase the risk for PPD (Guintivano et al., 2018). These authors state that, "If we consider a history of psychiatric disorders as the best current predictor for PPD, adverse life events may account for the next largest source of variation associated with the disorder" (Guintivano et al., 2018, p. 7).

Resiliency or the "ability to maintain equilibrium in the face of adversity" has been found to be a multidimensional protective factor that includes genetics, neurobiological, social, and psychological factors (Ozbay et al., 2010, p. 196). Resilience factors such as cognitive flexibility, positive reframing, and the ability to find meaning in adverse events are important but social support has been consistently associated with both positive mental and physical health in many studies (Lanius et al., 2010; Ozbay et al., 2010).

Since the trauma-informed care paradigm shifted clinical awareness away from individual pathology (*What's wrong with you?*) into the importance of lived experiences (*What happened to you?*) (SAMHSA, 2014), a history of childhood trauma is now considered a clinical imperative when working with depressed mothers as childhood trauma is associated with developing PPD and, for some, PTSD (Wonjung et al., 2016). An assessment of resiliency is also needed as mothers' depression can negatively impact infant bonding (Hairston et al., 2018), and if untreated, has been associated with developmental problems in the infant, other children in the family, the mother's partner, and overall poorer family functioning (Polmanteer et al., 2019).

Maternal Depression and Infant Development

Maternal depression is known to adversely affect infant development and security primarily because depression can diminish the nonverbal, implicit affect resonance that infants need for development. In contrast with bright, loving, and adoring eyes; lyrical voices with wide ranges that convey meaning, play, or new experiences; and dynamic facial expressions that infants can enjoy and begin to interpret, depressed mothers often have dull eyes, flat voices, and expressionless faces (see Newton, 2008). Depressed mothers have less infant-directed speech in general, are less animated, touch their infants less, and are more likely to speak in a flat voice than nondepressed mothers (Herrera et al., 2004; Sohr-Preston & Scaramella, 2006).

Depression in pregnancy is also a concern as the infant/parent relationship is thought to begin in the last trimester when infants can hear (Kisilevsky et al., 2003). Thus, perinatal (pregnancy, birth, and the first postpartum year) depression is a serious health risk for mothers, infants, and their families. Because depression impacts the mother's implicit world of eyes, facial expressions, voice prosody, touch, and gesture; that is, the nonverbal language all infants are born speaking, the infant is at particular risk. Clinical interventions need to address both the nonverbal implicit and narrative communication of the mother while assessing the impact of her depression on the infant. The author suggests that clinical inventions during the perinatal period require clinicians to have advanced training in affective neuroscience.

Since infant brain development is thought to be experience-dependent on the quality of the attachment relationship (Schore, 1994), the last trimester of pregnancy through the first two years of life are considered a right-hemisphere-sensitive period (Chiron et al., 1997; Mento et al., 2010), and synthesizing the fields of attachment and neurobiology is now a clinical necessity when working with mothers and infants. Although mothers' biological resources and health are generally clinically assessed, what is often not deeply evaluated is mothers' emotional resources. Understanding a mother's lived experience, her desires, stresses, and the expectations of motherhood from her family and culture are also needed. What has Lucretia experienced in her life? Did she have a secure attachment to her own mother? Did she experience any trauma? Does she have ongoing stressors that can affect the quality of her affective communication and happiness? Has she had previous bouts of depression and anxiety? How does her family system and culture view her? Is Miguel's father actively involved in his care? These questions are critical for successful intervention.

Intervention

Miguel is a cute seven-month-old infant with a thick head of black hair. He was carried into our intake session in a car seat by his 36-year-old mother Lucretia. His mother looked depressed, anxious, and irritable. She was referred to us by the Pediatric Developmental Services

Department at FHCSD[2] because at the time of screening mother was observed to raise her voice at the infant and say, "Now what do you want?" When the infant got fussy and began to cry,[1]

The mother was observed to say, "He cries just because." Miguel had exceptionally low affect in this first session and was silent. With ongoing attempts to speak with him using more baby-friendly affect, the clinician was able to elicit a slight smile toward the end of the first session. Miguel was a full-term baby, who was current on his well-baby visits. He was breastfed at birth but very soon changed to formula because, as his mother said, "He hurt me, and it just took too long to feed him." Mother was given a PHQ-9 and scored within the range for intake into the Maternal Depression Pilot.

As a FHCSD partner, NCAR received the referral for Lucretia and Miguel. The dyad was seen through the Maternal Depression Pilot (MDP) funded by First 5 San Diego/HDS/FHCSD. The MDP provides depressed mothers scoring within the mild to moderate ranges on the PHQ-9 (scores 5–14) with 14 sessions of therapy (7 individual and 7 dyadic). Mothers scoring within the severe range are referred directly to FHCSD Mental Health. Other MDP services include care coordination for scheduling and coordinating multiple services and providing needed necessities (such as bus tokens, diapers, and other tangibles), psychiatric appointments, and medications.

NCAR is specialized in the neuroscience of attachment. All assessments and interventions for all age groups are informed by Integrative Regulation Therapy (iRT, Newton, 2009/2013; 2017), a neurobiological evidence-informed scaffold for evidence-based psychodynamic therapies. What iRT adds is a focus on and use of the underlying brain processes, the different processing styles of the cerebral hemispheres, the different attachment organizations, and the nature of the implicit, nonconscious subcortical world of affect where the primary attachment experiences have been encoded (Damasio, 2018; Edelman, 2004; Panksepp, 2012). The use of iRT in infant/parent psychotherapy is especially important because the quality of the mother's ability to provide good-enough attunement and care within an evolutionary driven Primary Biological Entrainment Period associated with subcortical wiring is critical (Newton, 2020). For dyadic therapies, iRT scaffolds evidence-based Infant Parent Psychotherapy (IPP; Fraiberg, 1980; Fraiberg et al., 1975; Lieberman, 1992; Lieberman et al., 2000), and this is the approach we used to treat Lucretia and Miguel.

iRT requires postgraduate advanced training for clinicians to be able to work at deep affective levels within natural relational contexts that incorporate the mother's presenting concerns. Using a developmental history form tailored to assess trauma and early life availability of carers with other pretest measurers and intake impressions, we first proceed in making a *probable map* of the mother's neurobiological organization.

Probable maps specifically assess attachment impressions, self-statements, arousal ranges, how the mother is currently attempting to soothe herself, defenses, use of instincts, use of reflection, strength of agency, and hopes and desires (Newton, 2009/2013; Newton, 2017; 2021). Lucretia gave us the impression of a very depressed, angry mother who was frustrated with her life and with her infant. Lucretia had a trauma history that included a mother who was unavailable and harsh. Because she was the only girl in her family of origin, she was expected to care for her siblings.

Lucretia's attachment organization was somewhat on the dismissive spectrum with some use of denial and dissociation; however, she was angrily able to report her frustration with her husband and his family. There was no evidence that she accessed her own instincts nor was there evidence that she reflected on her life. She was, however, strong willed, which we considered a resiliency factor. After the initial clinical session (that is always dyadic so we can assess to what extent the infant's development has been affected), we decided to have an individual session with Lucretia to get the truth of her lived experience out in the open as we strongly suspected that Lucretia resented this unplanned fourth child.

In this next session, the iRT clinician empathized with Lucretia about how hard it must be for her given her circumstances. Lucretia responded by giving much angry information about how her husband takes his parents' side, they are dismissive of her, and how they make her feel like she is "a nothing." The clinician then said, "That is terribly hard, but I also see you said Miguel was not a planned pregnancy." Lucretia said strongly,

> *No, I was done having children after my second; my third wasn't planned either. I had plans for my life. I didn't want to just be a mother; I had to mother my own mother's children. I wanted to go back to school and study accounting and have my own money and my own career.*

The clinician continued to feel how much pain Lucretia was in, how trapped she felt and with little support that included active denigration. When she finished, the clinician asked, "Do you let yourself imagine how you can still go to school?" Lucretia gave a dismissing look at the clinician who then quickly responded, "but we would have to help your husband be more supportive of you and work on better boundaries around your in-laws." Now Lucretia started to listen more intently.

It was clear to us that Lucretia was extremely overwhelmed and angry with the responsibility of caring for her children. She also felt her husband and his family were not supportive. As we worked through several sessions on the realities of her life, we began to ask Lucretia if she felt Miguel could feel her agitation and unhappiness. She looked surprised. The clinician was able to say that infants can feel our unhappiness and our anger.

> *Sometimes if there is so much anger around them, they might get quiet and kind of reduce their movements and even their smiles, because they sense that things are a bit scary and not safe. This is how our biology works whether we are an infant or an adult. When things are scary, like if we suddenly were confronted with a scary person, we might initially freeze, be still, or scream.*

Lucretia identified with this as she came from a trauma background herself and was confronted with several scary people with no protection. When asked if she also felt depressed or anxious in her childhood, she said, "All the time!" Since the clinician could sense that Lucretia was starting to think about this, she continued, "I know you also experienced scary times when you were growing up and didn't have anyone to help you."

Lucretia started to settle into herself as the individual sessions proceeded. We knew that building resiliency in Lucretia and her son would require acknowledging Lucretia's deeper feelings and desires. She was also able to hold in her mind that maybe Miguel was experiencing her anger and rejection. One session she came in with the following observation.

> *I was feeding him, he always takes forever, and I started to get frustrated and angry, but I saw him turn away and move back in his highchair; I wondered if he could feel my anger. I felt sorry for him because I didn't want him to feel he's not important, like I feel.*

The clinician, seeing that she was now considering Miguel's feelings saw this as an opening and suggested that she bring him next time, "and we will work together to see who he is and what makes him smile and talk with us."

From attachment research, we know that avoidant children have mothers who were often harsh, negative, rejecting, don't like touch, and focused more on external achievements, not internal feelings (Main, 2000; Sroufe et al., 2005). iRT clinicians are trained to recognize this attachment organization and build a warm, affective relationship with the adult who also experienced rejection as a child. Our iRT clinician did this and did not get flustered by Lucretia's harsh anger but instead consistently stayed with her deeper self. Ongoing support for the clinician was given in supervision so that she felt guided and cared for being at the helm of this complex therapy. The clinician could admit that sometimes Lucretia scared her. She received the support of her peers in NCAR's clinical supervision group that focuses on reflection on one's own attachment organization and how it can interact with a client's organization.

Although we had a safety plan in place for Lucretia's suicidal ideation and considered a possible psychiatric referral for medications, it was becoming clearer that Lucretia was feeling better about herself and her baby as the truth of her inner desires was addressed, so we proceeded to help her with her husband and family system conflict by increasing her matter-of-fact assertiveness by using reversed role-plays (iRT intervention, clinician plays the role of client while client plays the role of the problematic other), reviewing the class schedule with her from a local community college, and simultaneously highlighting any dyadic interaction she had with Miguel that used affect, "Oh wow look at you two and that smile!"

Continuing along, we began to *platform* (iRT intervention that targets left-brain concept formation) a better understanding of attunement, affect, and synchrony; we tend to do this by using affect ourselves.

> *I love how you responded to his smile with your smile; you are in sync!*
> *Did you know that parent attunement and synchrony, like you just did,*
> *are associated with secure attachment?*

We also suggested singing with Miguel, but Lucretia was not willing to do this, so the clinician said, "We'll sing together" and began singing a song that Lucretia softly attempted, and Miguel loved. Although treatment goals were set in the beginning of this therapy to help Lucretia with self-care, we had many changes in goals due to the mother's positive responses. The latest goals concerned singing, playing, and narrating for Miguel what they were doing so he could not only feel his mother's connection, but could hear more language. Lucretia's goals moved into date nights with her husband while her in-laws took care of Miguel.

Alternating between individual sessions when needed and dyadic sessions, more of Lucretia's story came out. She stated she only wanted two children and was set to pursue her career when she became pregnant with her now nine-year-old daughter; she had a postpartum depression when she was born. But Lucretia began to see it was possible for her to pursue her goals for a career and still parent with more support from her husband. She said,

> *I know I'm old, but it makes me happier when I think I can have my own*
> *accounting business. I'm good at this you know. I also talked with my*
> *husband like we rehearsed (we rehearsed matter-of-fact statements) …*
> *well, actually I told my husband that he had to help with the kids more*
> *because I am going to pursue my career. And I want to have a place of our*
> *own, and if I start my business, we'll make more money.*

To her surprise, her husband was supportive.

We consider this therapy a success, and all post-test outcomes reflected this. Lucretia coded in the minimal, if any, range for depression and anxiety and reported less parenting stress. She was beginning to accept that she had four children and was now wondering if she should start a therapy with her nine-year-old. Her interactions were not 100% consistent but clearly Miguel showed signs of catching up in his development. He smiled more, had better coordinated movement, was crawling well and pulling up to stand by the end of treatment. He vocalized more and sought his mother's eyes and got them. Lucretia, feeling less depressed, was motivated to pursue the career she desired. As Lucretia was experiencing less stress, she showed more affect with Miguel and used a softer voice more times than not. Although she refused to get down on the mat to play with Miguel in the beginning of treatment, saying, "I don't play with him," by the end of treatment she was sitting on the mat with Miguel and clinician and narrating his play. It was still hard for her to fully participate in his play but given all, it was good enough. Miguel was referred for a speech evaluation before we started working with him, but Lucretia didn't think it was necessary. We continued to feel he would benefit from speech even though his vocalizations were improving. A second referral was made, and Lucretia was willing to consider this.

Summary and Recommendations for Policy Changes

Postnatal depression affects more than just the mother. We saw Lucretia's depression negatively affecting her infant's development and home environment. Given how she responded to the therapy, we did see her depression as protecting her from overwhelming feelings of loss of her own self-goals. Coupled with childhood trauma that appeared to result in a dismissive attachment organization, it became easier to know how (and how not) to connect with her. It was also clear that the wrap-around services helped.

Policy changes are needed to reduce the detriments associated with PDD. It is recommended that greater services be provided throughout the entire perinatal period to optimize health and development. Ongoing assessment for depression and anxiety during pregnancy is greatly needed with interventions provided in pregnancy, especially in the last trimester. A four-week basic course on the neurobiology of attachment that provides information about how bonding begins in the last trimester is recommended during the last two weeks of the second trimester and the first two weeks of the third. Any pregnant woman coding for depression and/or anxiety during pregnancy should be offered intervention services and with her partner if warranted.

Because women literally "carry the race," a deeper understanding of a woman's emotional life and lived experience prior to pregnancy is needed, especially when prior to pregnancy depression can increase the likelihood of depression in the perinatal period (Robertson et al., 2004). In my opinion, all mental health clinicians providing services to pregnant women and/or postpartum mothers and their infants need to have advanced training in the neurobiology of attachment organizations and how to relationally interact on both affective and narrative levels. This requires knowledge of typical infant development to assess the impact of the mother's depression on the infant. Increased financial resources for clinical training are needed.

We strongly recommend that any mother with PPD be provided with both individual and dyadic therapy. Since PPD can negatively impact infant development, systems with multiple coordinated levels for developmental support, such as speech and language, OT/PT, developmental groups, parenting classes, care coordination, etc., are needed as wrap-around services that can seamlessly work with clinical intervention. FHCSD has this level of care within systems that communicate relationally. The First 5/HDS/ FHCSD/NCAR MDP model should be considered the gold standard of care for treating mothers with PPD and their infants, and funding should be provided for its expansion.

At a societal level, relieving parents of financial stress by fully funding *The Family Leave and Medical Act of 1991* gives parents the time to care for their infants during the critical period of a mother's recovery and adjustment, parent–infant bonding, and infant brain development (Newton et al., 2015). Employers providing flextime during the postpartum period that allows parents to alternate work schedules around infant care is highly recommended. Since negative effects on infant development have been found when mothers work 30 hours a week or more during the first 9 months postpartum (Brooks-Gunn et al., 2002), an ideal configuration for infants and their parents is flexible parent employment supplemented with other invested family members and friends during the first postpartum year.

Much is known about PPD and its treatment. What is still missing is a fuller understanding of the emotional resources needed to parent a child. Many parents look forward to the birth of their child, yet still experience PPD. Other parents can have difficult feelings that are often not spoken about in deference to concepts of motherhood, family, and culture. Mental health clinicians focusing on maternal self-care while affectively communicating on both the nonverbal and verbal levels with both mother and infant can reduce PPD and improve infant attunement and synchrony, thereby changing the trajectory of PPD for both. The resulting resiliency can naturally increase mother's self-care and agency as well as improve her attachment with her infant. At her last session, Lucretia said, "I feel I have myself again, thanks." We walked high-stepping Miguel out with his mother who looked at him and smiled because he saw a similar Jack-in-the-Box he was playing with in session on the toy chest in the lobby. He pointed to it, smiled, and looked up at his mother who said, "Yes, that's like the one you played with." This is attunement and synchrony, and it makes all the difference in Miguel's development and security with his mother.

Interventions used during the postpartum period have often solely focused on the mother. Although mothers often do need their own individual therapy, we have found that treating both the mother, her bond with her infant, and her concerns found in her family system provide a more complete change and increase overall resiliency and biological health for all.

Notes

1. Lucretia and Miguel represent a composite case.
2. Family Health Centers San Diego (FHCSD) is a large, community-based non-profit organization dedicated to providing primary medical, reproductive, prenatal, pediatric, mental health, and other supportive care to largely low-income families in San Diego.

References

Brooks-Gunn, J., Han, W.-J., & Waldfogel, J. (2002). Maternal employment and child cognitive outcomes in the first three years of life: The NICHD study of early child care. *Child Development, 73*(4), 1052–1072.

Chiron, C., Jambaque, I., Nabbout, R., Lounes, R., Syrota, A., & Dulac, O. (1997). The right brain hemisphere is dominant in human infants. *Brain, 120*(6), 1057–1065.

Damasio, A. (2018). *The strange order of things: Life, feeling, and the making of cultures.* New York: Pantheon Books.

Edelman, G. M. (2004). *Wider than the sky: The phenomenal gift of consciousness.* New Haven, CT: Yale University Press.

Fraiberg, S. (1980). *Clinical studies in infant mental health.* New York: Basic Books.

Fraiberg, S., Adelson, E., & Shapiro, V. (1975). Ghosts in the nursery: A psychoanalytic approach to the problems of impaired infant-mother relationships. *Journal of the American Academy of Child Psychiatry, 14*(3), 387–421.

Gress-Smith, J. L., Luecken, L. J., Lemery-Chalfant, K., & Howe, R. (2012). Postpartum depression prevalence and impact on infant health, weight, and sleep in low-income and ethnic minority women and infants. *Maternal and Child Health Journal, 16*(4), 887–893.

Guintivano, J., Manuck, T., & Meltzer-Brody, S. (2018). Predictors of postpartum depression: A comprehensive review of the last decade of evidence. *Clinical Obstetrics and Gynecology, 61*(3), 591–603. https://doi.org/10-1097/GRF.0000000000000368

Hairston, I. S., Handelzalts, J. E., Assis, C., & Kovo, M. (2018). Postpartum bonding difficulties and adult attachment styles: The mediating role of postpartum depression and childbirth-related PTSD. *Infant Mental Health Journal, 39*(2), 198–208.

Herrera, E., Reissland, N., & Shepherd, J. (2004). Maternal touch and maternal child-directed speech: Effects of depressed mood in the postnatal period. *Journal of Affective Disorders, 81*(1), 29–39.

Kisilevsky, B. S., Hains, S. M. J., Lee, K., Xie, X., Huang, H., Hui, H., ... Wang, Z. (2003). Effects of experience on fetal voice recognition. *Psychological Science, 14*(3), 220–224.

Lanius, R. A., Vermetten, E., & Pain, C. (Eds.). (2010). *The impact of early life trauma on health and disease: The hidden epidemic.* Cambridge: Cambridge University Press.

Lieberman, A. F. (1992). Infant-parent psychotherapy with toddlers. *Development and Psychopathology, 4*(4), 559–574.

Lieberman, A. F., Silverman, R., & Pawl, J. H. (2000). Infant-parent psychotherapy: Core concepts and current approaches. In C. H. Zeanah, Jr. (Ed.), *Handbook of infant mental health* (2nd ed., pp. 472–484). New York: Guilford Press.

Main, M. (2000). The organized categories of infant, child, and adult attachment: Flexible vs. inflexible attention under attachment-related stress. *Journal of the American Psychoanalytic Association, 48*(4), 1055–1096.

Mento, G., Suppiej, A., Altoe, G., & Bisiacchi, P. S. (2010). Functional hemispheric asymmetries in humans: Electrophysiological evidence from preterm infants. *European Journal of Neuroscience, 31*(3), 565–574.

Newton, R. P. (2008). *The attachment connection: Parenting a secure & confident child using the science of attachment theory.* Oakland, CA: New Harbinger.

Newton, R. P. (2009 [2013]). Scaffolding the brain: A neurobiological approach to observation, assessment, and intervention. Integrative regulation therapy (iRT), Part A & B. Unpublished protocol. San Diego, CA: Center for Affect Regulation.

Newton, R. P. (2017). Scaffolding the brain: A neurobiological approach to observation, assessment, and intervention. Integrative regulation therapy (iRT), Part A & B [Kindle version]. *Retrievable.* Retrieved from https//amazon.com/Scaffolding -Brain-Neurobiology-Intervention

Newton, R. P. (2020). Scaffolding the brain: Infant parent psychotherapy during the primary biological entrainment period. *Journal of Infant, Child, and Adolescent Psychotherapy, 19*(1), 56–70. https://doi.org/10.1080/15289168.1717207

Newton, R. P. (2021). Scaffolding the brain: Key areas of evaluation in infant parent psychotherapy. *Journal of Infant, Child, and Adolescent Psychotherapy.* https://doi .org/10.1080/15289168.2021.1995690

Newton, R. P., Flowers, K., Hartwell, S., & Hervatin-Hergesheimer, C. (2015). *The NCAR work group on the neuroscience of attachment: The family leave Act. (2015).* San Diego, CA: Newton Center for Affect Regulation.

O'Hara, M. W., & McCabe, J. E. (2013). Postpartum depression: Current status and future directions. *Annual Review of Clinical Psychology, 9*, 379–407. https://doi.org /10.1146/annurev-clinpsy-050212-185612

Ozbay, F., Sharma, V., Kaufman, J., McEwen, B., Charney, D., & Southwick, S. (2010). Neurobiological factors underlying psychosocial moderators of childhood stress and trauma. In R. A. Lanius, E. Vermetten, & C. Pain (Eds.), *The impact of early life trauma on health and disease: The hidden epidemic* (pp. 189–199). Cambridge: Cambridge University Press.

Panksepp, J. (2012). Brain emotional systems and affective qualities of mental life. From animal affects to human psychotherapeutics. In D. Fosha, D. J. Siegel, & M. F. Solomon (Eds.), *The healing power of emotion: Affective neuroscience, development & clinical practice* (pp. 1–26). New York: W. W. Norton & Company.

Polmanteer, R. S. R., Keefe, R. H., & Brownstein-Evans, C. (2019). Trauma-informed care with women diagnosed with postpartum depression: A conceptual framework. *Social Work in Health Care, 58*(2), 220–235. https://doi.org/10.1080/00981389 .2018.1535464

Robertson, E., Grace, S., Wallington, T., & Steward, D. E. (2004). Antenatal risk factors for postpartum depression: A synthesis of recent literature. *General Hospital Psychiatry, 26*(4), 289–295.

Schore, A. N. (1994). Affect regulation and the origin of the self: The neurobiology of emotional development. Mahweh, NJ: Erlbaum.

Sohr-Preston, S. L., & Scaramella, L. V. (2006). Implications of timing of maternal depressive symptoms for early cognitive and language development. *Clinical Child and Family Psychology Review, 9*(1), 65–83.

Sroufe, L. A., Egeland, B., Carlson, E. A., & Collins, W. A. (2005). *The development of the person: The Minnesota study of risk and adaptation from birth to adulthood.* New York: Guilford.

Substance Abuse and Mental Health Services Administration (SAMHSA). (2014). *Trauma-informed care in behavioral health services.* Rockville, MD: SAMHSA.

Wonjung, O., Muzik, M., McGinnis, E. W., Hamilton, L., Menke, R. A., & Rosenblum, K. L. (2016). Comorbid trajectories of postpartum depression and PTSD among mothers with childhood trauma history: Course, predictors, processes and child adjustment. *Journal of Affective Disorders, 200*, 133–141. https://doi.org/10-1016/j .jad.2016.04.037

Chapter 2

A Biological Imperative to Thrive

Supporting Military Families with Young Children

Kim A. Flowers, Donna K. Hilt, and Audrey Hokoda

> *If we are to teach real peace in this world, and if we are to carry on a real war against war, we shall have to begin with the children.*
>
> *—Mahatma Gandhi*

Across the world, the American flag evokes diverse feelings, yet for many who serve in our United States military, it often kindles a heartfelt response of pride. This pride is born of a belief in the military values of selflessness, integrity, loyalty, excellence, and resiliency. To enter service is to enter a culture of community that offers something akin to the bonds that exist within families—connection and commitment. Being a part of something larger than oneself, set within the context of "family" and with access to the promise of adventure and military benefits, is appealing. Serving one's country while rearing young children, however, can be complicated. Each year, more than 90,000 infants are born into military families (Davis et al., 2012), as most female service members and spouses are under 30, a primary childbearing age. Of active duty families with children, the largest percentage (41%) have little ones, aged birth to five years (Profile of the Military, 2019). Like their

DOI: 10.4324/9781003046295-4

parents, these babies and young children experience both the benefits and the sacrifices inherent in military service; however, they do so during what we understand to be some of the most formative developmental stages in life.

How do early childhood mental health and allied professionals help military parents promote and protect their young children's well-being? This chapter will focus on strategies to support infants, toddlers, and preschoolers whose parent(s) are serving in the Armed Forces of the United States of America. We will highlight key aspects of military culture and the diversity found within, while paying special attention to the experience of pregnancy, maternal mental health, and the effects of deployment. We focus on ways to further the mental health and overall well-being of infants, young children, and their parents, guided by research on attachment, child development, and trauma-informed care. We explore best practices of primary, secondary, and tertiary levels of prevention and intervention within a socio-ecological model, and offer policy recommendations. Ultimately, our goal is to help both providers and policy makers alike with enhancing military infant, child, and family development, working with and supporting innate biological tendencies toward optimal life.

Understanding and Supporting America's Military Families

The media images are compelling: Young sailors, marines, and soldiers returning from overseas deployments, met by happy, tearful family members, many of them very young children and even infants, who are meeting their parents for the very first time. Mothers in combat fatigues reuniting with their children remind us of the realities of 21st-century warfare. In sharing these moments, we bear witness to the patriotism, strength, and resiliency of parents and children amid the extraordinary demands of military family life.

Unique to the military are recurrent deployments, requiring service members to be repeatedly gone for months at a time. Since September 11, 2001 (9/11), military families have experienced more frequent and longer deployments, challenging families' preparedness and resiliency (Agazio et al., 2014). When the United States is at war, mission readiness oftentimes demands a higher (24/7) work tempo over months of training and preparation. Each service member and their family belongs to a command (e.g., ship, squadron, unit) and are impacted by the orders and dictates of that command. Land and sea forces must be ready and able to deploy within 24 hours. As deployment draws near, military couples experience the stress of impending separation; couples may drift apart and argue more as they prepare for the inevitable pain of separation. Existing marital discord may be amplified, creating an emotionally charged environment that affects the whole family (Agazio et al., 2014).

Pregnancy, childbirth, and childrearing are unique periods in life where it has long been understood that the "village" is needed to support a woman's mental health and well-being. Whether an active duty servicewoman or dependent spouse, supports and stressors unique to the military experience may provide a protective buffer and also engender risk for perinatal depression (PND) and postpartum depression (PPD). Active duty women, especially those with low self-esteem, marital satisfaction, and social support, are at increased risk for PPD, with rates as high as 19.5% (Braun et al., 2016). Expectant women coping with the absence of their deployed-to-combat partners and active duty women who experience deployment are both at higher risk for PND (Klaman & Turner, 2016). PND can impact fetal development and result in low birth weight and preterm delivery (Jarde et al., 2016). Infants and toddlers of depressed mothers may be irritable and difficult to soothe, and their development may be impacted as PPD increases risk for attachment difficulties, less developmentally supportive parent–child interactions, and mothers' use of corporal punishment (Slomian et al., 2019).

New duty station assignments require families to relocate, sometimes as frequently as every two to three years. For young children, this means repeatedly adjusting to new homes, childcare providers, and friends. The loss of expected routines and familiar environments can be frightening for infants and toddlers who do not understand what is happening. For the young military child, normal developmental fears in the early years—harm to their body, separation anxiety, and the loss of love and approval of a parent—are magnified by events that interfere with their parents' physical and emotional availability (Lieberman & Van Horn, 2013). For parents maintaining the home front, sleep disorders, depression, anxiety, social isolation, fear that their spouse will be injured or killed, and the overwhelming experience of parenting alone may result in limited emotional and physical resources to respond appropriately and consistently to their young child (Lieberman & Van Horn, 2013). This can be detrimental, especially if it happens during the early years when infants and young children are forming secure attachment relationships, expressing and learning to manage positive and negative emotions, and exploring the environment to learn—all within the context of culture and community. This is the essence of what "infant mental health" is (Cohen et al., 2005).

Infant Mental Health: Theoretical Underpinnings

Through John Bowlby's early groundbreaking work (e.g., Bowlby, 1982) and others' work (e.g., Cassidy et al., 2013) on attachment, we understand that positive relationships are necessary for healthy human development. The early years are critical for young children, given the plasticity of early brain development and neurological processes that support secure attachments with caregivers and infant and toddler mental health (Osofsky & Chartrand, 2013). The quality of a child's first attachment relationships determines, in large part, how a child's brain develops during the first three years of life, how they feel about themselves and others (their internal working model [IWM]), and how well they will be able to regulate emotions and behavioral impulses. In turn, this development in social-emotional capacities shapes the brain and determines how much of the brain is available for learning and how well it will function (Newton, 2008).

Early pioneering work by Selma Fraiberg (Fraiberg et al., 1975) in the field of infant mental health illuminated the need for attention to the relationships between babies and their primary attachment figures. In *Ghosts in the Nursery*, Fraiberg helped providers understand that parents' own experiences of having been cared for in ways less than hoped for serves as a negative, implicit model for how to be with their own babies. The legacy of harsh, critical, or even abusive caregiving from previous generations could be observed in the current parent–child relationship, especially activated when under stress. Alicia Lieberman, in her seminal work, *Angels in the Nursery*, paved the way for understanding that the opposite could be true, as well (Lieberman et al., 2005). Nurturing and attuned caregiving serves as one of the most powerful of protective factors and involves mentalization or "mind-mindedness," the ability of a caregiver to see and think about the internal states of the child's body and mind (e.g., feelings, thoughts) (Fonagy et al., 2002). Being aware of one's own and one's child's physical and mental states and the interrelationship between the two is essential to forming a secure attachment (Slade, 2002).

When babies are born in optimal circumstances, parents are free from undue stress and available to engage in mind-mindedness. The ability to mentalize and be emotionally available, however, may be impacted by a caregiver's experience with trauma and depression (Stob et al., 2020). Stress that is prolonged, severe, or unpredictable (e.g., caregiver's depression, neglect, family violence) can impair the physical structure of the young child's brain and, ultimately, impact their regulatory system (Schore, 2001), sensitizing the neural pathways involved in anxiety and fear responses, literally over-developing the regions of the brain involved in these functions (Perry & Pollard, 1998). Meanwhile, other key areas of the brain responsible for complex thought (e.g., prefrontal cortex) may be underdeveloped (Schore, 2001). This combination of sensitization and underdevelopment can lead to young traumatized children having difficulties paying attention, regulating their emotions, and forming relationships. They may have difficulty with learning and memory, which can lead to diagnoses of learning disabilities. In addition, traumatized children may have behavioral and socio-emotional difficulties that place them at higher risk for expulsion from preschool (Meek & Gilliam, 2016; Perry, 1996).

Building Resilience in Military Children and Families

If we value our children, we must cherish their parents.

—*John Bowlby*

No parent, military or civilian, wishes adversity for their young child. Neither can they inoculate their little one from disappointment or stress. Families and other caregivers can serve to help develop and build resilience, a quality deeply valued by the military community, so that military children can handle the bumps and bruises that life brings. In the most simplistic sense, resiliency is one's ability to overcome adversity with better than expected outcomes. Resiliency theorists and child development experts note that the single most critical factor in whether a child develops resiliency or not is whether they have formed a stable, supportive, and committed relationship with a caring adult who is available and responsive to their needs. In doing so, the entrained stress-response system develops most positively. The child is then biologically hardwired for greater success when dealing with life's typical upsets, as well as traumatic experiences.

Ecological perspectives (e.g., Bronfenbrenner, 2005) remind us of the many influences within the community that can either support or undermine military families with young children. For example, growing up in a military family during a time of war may have a profound impact on the intricacy of development. What additional impact would there be if family-of-origin support floundered due to anti-war sentiment? Or if the community at large was protesting the war and those serving in it? What if one's parents were also experiencing severe mental illness? To build resilience in young military children, we must support their parents' mental health and their family's access to adequate resources such as parental employment, neighborhood safety, and affordable, high-quality childcare. These are examples of powerful eco-systemic contributors to resiliency.

All professionals, from policy makers to educators, physicians, and mental health specialists, can help build resilience in young children and strengthen their families by promoting protective factors (Center for the Study of Social Policy-CSSP, n.d.). CSSP's research-informed framework recommends building: (1) parental resilience, (2) social connections, (3) knowledge of parenting and child development, (4) concrete support in times of need, and (5) social and emotional competence of children. Professionals serving military families can implement trauma-informed approaches by recognizing the importance of building trust and providing safety and support (Substance Abuse and Mental Health Services Administration-SAMHSA, 2014). Trauma-informed professionals, mindful of the effects of trauma, work toward preventing re-traumatization. They focus on collaboration, providing parents with information and empowering choices to support them as they raise their young children.

Prevention and Intervention Services

Following recommendations by the National Child Traumatic Stress Network (NCTSN), organizations should implement services that are guided by trauma and attachment research and focus on strengthening protective factors, while responding to the unique needs of a diverse military community. Early childhood programs and services typically fall within one of three categories along a continuum of best practices: Primary prevention, secondary prevention, and tertiary intervention/treatment. Public primary prevention services are easily accessible and universally offered. Secondary prevention programs offer on-line education and support services to individuals and families at-risk such as Babies on the Homefront and Zero to Three. Secondary strategies can also include psycho-educational parent groups, dyadic playgroups, and home visitation/family support programs, such as the Department of Defense (DoD)-funded New Parent Support Program (NPSP). Typically serving at-risk families with children prenatal to age three or five years, home visitors strive to enhance attachment, educate parents about child development, and promote positive parenting practices. They offer anticipatory guidance and emotional support, provide developmental and mental health screenings, and link families to needed military and civilian resources before more serious issues develop. They also link military families to tertiary intervention services such as mental health treatment provided by licensed infant-family and early childhood mental health (IF-ECMH) professionals (Goodson et al., 2013).

Several evidence-based tertiary interventions (e.g., Families OverComing Under Stress—FOCUS; Parent Child Interaction Therapy—PCIT) have been adapted for military families (e.g., Beardslee et al., 2011; Lester, Klosinski, et al., 2016; Pemberton et al., 2013). With these therapies, trained clinicians help families heal from trauma and attachment disruptions (e.g., deployment, combat-related injuries, death) and build family resilience. An evaluation of FOCUS with military families shows reductions in parental depression and trauma symptoms, as well as anxiety in children (Lester, Liang, et al., 2016).

Family Support Programs: Home Visitation

Tracy, an infant-family and early childhood-trained home visitor, planned for her first visit to Juanita and Parker's home. The parents had a five-month-old baby, Joseph, and a four-year-old daughter, Maya. The family had recently moved to San Diego, after several relocations in the past four years. Parker had deployed a week ago, leaving Juanita alone as she raised a newborn and young child who was grieving the absence of her daddy while adjusting to a new sibling. Upon Tracy's arrival, Maya was screaming at her mother and Joseph was frantically crying. In tears, Juanita opened the door and apologized for their behavior, stating she was terrified the neighbors might report her to Navy housing.

Tracy partnered with Juanita to complete the first of several assessments and developmental screenings with Joseph, who spent a lot of time alone in his crib and playpen and had not yet tried to roll over. Initially, Juanita watched and cleaned during floor time with Joseph, as Tracy gave her guidance to support his development. At every visit, Tracy encouraged Juanita to sit on the floor and play with Joseph, emphasizing how he was looking and smiling at her. Over time, Juanita began sharing her personal struggles and insecurities about being a bad parent when her children "misbehaved." After months of working together, Juanita's confidence in her parenting choices grew and the children thrived. Eventually, she and Joseph came to the community playgroup where she met other parents with young children and made friends. Home visits continued until Joseph was almost three, but on that first day long ago, Juanita's decision to play with Joseph would be enough.

Knowledgeable about the unique challenges faced by young military families, Tracy followed recommended trauma-informed practices (NCTSN) as she focused on building trust, educating and modeling ways to support early childhood development, and promoting warm, attentive parenting. Tracy introduced dyadic play activities at almost every home visit. Indeed, Bowlby (1982) described how play or mutually enjoyable interactions within warm, responsive caregiver–infant relationships is critical to attachment. The gentle reciprocity of parent–child play during infancy and early childhood offers parents and children the chance to be fully attuned with each other and in the moment (Newton, 2008). Play also fosters children's development; it is through play that children naturally explore their environment (Ginsburg, 2007). Encouraging Juanita to notice and reciprocate Joseph's smiles and interactions with her promotes mind-mindedness and nurturing, sensitive caregiving. As Juanita engaged with Joseph in play, his motor, cognitive, and social-emotional skills improved and her confidence in her parenting grew.

Juanita agreed to join a culturally diverse, parent–child playgroup, where she saw other military parents struggling with their children's behaviors too. Together, parents learned play-based activities for supporting their children during deployment. Juanita also engaged in bibliotherapy, a helpful strategy that uses books such as *"Home Again"* to help caregivers support their children with the challenges experienced in military life. Eager to share her Mexican culture, she delighted in reading bilingual English/Spanish language books to Maya and Joseph, promoting their cultural identity and literacy skills.

As Joseph blossomed, Juanita and Tracy focused on Maya, who was acting out at home and in preschool. Research has shown that children experiencing a parental deployment may display regulatory issues through temper tantrums, defiance, clinginess, appetite changes, and sleep problems (Alfano et al., 2016). Juanita learned to recognize the meaning of Maya's acting out behaviors and use playful, interactive strategies that helped Maya develop self-regulation skills. Maya's behavior at home improved, but her defiance and tantrums put her at risk for preschool expulsion. Tracy referred the family to Children's Hospital, Developmental and Behavioral Health Services, for further assessment and dyadic treatment. With a newfound understanding of parenting, Juanita's distorted belief that she was a bad parent was successfully challenged. Increased knowledge about child development helped to strengthen her parenting confidence and improve her self-esteem. Juanita could then parent with more compassion. Family support services including home visitation, play groups, and referrals to early intervention were essential in helping Juanita and her children thrive.

Infant-Family and Early Childhood Mental Health Treatment

> Arthur listened as Jill shared how anxious she felt about Brandon's upcoming seven-month deployment. Marital conflict had escalated with his imminent departure. She worried about his safety and how the deployment would affect Marquis, their toddler. Marquis was evidencing signs of a speech and language delay, and some regulatory difficulties. He was tantruming for long periods of time, to include banging his head on the floor, and was primarily using gestures to communicate, with fewer words than would be expected for a 30-month-old. Family support was limited and complex, with Jill's depressed and abusive mother committing suicide when she was a teenager. Having given birth recently to newborn Bryson, Jill and her children carried the imprint of her childhood. She was struggling with PPD and anxiety to include intrusive thoughts of harming her children. She would not seek a psychiatric evaluation for medication but had been relying heavily on her husband's support—and now, her IF-ECMH therapist, Arthur.

A strong therapeutic alliance is fundamental to providing developmentally informed assessment and treatment. The quality of attachment relationships, along with Marquis's physical, cognitive, social, and emotional functioning needed to be understood. Developmental and family history, clinical observation, and direct evaluation were important components of the assessment process. An understanding of the family's larger ecosystem was a must, too. What stressors existed and what resources were available? What was the family's separation history? Was Brandon present and engaged in his children's births? Had there been a previous war-related physical or psychological injury? While assessment is ongoing, a comprehensive assessment helped formulate an initial treatment plan.

Military parents with unresolved histories of trauma may need adult mental health services prior to or in conjunction with IF-ECMH services. Jill, struggling with PPD and anxiety, had difficulty providing the responsive care that her young toddler and newborn needed. Referred because of risk to herself and her children, she started therapy to address her mental health. Skills-based psycho-education rooted in Cognitive Behavioral Therapy (CBT) helped her understand and manage her intrusive thoughts, improve her mood, and decrease her anxiety. When ready, Jill accepted a referral to a clinician specializing in treating trauma using Eye Movement Desensitization Reprocessing (EMDR) (Shapiro & Solomon, 2010).

In therapy, the couple learned about the emotional cycle of deployment, which helped frame their increasing marital distress. They gained insight into their children's needs and learned strategies to stay connected. Tracing Brandon's hand so that Marquis could pretend to "high five" him was a favorite. Arthur linked Brandon to a program for military families (United Through Reading, n.d.) and he recorded stories for his children to listen to when he deployed. Jill learned to use photos as transitional objects. She helped Marquis wear his dad's T-shirt, which held his smell, and use a cuddly blanket with family pictures imprinted from "Operation Kid Comfort" (Armed Services YMCA—ASYMCA, n.d.). Improved mentalization led to enhanced support and furthered healthy IWMs. Brandon deployed at greater ease with support in place for his family.

Following developmental screening, Arthur referred Marquis to the Regional Center for further assessment. Speech therapy was conveniently delivered in-home. Marquis began therapeutic childcare where he was immersed in a language-rich, nurturing environment that promoted emotional regulation. Jill gained respite and joined a military family playgroup which reduced isolation and helped repair her IWMs about relationships. Jill had "ghosts in her nursery," so to speak, and as she steadily gained support and insight, she interrupted the intergenerational transmission of insecure attachment and built family resiliency.

Play therapy promotes development and enables young children to work through their conflicts and master their fears, such as with the birth of a new sibling or the deployment of a parent. It can focus specifically on the child's development or functioning, or on improving relationships. Jill and Marquis's play sessions focused on strengthening attachment, promoting Marquis's communication skills, and facilitating the expression of feelings about his new sibling and father's deployment. Jill learned strategies to respond to Marquis's tantrums and help him with emotional regulation, and to read Bryson's cues and respond with attunement.

Whether providing treatment to facilitate the repair and integration of trauma, intervening to help engender secure attachment, or promoting child and family well-being from a prevention framework, providers are impacted by the emotional content and complexities of early childhood work and benefit from support. They need opportunities to step back from the work to think about all of the developing relationships, and the emotions and reactions that might be activated. Providers can feel stressed and overwhelmed themselves, which can lead to burnout or vicarious trauma (Perry, 2003). One important source of support comes in the form of reflective supervision.

Reflective Supervision to Support Providers

> *"What right does the Command have to send a marine to 'supervise' our home visit, to report details of progress back to him? Typical employers aren't involved in an employee's life like this, controlling every aspect!" Jayla found herself grateful to finally have time with her supervisor, needing to process the intense feelings, indeed, the protective urges that were aroused with this new development as she worked with a service member who admitted to having shaken one of her twin babies. Gratefully, the baby had not been physically injured, but now the young marine's life was being both monitored and controlled at a high level— and her own activation was causing her to think less clearly. As Jayla shared her feelings, she found herself calming down. Her supervisor helped her explore how, in a parallel way, she too had felt vulnerable while being "supervised" during a session. Who else in this story of relationships might be feeling vulnerable? What might each baby's experience be? And their young mother's? In reflective supervision, she found herself understanding the concern and sense of responsibility the Command might be feeling, too. Her ability to think more objectively and inclusively was reinstated. What did she think the Command knew or understood about therapy? With this question, she wondered if it might be helpful to explain how treatment worked and how the marine's "supervising" presence could negatively impact the process.*

The work of early childhood providers is complex. Psychoanalyst Donald Winicott's famous statement, "A baby cannot exist alone" (Lehmann, 2015) implies that each one of us was once just that, a baby, for better or worse cared for and completely dependent upon an adult. Our own IWMs about who we are and how relationships work are strongly colored by this early caregiving experience—and readily present as we work to skillfully support parents and their children. This, in addition to the presence of trauma, and the intricate nature of dyadic, family, and systems work, begs us to forgo the notion that providers can simply churn out services without an opportunity to pause and reflect on the powerful and sometimes subtle undercurrents of the social-emotional and

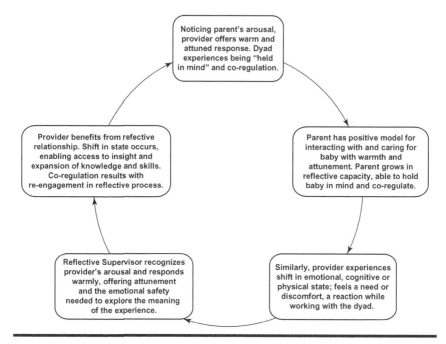

Figure 2.1   Parallel Process of Reflective Supervision.

implicit embodied realm. Reflective supervision is a distinct form of supervision, not to be confused with administrative or clinical supervision, with an emphasis on co-regulation, increased self- and other-awareness, and the shared exploration of diverse perspectives and relationships (Flowers & Burgeson, 2015). All emerging relationships are attended to between baby or young child, parent, provider, and supervisor with an understanding of the importance of the parallel process between them (see Figure 2.1). In this relational context, providers seek to understand the cultural beliefs, values, practices, and histories that are in operation, including their own. "Reflection-on-action" involves thinking through past experiences and emotional content in preparation for subsequent experiences; "reflection-in-action" makes use of this newfound understanding to analyze and modify one's response real-time, to think and respond more effectively in the moment (Schon, 1983).

Reflective supervision offers many benefits to organizations and the individuals they employ. These include the integration of emotion and reason; reduction of burnout, secondary, or vicarious trauma; and the promotion of professional development and a reflective organizational culture. Early childhood professionals concur, reporting decreases in work-related stress, and increases in self-efficacy for managing their emotions and reflecting on how their emotional responses influence their work with young children and families (Frosch et al., 2018).

Reflective supervision must be prioritized as it enables access to deep reflection, which promotes the wisdom necessary to skillfully work with complex and often unconscious material. It is part of a larger body of recommended actions necessary to support military families with young children and the providers who serve them.

Recommendations: United in Service for Military Families with Young Children

There can be no keener revelation of a society's soul than the way in which it treats its children.

—Nelson Mandela

Many active duty personnel simultaneously serve our country and raise young children, and it is imperative that as a society we support them and promote their families' well-being. Military families make many sacrifices and face unique stressors such as deployment, reunion, and frequent relocation. For a young child, the physical and emotional absence of a parent across the milestones and developmental stages of their life is a significant sacrifice (Lester et al., 2010). This chapter described military culture, relevant early childhood theory and research, and evidence-based, trauma-informed strategies that professionals can use to help military families with their young children. With adequate, flexible, and stable funding to invigorate and sustain primary and secondary prevention programs and tertiary interventions specific to IF-ECMH, we can, as a society, better support military families with young children and the providers who serve them.

Six key policy and practice recommendations are:

1. **Destigmatize services and promote participation in prevention programs where attention is given to critical periods when military families may need more support and linkages to tertiary services.**

In a culture where strength is much celebrated, help-seeking is laden with stigma. Approximately 60% of service members who would benefit from mental health treatment do not receive it due to stigma (Sharp et al., 2015). Therefore, active promotion of help-seeking attitudes within military personnel is a must. Benefits of home visitation programs, adapted for military families with young children, include decreased parental stress, depression, and anxiety (see Adelstein et al., 2019; DeVoe et al., 2017). Home visitors deliver trauma-informed services aligned with critical periods in military families' lives (e.g., deployment and reintegration) and in the comfort of families' homes, eliminating typical barriers to access (e.g., lack of transportation or childcare). They link families to needed resources (e.g., family playgroups, breastfeeding support) as well as tertiary-level services provided by licensed mental health professionals. Positive outcomes associated with regularly scheduled visits include early screening, identification, and treatment of maternal depression and child developmental delays; increased rates of breastfeeding and maternal education, enhanced social support, reduced rates in child maltreatment, and healthier parent–child interactions. Policy decisions and funding should also be directed toward critical times and events such as pregnancy, childbirth, and postpartum. DoD policies, for example, that allow for lengthy deferred deployments after the birth of a baby support parental mental health and attachment.

2. **Ensure a robust, well-trained, multidisciplinary workforce that demonstrates knowledge, experience, competence, and collaboration in working with infants, young children, and their military families.**

Providers from diverse fields such as politics, education, non-profit organizations, and health and childcare should be educated about military culture and family life, and the impact of deployment on all family members. Furthermore, civilian and military providers alike should receive specialized training in early identification of attachment difficulties in young children, and other stressors and traumas associated with the military (e.g., maternal depression, single parenting, social isolation). With approximately 70% of military families living off-base in civilian communities (Ross et al., 2015), teachers working in preschools, for example, should be trained on the effects of trauma and deployment on young children (e.g., temper tantrums, aggression, withdrawal) (Alfano et al., 2016) that put them at risk for expulsion from preschool or problems with mental health that continue into adulthood. Particularly in areas with a large military population (e.g., San Diego), collaboration between military and civilian providers has enabled increased access to multidisciplinary services, such as childcare and developmental services (e.g., speech, occupational, and physical therapies). Providers should be familiar with each other's services, capabilities, and limitations.

3. **Increase recognition of and support for all military parents and parents-to-be, including active duty fathers, and others regardless of race, ethnicity, religion, gender, gender identity, sexual orientation, nationality, or special needs.**

Under the DoD's broad umbrella of diversity and inclusion in the 21st century are America's military families. America's military reflects the ethnic, racial, cultural, and gender diversity of its people. DoD statistics report that 68.8% of active duty personnel identified as white and 31.3% identified as racial and ethnic minorities (Profile of the Military, 2019). This diversity includes families with unique identities, lifestyles, and needs. The DoD sponsors the Exceptional Family Member Program (EFMP), which supports military family members who have educational, medical, and mental health needs. Military parents can access civilian organizations that support foreign military spouses (Foreign Military Spouse Association), as well as advocate for lesbian, gay, bisexual, transgender, and queer (LGBTQ) families (American Military Partner Association). Services are also needed to address the confusion and sense of alienation many active duty fathers experience with their young children after deployment (Walsh et al., 2014). Continued policy development to ensure the well-being of all active duty members' families is understood by the DoD as a critical component of force readiness (DoD Board on Diversity and Inclusion, 2020).

4. **Collect and evaluate military family-specific data to address any gaps or challenges and ensure evidence-based practices specific to services provided to infants, young children, and their military families.**

Determining military families' utilization patterns and assessing whether additional services are needed and/or barriers to access removed is an important first step for enhancing resiliency and well-being in young children and their parents. For example, particular attention should be paid to identifying needs and understanding whether adequate services to meet these needs are available at military installations in rural areas or for those stationed overseas. Armed with a clear understanding of the data, innovative solutions can be developed or additional resources may be assigned to improve access to necessary services. IF-ECMH researchers and providers must also work together to research the use of evidence-based practices (EBPs) to ensure their efficacy with military families. Modifications to the delivery of services to meet the needs of families embedded within the military system and culture, as well as the larger ecosystem, must be soundly rooted in evidence. Providers must know how to select and implement EBPs, to include these military-specific modifications. Databases and clearinghouses (e.g., California Evidence-Based Clearinghouse for Child Welfare, n.d.) that detail EBPs should include military-specific data as young military children and their families deserve nothing less than rigor in the scientific evidence to support them.

5. **Engage and convene military and civilian stakeholders to identify areas of shared mission alignment and build successful strategic partnerships across exosystems.**

Ideally, military and civilian community leaders will increasingly partner, leveraging resources for effective wrap-around services that provide medical, psychological, educational, social, and practical support to military families.

Aligning in areas of common purpose and pooling tangible resources, such as funding, and intangible resources, such as the exchange of prenatal, infant, and early childhood knowledge, will result in improved services. To effectively do so, stakeholders must invest in understanding larger exosystemic impacts on military families. The Maternal and Infant Support Team (MIST) at Naval Hospital Camp Pendleton provides a unique example of civilian and military collaboration to influence positive outcomes (Weis & Elmore, 2017). When NHCP implemented postnatal depression screening with new mothers, MIST members—NPSP, ASYMCA, and Marine Corps Community Services Child Development Centers—partnered to develop and implement the "Moms in Transition" support group with concurrent childcare for symptomatic mothers. Leveraging resources helped meet an identified need, surely bolstering family readiness at a time of major transition in young military families. The San Diego Military Family Collaborative offers a community-based model including representatives from over 50 diverse military and civilian organizations. They share a common mission to support and strengthen "the military-connected community through education, advocacy, and engagement" (San Diego Military Family Collaborative, n.d.). Their Military Transition Spouse Edition Action Team, for example, specifically supports military families transitioning to civilian life, a critical period in the lifecycle of the military family made easier through strategic partnerships.

6. **Implement regular and ongoing reflective supervision in programs as a highly valued form of trauma-informed care and provider self-care given the critical and complex nature of the work.**

Reflective supervision is critical for exploring and understanding emerging relationships: Supervisor with provider, provider with parent, and parent with baby or young child. Meeting regularly over time with a trusted reflective partner is key to IF-ECMH providers' effectiveness in their roles. Working with traumatized military families is difficult emotional work and can trigger vicarious traumatic reactions. The provision of emotional and physical safety, non-judgment, collaboration, and empowerment—the critical and foundational practices of reflective supervision—also aligns with strategies for preventing and addressing workplace stress. In addition to reflective supervision, trauma-informed organizations should offer extensive workforce development on concepts such as burnout, compassion fatigue, and vicarious trauma—and incorporate policies that promote safety and respect for families and the providers who partner with them. Assessing, monitoring, and improving trauma-informed self-care practices of providers is a strategy that can be used to help ensure this (Salloum et al., 2019), one that is part of mainstream practice in reflective supervision. Organizations should have the training, resources, and commitment to support it, this space to slow down, step back from, and reflect upon experience. Reflective supervision promotes provider well-being and enhances skill, key factors in the delivery of high-quality services.

Conclusion

In conclusion, infants and young children are biologically hardwired to form relationships with their caregivers. Attachment relationships serve to promote children's survival and the survival of our species, but this is not the sole reason relationships are critically important. Secure relationships, specifically, serve as a protective factor for children. Developmental science helps us to understand that military families with infants and young children will thrive with the right kinds of and enough support to promote early developing relationships. Human biology is primed and wont to thrive in the best of conditions. Bronfenbrenner's ecosystemic theory (Bronfenbenner, 2005) reminds us of the important impact and work of "the village." Preventing and addressing family separations, reducing stress, promoting whole family well-being, engaging robust social support systems, and treating the effects of trauma, to include mental health disorders, is crucial to this. When military children and their families flourish, world peace, as envisioned by the renowned activist Mahatma Gandhi, will be one step closer for us all.

References

Adelstein, S., Longo, F., & Shakesprere, J. (2019, March). *Home visiting for military families: An overview of innovative programs.* National Home Visiting Resource Center Innovation Roundup Brief. Arlington, VA: James Bell Associates and Urban Institute.

Agazio, J., Goodman, P., & Padden, D. L. (2014). Impact of deployment on military families. In P. W. Kelley (Ed.), *Annual review of nursing research, 32: Military and veteran innovations of care* (Vol. 32, pp. 109–133). New York: Springer Publishing Company.

Alfano, C. A., Lau, S., Balderas, J., Bunnell, B. E., & Beidel, D. C. (2016). The impact of military deployment on children: Placing developmental risk in context. *Clinical Psychology Review, 43*, 17–29. Retrieved from https://doi-org.libproxy.sdsu.edu/10.1016/j.cpr.2015.11.003

Armed Services YMCA. (n.d.). *Operation kid comfort.* Retrieved from https://www.asymca.org/operation-kid-comfort

Beardslee, M. D., Lester, P., Klosinski, L., Saltzman, W., Woodward, K., Nash, W., … Leskin, G. (2011). Family-centered preventive intervention for military families: Implications for implementation science. *Prevention Science, 12*(4), 339–348.

Bowlby, J. (1982). *Attachment and loss: Vol. 1. Attachment* (2nd ed.). New York: Basic Books.

Braun, L. A., Kennedy, H. P., Womack, J. A., & Wilson, C. (2016). Integrative literature review: U.S. Military women's genitourinary and reproductive health. *Military Medicine, 181*(1), 35–49. https://doi.org/10.7205/MILMED-D-15-00242

Bronfenbrenner, U. (2005). *Making human beings human: Bioecological perspectives on human development.* Thousand Oaks, CA: Sage Publications.

CA Evidence-Based Clearinghouse Child Welfare. https://www.cebc4cw.org/

Cassidy, J., Jones, J. D., & Shaver, P. R. (2013). Contributions of attachment theory and research: A framework for future research, translation, and policy. *Development and Psychopathology, 25*(4, Pt 2), 1415–1434. https://doi.org/10.1017/S0954579413000692

Center for the Study of Social Policy. (n.d.). *Strengthening families.* Retrieved from https://cssp.org/our-work/project/strengthening-families/

Cohen, J., Onunaku, N., Clothier, S., & Poppe, J. (2005). *Helping young children succeed: Strategies to promote early childhood social and emotional development.* Washington, DC: National Conference of State Legislatures.

Davis, B. E., Blaschke, G. S., & Stafford, E. M. (2012). Military children, families and communities: Supporting those who serve. *Pediatrics, 129*(Suppl. 1), Issue Supplement 1. https://doi.org/10.1542/peds.2010-3797c

DeVoe, E. R., Paris, R., Emmert-Aronson, B., Ross, A., & Acker, M. (2017). A randomized clinical trial of a postdeployment parenting intervention for service members and their families with very young children. *Psychological Trauma: Theory, Research, Practice, and Policy, 9*(Suppl. 1), 25–34. Retrieved from https://doi-org.libproxy.sdsu.edu/10.1037/tra0000196

DoD. (2020). Department of defense board on diversity and inclusion report: Recommendations to improve racial and ethnic diversity and inclusion in the military. Washington, D.C.

Flowers, K., & Burgeson, M. (2015). *Reflective supervision: A resource for those supporting infants, toddlers, preschoolers and their families with early childhood mental health.* San Diego, CA: Members of the Early Childhood Mental Health Leadership Collaborative.

Fonagy, P., Gergely, G., Jurist, E. L., & Target, M. (2002). *Affect regulation, mentalization, and the development of the self.* New York: Other Press.

Fraiberg, S., Adelson, E., & Shapiro, V. (1975). Ghosts in the nursery. A psychoanalytic approach to the problems of impaired infant-mother relationships. *Journal of the American Academy of Child and Adolescent Psychiatry, 14*(3), 387–421.

Frosch, C. A., Varwani, Z., Mitchell, J., Caraccioli, C., & Willoughby, M. (2018). Impact of reflective supervision on early childhood interventionists' perceptions of self-efficacy, job satisfaction, and job stress. *Infant Mental Health Journal, 39*(4), 385–395. https://doiorg.libproxy.sdsu.edu/10.1002/imhj.21718

Ginsburg, K. R. (2007). The importance of play in promoting healthy child development and maintaining strong parent-child bond. *Journal of American Academy of Pediatrics, 119*(1), 183–185.

Goodson, B. D., Mackrain, M., Perry, D. F., O'Brien, K., & Gwaltney, M. K. (2013). Enhancing home visiting with mental health consultation. *Pediatrics, 132*(Suppl. 2), 180–190. https://doi.org/10.1542/peds.2013-1021S

Jarde, A., Morais, M., Kingston, D., Giallo, R., MacQueen, G. M., Giglia, L., … McDonald, S. D. (2016). Neonatal outcomes in women with untreated antenatal depression compared with women without depression: A systematic review and meta-analysis. *JAMA Psychiatry, 73*(8), 826–837. https://doi.org/10.1001/jamapsychiatry.2016.0934

Klaman, S. L., & Turner, K. (2016). Prevalence of perinatal depression in the military: A systematic review of the literature. *Maternal and Child Health Journal, 20*(Suppl. 1), 52–65. Retrieved from https://doi-org.libproxy.sdsu.edu/10.1007/s10995-016-2172-0

Lehmann, J. (2015). There is no such thing as a baby. The mother-child couple at the center of Winnicott's practice. *Journal de la psychanalyse de l'enfant, 2*(2), 181–202. https://doi.org/10.3917/jpe.010.0181

Lester, P., Klosinski, L., Saltzman, W., Milburn, N., Mogil, C., & Beardslee, W. (2016). Families overcoming under stress (FOCUS): A family-centered preventive intervention for families facing trauma, stress, and adversity: Implementation with military families. In M. J. Van Ryzin, K. L. Kumpfer, G. M. Fosco, & M. T. Greenberg (Eds.), *Family-based prevention programs for children and adolescents: Theory, research, and large-scale dissemination* (pp. 229–255). New York and London: Psychology Press.

Lester, P., Liang, L.-J., Milburn, N., Mogil, C., Woodward, K., Nash, W., … Saltzman, W. (2016). Evaluation of a family-centered preventive intervention for military families: Parent and child longitudinal outcomes. *Journal of the American Academy of Child and Adolescent Psychiatry, 55*(1), 14–24. Retrieved from https://doi-org.libproxy.sdsu.edu/10.1016/j.jaac.2015.10.009

Lester, P., Peterson, K., Reeves, J., Knauss, L., Glover, D., Mogil, C., … Beardslee, W. (2010). The long war and parental combat deployment: Effects on military children and at-home spouses. *Journal of the American Academy of Child and Adolescent Psychiatry, 49*(4), 310–320. https://doi.org/10.1097/00004583-201004000-00006

Lieberman, A. F., Padrön, E., Van Horn, P., & Harris, W. W. (2005). Angels in the nursery: The intergenerational transmission of benevolent parental influences. *Infant Mental Health Journal, 26*(6), 504–520. https://doi.org/10.1002/imhj.20071

Lieberman, A. F., & Van Horn, P. (2013). Infants and young children in military families: A conceptual model for intervention. *Clinical Child and Family Psychology Review, 16*(3), 282–293. Retrieved from https://doi-org.libproxy.sdsu.edu/10.1007/s10567-013-0140-4

Meek, S. E., & Gilliam, W. S. (2016). Expulsion and suspension in early education as matters of social justice and health equity. *NAM Perspectives*. Discussion Paper. National Academy of Medicine. https://doi.org/10.31478/201610e

Newton, R. P. (2008). *The attachment connection: Parenting a secure and confident child using the science of attachment theory.* Oakland, CA: New Harbinger Publications.

Osofsky, J. D., & Chartrand, M. M. (2013). Military children from birth to five years. *Future of Children, 23*(2), 61–77. https://doi.org/10.1353/foc.2013.0011

Pemberton, J. R., Kramer, T. L., Borrego, J., Jr., & Owen, R. R. (2013). Kids at the VA? A call for evidence-based parenting interventions for returning veterans. *Psychological Services, 10*(2), 194–202. Retrieved from https://doi-org.libproxy.sdsu.edu/10.1037/a0029995

Perry, B. D. (1996). *Maltreated children: Experience. Brain development and the next generation.* New York and London: W.W. Norton.

Perry, B. D. (2003). *The cost of caring: Secondary traumatic stress and the impact of working with high risk children and families.* Houston, TX: Child Trauma Academy.

Perry, B. D., & Pollard, R. (1998). Homeostasis, stress, trauma, and adaptation: A neurodevelopmental view of childhood trauma. *Child and Adolescent Psychiatric Clinics of North America, 7*(1), 33–51.

Profile of the Military Community. (2019). Retrieved from https://download .militaryonesource.mil/12038/MOS/Reports/2019-demographics-report.pdf

Ross, A., Belknap, A., O'Neill, K., & Landsverk, J. (2015). Home visiting program readiness to serve military families with very young children. Retrieved from http://www.hvresearch.org/harc-projects.html

Salloum, A., Choi, M. J., & Stover, C. S. (2019). Exploratory study on the role of trauma-informed self-care on child welfare workers' mental health. *Children and Youth Services Review, 101*, 299–306. https://doi.org/10.1016/j.childyouth.2019.04.013

Schön, D. A. (1983). *The reflective practitioner: How professionals think in action.* New York: Basic Books.

Schore, A. N. (2001). The effects of early relational trauma on right brain development, affect regulation, and infant mental health. *Infant Mental Health Journal, 22*(1–2), 201–269. https://doi.org/10.1002/1097 -0355(200101/04)22:1<201::AID-IMHJ8>3.0.CO;2-9

SD Military Family Collaborative.https://sdmilitaryfamily.org/

Shapiro, F., & Solomon, R. M. (2010). *Eye movement desensitization and reprocessing.* https://doi.org/10.1002/9780470479216.corpsy0337

Sharp, M. L., Fear, N. T., Rona, R. J., Wessely, S., Greenberg, N., Jones, N., & Goodwin, L. (2015). Stigma as a barrier to seeking health care among military personnel with mental health problems. *Epidemiologic Reviews, 37*, 144–162. https://doi.org/10 .1093/epirev/mxu012

Slade, A. (2002). Keeping the baby in mind: A critical factor in perinatal mental health. *Zero to Three, 22*, 10–16.

Slomian, J., Honvo, G., Emonts, P., Reginster, J. Y., & Bruyère, O. (2019). Consequences of maternal postpartum depression: A systematic review of maternal and infant outcomes. *Women's Health, 15*, 1745506519844044. https://doi.org/10.1177 /1745506519844044

Stob, V., Slade, A., Adnopoz, J., & Woolston, J. (2020). The family cycle: Breaking the intergenerational transmission of trauma through mentalizing. *Journal of Infant, Child, and Adolescent Psychotherapy, 19*(3), 255–270. https://doi.org/10.1080 /15289168.2020.1786762

Substance Abuse and Mental Health Services Administration. (2014). *SAMHSA's concept of trauma and guidance for a trauma-informed approach.* HHS Publication No. (SMA) 14-4884. Rockville, MD: Substance Abuse and Mental Health Services Administration.

United Through Reading. (n.d.). Retrieved from https://www.unitedthroughreading.org

Walsh, T. B., Dayton, C. J., Erwin, M. S., Muzik, M., Busuito, A., & Rosenblum, K. L. (2014). Fathering after military deployment: Parenting challenges and goals of fathers of young children. *Health and Social Work, 39*(1), 35–44. https://doi.org/10 .1093/hsw/hlu005

Weis, K. L., & Elmore, K. O. (2017). Military prenatal intervention models. In M. A. Thiam (Ed.), *Perinatal mental health and the military family identifying and treating mood and anxiety disorders* (1st ed., pp. 151–165). Routledge.

Chapter 3

Prevalent but Hidden

Sexual Abuse, Its Impact, and the Healing Process for Children and Parents

Shulamit N. Ritblatt and Miranda Cruz

> *Missy has suffered five years of sexual abuse in her childhood by her grandfather. At the beginning, Missy loved being with her grandpa. He was funny and they spent time playing. As Missy turned three years old, things changed. Her grandpa's touch has become uncomfortable. He started touching her private parts when he was bathing her. Then his fingers started to penetrate her private parts and hurt her. Each time, her grandpa gave her a present or a candy and told her to keep their secret.*

Child sexual abuse happens worldwide to an estimated 9 out of 100 girls and 3 out of 100 boys (Barth et al., 2013; Halvorsen et al., 2020). In the US, about 1 in 4 girls and 1 in 13 boys experience child sexual abuse at some point in childhood (CDC, 2020). Child sexual abuse is

> a type of maltreatment that refers to the involvement of the child in sexual activity to provide sexual gratification or financial benefit to the perpetrator, including contacts for sexual purposes, molestation,

DOI: 10.4324/9781003046295-5

statutory rape, prostitution, pornography, exposure, incest, or other sexually exploitative activities.

(US Department of Health & Human Services, Children's Bureau, 2020)

It harms girls and boys from all walks of life, communities, and socioeconomic backgrounds, whose offenders include trusted family members, strangers, men and women of all ages, sexual orientations, SES, and cultural backgrounds (Murray et al., 2014).

Who Is the Perpetrator?

There is a paucity of studies examining the differences between intra-familial versus inter-familial sexual abuse. However, the research findings indicate that there are added stressors when the perpetrator is a family member. These stressors range from the need to remove the child and other siblings from the home, the breach of trust within the family system, the child's guilt about revealing the abuser, the strain it puts on couple relationships, and financial hardships when one breadwinner is being forced out (Murray et al., 2014; Seto et al., 2015). Furthermore, when a child is violated by a parent, relative, coach, or clergy, the ability to confront the perpetrator or end the relationship with them may not be a viable option for the child or the bystander. In these cases, victims and/or bystanders might continue accessing the resources provided by the abuser and preserving the relationships with them while adapting "Betrayal Blindness" (Delker et al., 2018; Freyd & Birrell, 2013; Freyd et al., 2007). Hence, the child victim might experience continued abuse as well as a double betrayal not only from the perpetrator, but also from family members (bystanders) who instead of protecting him/her are siding with the perpetrator.

> When Missy started going to school, her grandpa would pick her up and bring her home until her mom, who recently divorced, arrived from work. Her grandpa started to be more explicit in his sexual acts. At the beginning, he forced her to touch his private parts; then he forced her to have oral sex until he penetrated her. Missy started to steal things at school and home, she lied constantly, and was a low-performing student. Her mom felt overwhelmed by Missy's challenging behaviors and felt frustrated with her.

Impact of the Abuse on Children and Their Families

Sexual abuse experiences in childhood have negative long-term effects on individual development and life functioning (Coles et al., 2015; Halvorsen et al.,

2020; Hillberg et al., 2011). These negative outcomes are associated with conduct problems, poor social functioning and physical health, mental illnesses such as mood disorders, disassociation, Post-Traumatic Stress Disorder, personality disorders, and substance abuse, problems in sexual development and intimacy, harmful sexual behaviors, inability to maintain long-term relationships and attachment, disabilities, and early mortality (Adams et al., 2018; Putnam, 2003). Research findings indicate that there is a direct correlation between the severity of the abuse and the gravity of negative effects (Felitti et al., 1998; Larkin et al., 2014; Kwako et al., 2010; Mckibbin et al., 2017; Murray et al., 2014; Van Niel et al., 2014).

When the perpetrator is a primary caregiver, as in Missy's case, the negative outcomes are known to be more severe and damaging. The child experiences loss of trust and lacks a sense of safety, which leads to insecure disorganized attachment (Halvorsen et al., 2020; Kwako et al., 2010). According to Hayes (1987), to avoid unpleasant thoughts and memories of events and reduce the pain, the child uses emotional avoidance behaviors such as disassociation, self-mutilation, substance abuse, and binge eating. These emotional suppression behaviors are adaptive survival strategies used by sexual abuse survivors dealing with their history of abuse and trauma (Polusny & Follette, 1995).

Many times, Missy wanted to tell her mom about the abuse but was afraid. When she started second grade, her teacher, noticing her social interactions, behaviors, and poor academic functioning, asked to have a meeting with both Mom and Missy. During the meeting, Missy was sitting with her head down when the teacher noticed that she was obsessively covering the cuts on her wrists. The teacher asked Missy what happened to her wrists and how did she get these cuts. The teacher looked at Mom and asked her if she knew anything about these cuts. Missy's heart started racing and she felt trapped. The soft tone of voice and warmth of the teacher and the way her mom took her hand and held it in hers awakened something in Missy. Suddenly, she burst into tears and disclosed her sexual abuse experiences with her grandpa and talked about her self-harming behaviors.

Barriers and Facilitators to Disclosing Sexual Abuse in Childhood and Adolescence

According to research, the average time for victims to disclose their abuse is between 17.2 and 21.4 years (Easton, 2019; Halvorsen et al., 2020). The longer the delay in the disclosure, the more severe are the symptoms (Easton, 2013; 2019; Hillis et al., 2016; Mills et al., 2016; Stoltenborgh et al., 2015); 60–70% of survivors disclose when they are adults and 27.8% do not disclose their abuse

(Lemaigre et al., 2017). Disclosure within a year of the abuse is found to be a protective factor against mental and emotional symptoms and it helps rebuild trust and sense of safety (Easton, 2019).

One main barrier to disclosure is that children often do not understand or are unable to verbalize their experiences (Schönbucher et al., 2012; Teicher et al., 2016). From an ecological perspective, children's characteristics, family dynamics within the contexts of community, culture, and societal attitudes interplay in the disclosure and its timing (Alaggia et al., 2019). Cultural norms affect the way families react to the disclosure and how they proceed. These include the roles of modesty; taboos and shame; and sexual scripts that normalize and justify child sexual abuse (Fontes & Plummer, 2010).

A recent analysis of 20 studies on disclosure (Brennan & McElvaney, 2020) identifies six essential disclosure facilitators: Having trust in someone, perceiving the situation as abnormal, feeling powerless to face the emotional distress alone, wishing that something will be done to stop the abuse, anticipating that something will be done about it following the disclosure, and being asked about what is going on. Another thematic analysis of 33 studies looking at the disclosure experiences of children and adults found that "being asked" promotes disclosure (Alaggia et al., 2019). Missy was asked by her teacher about the cuts on her wrists, and this triggered the disclosure of the abuse.

When the abuser is a family member, as in Missy's case, the child may feel ambivalent regarding disclosure, a sense of guilt and self-blame which may lead to delayed disclosure (Herman, 1992; Fisher, 2017; Lemaigre et al., 2017; Magnusson et al., 2017; Murray et al., 2014). This is especially so when the child experiences "Betrayal Blindness," which involves repressed or diminished awareness of betrayal within close relationships for the individual to survive the trauma inflicted by a trusted adult (Delker & Freyd, 2017). Missy has experienced a dissonance between the expectation that her grandpa will love and protect her from any harm and his actual behavior and abuse. Now that she disclosed the abuse, she and her mom will feel betrayed. Many times, due to violence, threats, fear of not being believed, or shame, children comply with the secrecy pacts they form with the abuser (Foster, 2017a; 2017b; Foster & Hagedorn, 2014; Krähenbühl, 2011; Morrison et al., 2018; Schaeffer et al., 2011). Research indicates that age and gender play a role in disclosure behaviors: Older children are more likely to disclose than younger children, more specifically, children from middle childhood ages disclose the earliest (McElvaney et al., 2020; Murray et al., 2014); and boys are more hesitant and ashamed to share about their abuse than girls (Easton, 2013; Easton et al., 2014; Leander, 2010; Lippert et al., 2009; Schaeffer et al., 2011).

How Survivors Become Resilient

Social support is an essential protective factor against the negative outcomes of the abusive experiences (Delker, et al., 2018; Moak & Agrawal, 2010). Family members' response to the disclosure is critical to the healing process of the child. If the family members are punitive and fail to intervene and express disbelief and blame the child, it worsens the impact of the trauma. Lemaigre et al. (2017), in their review of studies pertaining to disclosure, concluded that asking the child directly while actively listening is the needed condition for disclosure to take place. Children's educators often must deal with the child's sexual abuse disclosure (Tener & Sigad, 2019). As in the case of Missy, her teacher was the first one to notice that Missy's behavior and functioning were indicators of underlying stressors and experiences. Relationships are key to providing a sense of safety and trust for the child victim. Believing children facilitates disclosure and provides opportunities for intervention and healing (McElvaney et al., 2020).

> *The teacher made a report to child protective services about the abuse. The police came and arrested Grandpa the same day of the disclosure. Following the disclosure, Missy's mom was flabbergasted. She became very depressed, lost her appetite, and became very agitated. She started having restless sleep and experienced repeated night terrors in her dreams. She was very angry with herself and blamed herself for what had happened to Missy, her daughter. For years, as a young child, she remembered her father's abuse of her, and she kept quiet all these years. When she sat with Missy at the meeting with the teacher she realized that she needs to put a stop to the reoccurring history of abuse. When the social worker from child welfare called and then met with her, Mom shared the history of the abuse and asked for guidance on how to help her daughter.*

When a child discloses experiencing sexual abuse, as in Missy's case, several community systems start getting involved with the family for a long period of time. Among the agencies involved are: Child protective services, medical and mental health teams, law enforcement and legal teams, child welfare and foster care services, among many others. Coordination among all these agencies is paramount to the treatment and healing of the child (Murray et al., 2014).

According to Ungar (2019), human resilience is defined

> as the capacity of a biopsychosocial system (this can include an individual person, a family, or a community) to navigate to the resources necessary to sustain positive functioning under stress as well as the capacity of systems to negotiate for resources to be provided in ways that are experienced as meaningful.

(p. 2)

Hence, resources of the resilience process include attachment, attribution style, social support, community cohesion, and human rights (Ungar, 2019).

Social support, one of the factors contributing to resilience, can affect the developmental trajectories of children who experienced sexual abuse (Murray et al., 2014). Following the disclosure, maternal support is found to be a significant predictor to the adjustment and healing of the child (Zajac et al., 2015). The validation and recognition of the trauma by the mother are the mobilizers in the child's recovery process and it depends on the mental health and emotional availability of the mother. A mother's history of sexual abuse may hinder her emotional availability (Daignault et al., 2018). Research findings indicate that 35–65% of mothers of children who experienced sexual abuse were sexually victimized (Hébert et al., 2007) and they suffer related outcomes such as depression, PTSD, and anxiety (Daignault et al., 2018). The child's disclosure might intensify these symptoms and affect the way the mother can provide support to her child. Missy's mom disclosed her sexual abuse experiences by her father after she had learned about her daughter's abuse. It is critical to provide family system support and therapy to address the intergenerational experiences of abuse.

Post-traumatic growth is an indication of healthy and resilient coping. It is different from resilience as it relates to a positive psychological growth in the wake of traumatic experiences. It is a permanent change in the individual. There are five domains of growth: Relationships with others, new possibilities, personal strength, spiritual change, and appreciation for life.

> *Missy felt guilty seeing her mom suffering and her grandpa in jail. She worried that her mom is angry with her. The social worker met with her and listened to her story. She asked her questions and was very nice and reassuring. She asked her to draw everything that happened to her. The social worker told her that she is not responsible for what happened to her. Missy started to feel better only after her mom talked to her and told her that her grandpa needed to be punished for what he had done to them both. Missy and her mom started dyadic therapy.*

Using Trauma-Informed Practices in Interventions with Children and Families

Treatment modalities that are used to work with individuals with histories of sexual abuse include individual, dyadic, family, and group therapies. The two most prevalent modes of treatments include individual therapy such as Trauma-Focused Cognitive Behavioral Therapy (TF-CBT) or Cognitive

Processing Therapy (CPT) and family therapy (Murray et al., 2014). All these modalities of treatment were adapted from the work with other PTSD populations. They include relaxation techniques, emotional coaching, understanding developmental histories, parent education and guidance, while mainly addressing inaccurate attributes about the role the victim played in causing the event. The different reviews of studies concluded that there is no conclusive evidence that one method is better than the others (Benuto & O'Donohue, 2015; Lev-Wiesel, 2008; Narang et al., 2019).

When addressing child sexual abuse, the treatment needs to include prevention and intervention. Prevention focuses on educating children about personal safety, more specifically body safety. Kid Learning About Safety (KLAS) is an example for a parent/child psycho-educational program. During the 16 sessions of the program, children and their parents are engaged in learning how to be safe (Kenny, 2010).

The intervention must address the individual child within the larger context of the family, its history, and the community. It requires a multidisciplinary team approach (Lev-Wiesel, 2008). Due to the prevalence of dissociative experiences and the repression of traumatic experiences, it is important to incorporate creative arts and projective play when working, especially with children. The use of art (drawing, painting, clay, music) offers a safe, non-verbal psychological space where the individual can organize their inner subjective world and connect it, bridge it with the objective reality. For example, Katz and Hamama (2013) found that drawing, a projective tool, is an effective way to facilitate the interview process with children retrieving the information and their narrative about their experiences of trauma. The social worker who interviewed Missy (in our case example) also used drawings and projective techniques to facilitate the verbal narrative of the abuse.

Support to the family and the non-offending members is essential to the recovery of the child (van Toledo & Seymour, 2013). Peer family advisors are found to be trustworthy and credible because of their personal lived experience. These types of services are cost-effective and are more accessible to parents of different cultural groups who do not wish to receive mental health services (Hoagwood, et al. 2010). Positive social support can buffer against negative effects of trauma and therefore can be an effective approach.

Thematic and systematic review of peer-led group interventions found that survivors' benefits include stabilization of emotions and reduction of isolation, processing of the trauma and reintegration. Participants indicated positive interpersonal and psychological well-being (Konya et al., 2020). However, the paucity of research on the effectiveness of peer support for victims/survivors of sexual abuse emphasizes the need for more data to assess its benefits (Gregory, et al., 2021).

Peer-Mentor Programs

> *After attending several therapy sessions, Missy's mom shared with the social worker that she does not see any improvement in Missy, who is very withdrawn and cries herself to sleep every night. The social worker suggested that they join a peer-mentor program led by a lived-experience survivor who specializes in working with young children and their family members.*

Missy and her mom selected to join the peer-mentor-based program led by a lived-experience coach to help them throughout the recovery process. They learned that the intervention consists of dyadic, individual, and group sessions utilizing verbal and non-verbal processes and strategies. Missy's mom joined the parents' support group while Missy received individual sessions.

In the first encounters, the coach assessed Missy in the presence of her mom using seven essential profiling determinants (see Figure 3.1) that help indicate which are the adaptive ways Missy is coping with the traumatic experiences and provide information needed to develop the healing treatment plan. The seven profiling components and the needed information for each include:

Sensory orientation: How does the child handle physical sensory input? How sensitive is the child to sensory information?

Movement and energy: What is the child's activity level? Is the child always on the go?

Developmental stage: What is the child's developmental level of understanding and articulation?

Behavioral and mental health: How does the child cope/react to the traumatic experiences? What behaviors does the child exhibit? What is the child's survival response (fight, flight, or freeze)? What are the mental states/moods of the parents?

Relationship's quality and interaction: What is the quality of child/parent attachment as demonstrated in their interactions?

Environmental elements: The neighborhood and home environment; their resources and level of safety.

Cultural diversity and family dynamics: How does culture impact the way the family react to the disclosure? What is the family power structure? What type of parenting style is used?

Observations throughout the sessions provide information about the way the individual experiences the trauma and responds to it. Developing an understanding for the person, and not only their trauma, helps engage and educate the psychological brain to alter misperceptions.

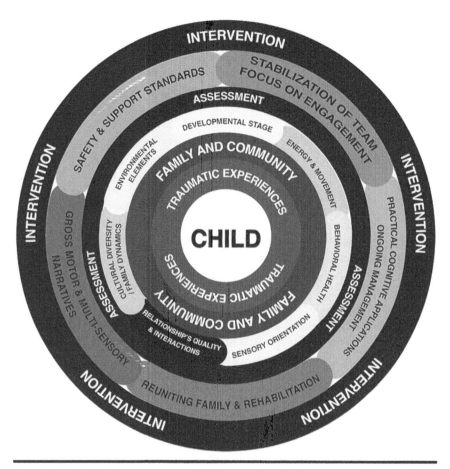

Figure 3.1   Process of Assessment and Intervention for Children Experiencing Sexual Abuse Trauma.

The intervention then is tailored to meet the specific profile of the child and his/her family in conjunction with a more active social support network and guidance. The individual intervention program for Missy includes five essential steps (see Figure 3.1) that are crucial to building brain development past traumatic interruption, allowing the psyche to also develop post-trauma:

(1) Stabilization of team commitment focusing on engagement: The first step in joining together in the therapeutic process; setting an agreement and understanding of the traumatic experiences, symptoms, behaviors, and the goals for the sessions; (2) Safety and Support Standards: The relational space is defined between the coach and the individual/family with clear empathic understanding of the traumatic experiences and the need for safety. Role-playing to re-processing the experiences to change attribution and cognitive thinking; (3) Gross Motor

and Multi-Sensory Narratives: It is critical to connect body and mind to deal with the trauma. Therefore, memories are the muscles that need practice to repair cognitive misconceptions and self-blame. Using multi-sensory approaches in conjunction with cognitive therapy support the healing and reduce the emotional and cognitive interruptions due to PTSD triggers; (4) Family Reuniting and Rehabilitation: Focuses on bringing the members together and working on processing the ways the family handles different behaviors, interactions, relationships, secrets, and disclosure; (5) Practical Cognitive Applications with Ongoing Management: Fostering and managing emotional and mental health practices to maintain continuous healing process and recovery.

This is a multi-sensory approach used to work through emotional and cognitive interruptions. Through practical application of life skills and healing, a survivor becomes resilient, creating the ability to plan and continue self-care, growth, and development in all areas, emotional, cognitive, and behavior application. Building the block of recognizing self-indicators of environmental triggers, peer triggers, and sensory triggers leading to self-knowledge of PTSD episodes and how to handle them as one would do with a muscle pain.

Trauma-informed practices were utilized during the sessions with Missy. Music, movement, drawing, painting, and play were used to establish trust, a sense of safety to connect with the trauma and the emotions, and process them (Katz & Hamama, 2013). Essential oils and dimmed lights helped soothe Missy and contributed to her level of comfort with the coach.

> *Missy is in the session with the coach and she recalls the experiences with her grandpa and reflects: "The one thing I don't like about remembering is that it feels it is happening again." The coach validated her feelings and suggested to do an activity "My Family My Feelings" (taken from Circle of Education® EduPod 18:2, Ritblatt, 2013: The activity, creating a booklet depicting family members and the different feelings we have associated with each one of them). While making the booklet, Missy listens to a special song about feelings. In the booklet, she portrayed her mom as the superhero, the grandpa as a monster, and herself as a very small crying child. After being quiet for a while, Missy is recalling the ways her grandpa groomed her and then took advantage of her. She is identifying the anger and frustration that she feels. She talks about her difficulty trusting people around her. She looks up to the coach and asks if she can just hold her hand. Missy felt calm and safe having an adult, her coach, touching her hand so gently.*

Following individual meetings with the coach, Mom joined a support group led by the lived-experience coach. Being in a group with other parents, who shared their own history of sexual abuse as well as their children's, was an important motivator for Mom to come regularly and feel safe to share without feeling ashamed and guilty. Konya et al. (2020), in their review of peer-led groups for survivors concluded that: In these groups, participants can connect with their feelings, give themselves permission to talk about the abuse and accept it, gain a sense of personal empowerment with less self-blame and shame, and feel validated and less socially isolated.

The adults' support group sessions started with soft music and essential oils filling the air. Fresh coffee and cookies were available for attendees. Each participant opened their personal journal and started writing in it how they feel and what is on their mind. Then, each shared what they wrote and the discussion and reflective process continued to evolve as they responded and shared. When one started to open-up and "touch" their pain; the coach guided the responses to meet the emotional state of the sharer. The coach facilitated the sessions organizing group activities, art projects, and games; offering quotes, poems, or segments of readings as well as sharing video clips or music videos to evoke responses. Parents talked about their child's struggle and progress, shared laughs and shed tears.

At home, Mom started to spend more time with Missy, playing, singing, reading, and talking. Mom saw a major improvement in Missy's moods and self-esteem. She was eating and sleeping well and could complete her school work successfully with very little help. When Mom was invited to join the sessions with Missy after several months of parallel intervention plans, they both felt excited and looked forward to their joint session:

> *Missy and Mom joined the session. The coach prepared art supplies and a large white paper and suggested that they both listen to the song about parent/child relationship (song "I love you when" taken from the Circle of Education ® program) and while listening scribble together on a piece of paper. Mom and Missy filled the paper with scribbles. Then the coach asked them to transform the scribbles to "meaningful things" according to whatever they "see" in the shape or figure that is on the paper by adding colors and drawing additional parts to make a scribble to look like, for example, a person or the sun. They both worked very carefully at the beginning trying not to invade the other's space. But as they listened to the lyrics and the music, they made eye contact, smiled, and started giving suggestions and directions to each other. The coach narrated their process and validated their actions as well as their feelings. When the song was done, and the scribbles "came to life," Missy ran towards her mom and hugged her tightly and said: "You are my hero." Mom held her and whispered to her: "You are my hero, my little one! You had the courage to stop the cycle of abuse! I love you! We will survive and prevail!"*

Discussion and Recommendations

Sexual abuse is a prevalent trauma experienced by many around the world and has detrimental long-term health consequences. This calls for attention to the needs of the survivors and their families, as well as a call for prevention. The Administration for Children and Families, in their 2018 Prevention Resource Guide (US Department of Health & Human Services, 2018), stated that the focus on early prevention is essential and less costly than offering intervention services. Many states have passed a law to include sexual abuse prevention in the public schools for K–12 students (Prevent Child Abuse America 2015). Many curricula have been used in schools to educate children about sexual abuse and body safety. They differ in their focus on the age group, materials, length of program, and mode of delivery. Evaluation studies of school-based prevention programs indicated that there are small gains in safety knowledge, self-protection skills, perception of risk, and disclosures; and they do not provide information if these gains decrease the likelihood of child sexual abuse from happening (Rudolph & Zimmer-Gembeck, 2018; Walsh et al., 2018).

Many of the survivors do not reveal and disclose their abuse due to shame, fear, and lack of trust. The trauma of those who disclose the abuse might intensify due to the negative reactions of the ones they shared their trauma with. Access to trusting adults was found to facilitate closure of the abuse by the child (Alaggia et al. 2019; Brennan & McElvaney, 2020). Teachers can be perceived by children experiencing sexual abuse as safe, trustworthy adults. Educational institutions need to prepare their teachers, who are in an ongoing daily contact with children, to discuss with their students the importance of feeling safe with the people around, as a preventative measure, and learn to identify warning signs in those who are experiencing abuse to provide trauma-informed intervention.

When a disclosure takes place, the survivor and the family are in dire need of support. Establishing hotlines for parents or family members who are seeking support and guidance following a disclosure about sexual abuse is essential. Anonymity was identified in research as critical to facilitate the support (Andalibi et al., 2018). It might be easier to support parents and family members using social media such as SMS. For example, findings from a study on the use of crisis SMS (Short Message Service) services by young adults, survivors indicated that the social media platform can be a valuable way of engagement and support (Schwab-Reese et al., 2019).

Receiving support and intervention from others who have experienced sexual abuse and were able to overcome and grow can be a better model of treatment to many than clinical interventions. Konya et al. (2020) examined the effectiveness of peer-led, group-based interventions as the healthcare system cannot meet the enormous needs of all affected individuals. They concluded that the outcomes of these groups on participants are very positive to their psychological and physical well-being. Participants in these groups have long-term relationships with other group members which contributes to their reciprocal healing.

Public policy needs to recognize the importance of protective factors to build safeguards to promote strengths-based capacities in the individual caregiver, the child, family, and community to ensure the safety and well-being of the child and the family. It is critical to use an ecological framework when addressing prevention and intervention policies targeting child sexual abuse.

References

Adams, J., Mrug, S., & Knight, C. D. (2018). Characteristics of child physical and sexual abuse as predictors of psychopathology. *Child Abuse and Neglect*, *86*, 167–177.

Alaggia, R., Collin-Vézina, D., & Lateef, R. (2019). Facilitators and barriers to child sexual abuse (CSA) disclosures: A research update (2000–2016). *Trauma, Violence and Abuse*, *20*(2), 260–283. https://doi.org/10.1177/1524838017697312

Andalibi, N., Haimson, L. O., De Choudhury, M., & Forte, A. (2018). Social support, reciprocity, and anonymity in responses to sexual abuse disclosures on social media. *ACM Transactions on Computer-Human Interaction*, *25*, 5, Article 28.

Barth, J., Bermetz, L., Heim, E., Trelle, S., & Tonia, T. (2013). The current prevalence of child sexual abuse worldwide: A systematic review and meta-analysis. *International Journal of Public Health*, *58*(3), 469–483. https://doi.org/10.1007/s00038-012 -0426-1

Benuto, T. L., & O'Donohue, W. (2015). Treatment of sexually abused child: Review and synthesis of recent meta-analyses. *Children and Youth Review*, *56*, 52–60.

Brennan, E., & McElvaney, R. (2020). What helps children tell? A qualitative meta-analysis of child sexual abuse disclosure. *Child Abuse Review*, *29*(2), 97–113.

CDC. (2020). Retrieved from https://www.cdc.gov/violenceprevention/childabusea ndneglect/childsexualabuse.html

Coles, J., Lee, A., Taft, A., Mazza, D., & Loxton, D. (2015). Childhood sexual abuse and its association with adult physical and mental health. *Journal of Interpersonal Violence*, *30*(11), 1929–1944. https://doi.org/10.1177/0886260514555270

Daignault, I. V., Hebert, M., Cyr, M., Pelletier, M., & McDuff, P. (2018). Correlates and predicators of mothers' adaptation and trauma symptoms following the unveiling of the sexual abuse of their child. *Journal of Interpersonal Violence*, *36*(11–12), 1–25. https://doi.org/10.1177/0886260518808849

Delker, B. C., & Freyd, J. J. (2017). Betrayed? That's me: Implicit and explicit betrayed self-concept in young adults abused as children. *Journal of Aggression, Maltreatment and Trauma*, *26*(7), 701–716.

Delker, B. C., Smith, P. C., Rosenthal, M. N., Bernstein, R. E., & Freyd, J. J. (2018). When home is where the harm is: Family betrayal and posttraumatic outcomes in young adulthood. *Journal of Aggression, Maltreatment and Trauma*, *27*(7), 720–743. https://doi.org/10.1080/10926771.2017.1382639

Easton, S. D. (2013). Disclosure of child sexual abuse among adult male survivors. *Clinical Social Work Journal, 41*(4), 344–355. https://doi.org/10.1007/s10615-012 -0420-3

Easton, S. D. (2019). Childhood disclosure of sexual abuse and mental health outcomes in adulthood: Assessing merits of early disclosure and discussion. *Child Abuse and Neglect, 93*, 208–214.

Easton, S. D., Saltzman, L., & Willis, D. G. (2014). "Would you tell under circumstances like that?": Barriers to disclosure of child sexual abuse for men. *Psychology of Men and Masculinity, 15*(4), 460–469. https://doi.org/10.1037/a0034223

Felitti, V. J., Anda, R. F., Nordenberg, D., Williamson, D. F., Spitz, A. M., Edwards, V., & Marks, J. S. (1998). Relationship of childhood abuse and household dysfunction to many of the leading causes of death in adults: The adverse childhood experiences (ACE) study. *American Journal of Preventive Medicine, 14*(4), 245–258. https://doi .org/10.1016/S0749-3797(98)00017-8

Fisher, J. (2017). *Healing the fragmented selves of trauma survivors.* New York: Routledge.

Fontes, L. A., & Plummer, C. (2010). Cultural issues in disclosures of child sexual abuse. *Journal of Child Sexual Abuse, 19*(5), 491–518. https://doi.org/10.1080/10538712 .2010.512520

Foster, J. M. (2017a). It happened to me: A qualitative analysis of boys' narratives about child sexual abuse. *Journal of Child Sexual Abuse, 26*(7), 853–873. https://doi.org /10.1080/10538712.2017.1360426

Foster, J. M. (2017b). The fears and futures of boy victims of sexual abuse: An analysis of narratives. *Journal of Child Sexual Abuse, 26*(6), 710–730. https://doi.org/10.1080/ 10538712.2017.1339223

Foster, J. M., & Hagedorn, W. B. (2014). Through the eyes of the wounded: A narrative analysis of children's sexual abuse experiences and recovery process. *Journal of Child Sexual Abuse, 23*(5), 538–557. https://doi.org/10.1080/10538712.2014.918072

Freyd, J. J., & Birrell, P. J. (2013). *Blind to betrayal.* Hoboken, NJ: John Wiley & Sons, Inc.

Freyd, J. J., DePrince, A. P., & Gleaves, D. H. (2007). The state of betrayal trauma theory: Reply to McNally—Conceptual issues and future directions. *Memory, 15*(3), 295–311. https://doi.org/10.1080/09658210701256514

Gregory, A., Johnson, E., Feder, G., Campbell, J., Konya, J., & Perot, C. (2021). Perceptions of peer support for victim-survivors of sexual violence and abuse: An exploratory study with key stakeholders. *Journal of Interpersonal Violence*, 1–30. https://doi.org/10.1177/08862605211007931

Halvorsen, J. E., Solberg, E. T., & Stige, S. H. (2020). "To say it out loud is to kill your own childhood." – An exploration of the first person perspective of barriers to disclosing child sexual abuse. *Children and Youth Services Review, 113*, 104999.

Hayes, S. C. (1987). A contextual approach to therapeutic change. In N. S. Jacobson (Ed.), *Psychotherapists in clinical practice: Cognitive and behavioral perspectives* (pp. 327–387). New York: Guilford Press.

Hébert, M., Daigneault, I., Collin-Vézina, D., & Cyr, M. (2007). Factors linked to distress in mothers of children disclosing sexual abuse. *Journal of Nervous and Mental Disease, 195*(10), 805–811.

Herman, J. (1992). *Trauma and recovery. The aftermath of violence - From domestic abuse to political terror* (3. utg.). New York: Basic Books.

Hillberg, T., Hamilton-Giachritsis, C., & Dixon, L. (2011). Review of meta-analyses on the association between child sexual abuse and adult mental health difficulties: A systematic approach. *Trauma, Violence, and Abuse, 12*(1), 38–49. https://doi.org/10 .1177/ 1524838010386812

Hillis, S., Mercy, J., Amobi, A., & Kress, H. (2016). Global prevalence of past-year violence against children: A systematic review and minimum estimates. *Pediatrics, 137*(3). https://doi.org/10.1542/peds.2015-4079

Hoagwood, K. E., Cavaleri, M. A., Olin, S. S., Burns, B. J., Slaton, E., Gruttadaro, D., & Hughes, R. (2010). Family support in children's mental health: A review and synthesis. *Clinical Child and Family Psychology Review, 13*(1), 1–45.

Katz, C., & Hamama, L. (2013). "Draw me everything that happened to you": Exploring children's drawings of sexual abuse. *Children and Youth Services Review, 35*(5), 877–882.

Kenny, M. C. (2010). Child sexual abuse education with ethnically diverse families: A preliminary analysis. *Children and Youth Services Review, 32*(7), 981–989.

Konya, J., Perôt, C., Pitt, K., Johnson, E., Gregory, A., Brown, E., ... Campbell, J. (2020). Peer-led groups for survivors of sexual abuse and assault: A systematic review. *Journal of Mental Health.* https://doi.org/10.1080/09638237.2020.1770206

Krähenbühl, S. (2011). Tell me what happened: Structured investigative interviews of child victims and witnesses by Michael E. Lamb, Irit Hershkowitz, Yael Orbach and Phillip W. Esplin. *Legal and Criminological Psychology, 16*(1), 189–190. https:// doi.org/10. 1002/9780470773291

Kwako, L. E., Noll, J. G., Putnam, F. W., & Trickett, P. K. (2010). Childhood sexual abuse and attachment: An intergenerational perspective. *Clinical Child Psychology and Psychiatry, 15*(3), 407–422.

Larkin, H., Felitti, V., & Anda, R. (2014). Social work and adverse childhood experiences research: Implications for practice and health policy. *Social Work in Public Health, 29*(1), 1–16. https://doi.org/10.1080/19371918.2011.619433

Leander, L. (2010). Police interviews with child sexual abuse victims: Patterns of reporting: Avoidance and denial. *Child Abuse and Neglect, 34*(3), 192–205. https://doi .org/10.1016/j.chiabu.2009.09.011

Lemaigre, C., Taylor, E. P., & Gittoes, C. (2017). Barriers and facilitators to disclosing sexual abuse in childhood and adolescence: A systematic review. *Child Abuse and Neglect, 70*, 39–52. https://doi.org/10.1016/j.chiabu.2017.05.009

Lev-Wiesel, R. (2008). Child sexual abuse: A critical review of intervention and treatment modalities. *Children and Youth Services Review, 30*(6), 665–673.

Lippert, T., Cross, T., Jones, L., & Walsh, W. (2009). Telling interviewers about sexual abuse: Predictors of child disclosure at forensic interviews. *Child Maltreatment, 14*(1), 100–113. https://doi.org/10.1177/1077559508318398

Magnusson, M., Ernberg, E., & Landström, S. (2017). Preschoolers' disclosures of child sexual abuse: Examining corroborated cases from Swedish courts. *Child Abuse and Neglect, 70*, 199–209. https://doi.org/10.1016/j.chiabu.2017.05.01

McElvaney, R., Moore, K., O'Reilly, K., Turner, R., Walsh, B., & Guerin, S. (2020). Child sexual abuse disclosures: Does age make a difference? *Child Abuse and Neglect, 99*, 104–121.

McKibbin, G., Humphreys, C., & Hamilton, B. (2017). "Talking about child sexual abuse would help me": Young people who sexually abused reflection preventing harmful sexual behavior. *Child Abuse and Neglect, 70*, 210–221.

Mills, R., Kisely, S., Alati, R., Strathearn, L., & Najman, J. (2016). Self-reported and agency-notified child sexual abuse in a population-based birth cohort. *Journal of Psychiatric Research, 74*, 87–93. https://doi.org/10.1016/j.jpsychires.2015.12.021

Moak, Z. B., & Agrawal, A. (2010). The association between perceived interpersonal social support and physical and mental health: Results from the national epidemiological survey on alcohol and related conditions. *Journal of Public Health, 32*(2), 191–201.

Morrison, S. E., Bruce, C., & Wilson, S. (2018). Children's disclosure of sexual abuse: A systematic review of qualitative research exploring barriers and facilitators. *Journal of Child Sexual Abuse, 27*(2), 176–194. https://doi.org/10.1080/10538712.2018

Murray, L. K., Nguyen, A., & Cohen, J. A. (2014). Child sexual abuse. *Child and Adolescent Psychiatric Clinics of North America, 23*(2), 321–337. https://doi.org/10.1016/j.chc.2014.01.003

Narang, J., Schwannauer, M., Quayle, E., & Zoe Chouliara, Z. (2019). Therapeutic interventions with child and adolescent survivors of sexual abuse: A critical narrative review. *Children and Youth Services Review, 107*, 104559.

Polusny, M. A., & Follette, V. M. (1995). Long-term correlates of child sexual abuse: Theory and review of the empirical literature. *Applied and Preventive Psychology, 4*(3), 143–166.

Prevent Child Abuse America (Prepared by Jetta Bernier). (2015). *State and federal legislative efforts to prevent child sexual abuse: A status report.* Retrieved from http://preventchildabuse.org/images/docs/PCA_MK_CSAstatusreport.pdf

Putnam, F. W. (2003). Ten-year research update review: Child sexual abuse. *Journal of the American Academy of Child and Adolescent Psychiatry, 42*(3), 269–278.

Ritblatt, S. N. (2013). My family my feelings. *EduPod, 18*, 2. Circle of Education. delibrainy, San Diego, CA.

Rudolph, J., & Zimmer-Gembeck, M. J. (2018). Reviewing the focus: A summary and critique of child-focused sexual abuse prevention. *Trauma, Violence and Abuse, 19*(5), 543–554.

Schaeffer, P., Leventhal, J. M., & Asnes, A. G. (2011). Children's disclosures of sexual abuse: Learning from direct inquiry. *Child Abuse & Neglect: The International Journal, 35*(5), 343–352. https://doi.org/10.1016/j.chiabu.2011.01.014

Schönbucher, V., Maier, T., Mohler-Kuo, M., Schnyder, U., & Landolt, M. A. (2012). Disclosure of child sexual abuse by adolescents: A qualitative in-depth study. *Journal of Interpersonal Violence, 27*(17), 3486–3513. https://doi.org/10.1177/0886260512445380

Schwab-Reese, L., Kanuri, N., & Cash, S. (2019). Child maltreatment disclosure to a text messaging–based crisis service: Content analysis. *JMIR mHealth and uHealth, 7*(3), e11306.

Seto, M. C., Babchishin, K. M., Pullman, L. E., & McPhail, I. V. (2015). The puzzle of intrafamilial child sexual abuse: A meta-analysis comparing intrafamilial and extrafamilial offenders with child victims. *Clinical Psychology Review, 39*, 42–57.

Stoltenborgh, M., Bakermans-Kranenburg, M. J., Alink, L. R. A., & van Ijzendoorn, M. H. (2015). The prevalence of child maltreatment across the globe: Review of a series of meta-analyses. *Child Abuse Review, 24*(1), 37–50. https://doi.org/10.1002/car

Teicher, M. H., Samson, J. A., Anderson, C. M., & Ohashi, K. (2016). The effects of childhood maltreatment on brain structure, function and connectivity. *Nature Reviews Neuroscience, 17*(10), 652–666. https://doi.org/10.1038/nrn.2016.111

Tener, D., & Sigad, L. (2019). "I felt like I was thrown into a deep well": Educators coping with child sexual abuse disclosure. *Children and Youth Services Review, 106,* 104465.

Ungar, M. (2019). Designing resilience research: Using multiple methods to investigate risk exposure, promotive and protective processes, and contextually relevant outcomes for children and youth. *Child Abuse and Neglect, 96,* 1–8. https://doi.org/10.1016/j.chiabu.2019.104098

US Department of Health & Human Services, Administration for Children and Families, Administration on Children, Youth and Families, Children's Bureau. (2018). *2018 prevention resource guide.* Retrieved from https://www.childwelfare.gov/pubPDFs/guide_2018.pdf

US Department of Health & Human Services, Administration for Children and Families, Administration on Children, Youth and Families, Children's Bureau. (2020). *Child maltreatment, 2018.* Retrieved from https://www.acf.hhs.gov/media/press/2020/2020/child-abuse-neglect-data-released

van Niel, C., Pachter, L. M., Wade, R., Felitti, V. J., & Stein, M. T. (2014). Adverse events in children: Predictors of adult physical and mental conditions. *Journal of Developmental and Behavioral Pediatrics, 35*(8), 549–551. https://doi.org/10.1097/DBP.0000000000000102

van Toledo, A., & Seymour, F. (2013). Interventions for caregivers of children who disclose sexual abuse: A review. *Clinical Psychology Review, 33*(6), 772–781.

Walsh, K., Zwi, K., Woolfenden, S., & Shlonsky, A. (2018). School-based education programs for the prevention of child sexual abuse: A cochrane systematic review and meta-analysis. *Research on Social Work Practice, 28*(1), 33–55.

Zajac, K. M., Ralston, E., & Smith, D. W. (2015). Maternal support following childhood sexual abuse: Associations with children's adjustment post-disclosure and at 9-month follow-up. *Child Abuse and Neglect, 44,* 66–75.

Chapter 4

Developing Child Resiliency through Art Intervention

A Strengths Perspective

Teresa Grame

> *A way to externalize all that I carried within, art became the venue by which I was able to find my voice*[1]
>
> —*Josie Méndez-Negrete*

A sociologist, associate professor of Mexican American studies, and clinical social worker, Méndez-Negrete draws from personal experience to help trauma survivors heal. In her youth, she was separated from her community in Mexico by her abusive father. During this time in her life, she expressed her feelings through writing, poetry, and drawings inspired by traditional arts the women in her family shared with her as a child. As an adult survivor, she embraced her love of the arts and uses her gifts to empower others (Méndez-Negrete, 2013). Méndez-Negrete's experience highlights how art and creativity maintain hope in the darkest times.

For many children and their caregivers, it has not been safe to express their voice, and doing so may directly jeopardize their physical and emotional safety (Hinz, 2020). Despite the hurtful impact of trauma, children find ways of tapping into avenues of self-expression as a way of surviving. The healing power of

DOI: 10.4324/9781003046295-6

creative expression provides the foundation for a trauma-informed and strength-based approach to art intervention (National Center for Trauma-Informed Care, as cited in Steele & Malchiodi, 2012). In this chapter the reader will witness one family's journey of strength and learn the ways practitioners apply therapeutic arts to support trauma recovery.

Case Story: Pamela, Sandra, and Harvey

For 38-year-old Pamela and her two children—13-year-old Sandra and 7-year-old Harvey (fictitious names)—creative arts drew upon their family and cultural resources.[2] When Pamela met with a therapist, it was the first time she shared the details of her family's long history of trauma.

Pamela married the children's father, her first husband, at a young age. He was emotionally and physically abusive to her, beginning during her pregnancy with Sandra. With the encouragement of a close friend from her church group, Pamela left the home with her two children to start a new life. Pamela married her second husband two years later. Sandra subsequently told her mother that her stepfather was sexually abusing her. Pamela immediately contacted the police, prompting a criminal investigation that would require Sandra to testify in court. Pamela questioned why she did not recognize the signs of sexual abuse before.

During the initial assessment appointment, Pamela's therapist talked with her about common responses to trauma and created a safe space for her to speak about the abuse. Pamela's therapist pointed out that, in seeking help, she demonstrated her strong determination to break the cycle of abuse for herself and for her children.

The therapist recommended Pamela begin individual therapy to help her to cope with her own trauma. Sandra and Harvey engaged in individual sessions to express their thoughts and feelings as they began their trauma recovery journey. Parent–child sessions were included because of the family's strong bonds. Art therapy was chosen as the primary modality with Sandra and Harvey because creative expression would help establish safety, strengthen relationships, and allow for the incorporation of the family's many strengths.

Art Therapy: A Trauma-Informed and Strength-Based Approach

Art therapy embodies the elements of a trauma-informed and strength-based approach, addresses the critical role of attachment in recovery from relational trauma, and applies neurobiological knowledge (National Center for

Trauma-Informed Care as cited in Steele & Malchiodi, 2012; Chapman, 2014). The American Art Therapy Association (AATA) defines the field of art therapy as an "integrated mental health and human services profession" (AATA, 2017). The art therapist facilitates active artmaking with individuals, families, groups, and communities within a psychotherapeutic relationship. Art therapists are master-level clinicians who receive education and supervised training to develop specialized knowledge about artmaking, creativity, and applied psychological theory. Their roles include conducting assessments to identify individual, family, and community needs as well as selecting interventions to achieve personal, relational, and community goals.

Each time a practitioner holds a space for self-expression, they honor a child and family's growing resiliency. This resiliency is reflected in the act of putting colors, shapes, or images down on paper. The vital role of creativity in the development of resiliency and growth is supported by art therapy research (Prescott et al., 2008; Mohr, 2014; Hass Cohen et al., 2018; Metzl, 2009).

Incorporating a wide range of art materials and interventions tailored to individual needs and strengths is key to trauma recovery (Hinz, 2020) and was a major consideration in Sandra and Harvey's therapy. The therapists working with Sandra and Harvey chose from a variety of art materials and digital media options. Art materials range from very resistive, requiring pressure to apply, and those that are more fluid and flow easily and quickly. Examples of resistive, two- and three-dimensional materials are pencils and wood. Fluid, two- and three-dimensional materials include paints and wet clay (Kagin & Lusebrink, 1978). Resistive materials tend to provide a sense of control to trauma survivors and fluid materials tend to encourage more spontaneous and expressive interaction, while each person experiences art media differently (Hinz, 2020). For this reason, Sandra and Harvey's therapists made sure to observe their individual responses to art activities.

The remainder of this chapter will demonstrate how art was used to identify strengths and how trauma-informed, arts-based activities were tailored to meet the children's needs in each stage of trauma recovery. The chapter will also highlight interventions which were selected for Pamela's family from a wide range of creative therapy tools available to practitioners.

Art Interventions in the Journey from Trauma to Resiliency

Sandra and Harvey's therapists considered the stages of trauma recovery when determining therapeutic goals. Herman (1997) identified three stages of trauma recovery, which collectively allow for a flexible and responsive approach to art intervention based on an understanding of children's needs and strengths over time. A strength-based approach to art intervention considers that strengths exist at all stages of trauma recovery and are made visible through art (Wilkinson & Chilton, 2018).

The stages of trauma recovery, described in the following sections, were considered when choosing art interventions for Sandra and Harvey. This process began with an assessment of needs and strengths informed by each child's interaction with art materials as they built a safe relationship with their therapist. As the children moved through the stages, ongoing observation of how Sandra and Harvey responded to treatment protected against re-traumatization and guided movement from trauma to resiliency.

The Safety Stage

Stage one of trauma recovery, characterized by the development of a safe therapeutic relationship, provides the foundation for the recovery process (Herman, 1997). In addition to establishing safety, practitioners assess children's strengths and weaknesses (Hinz, 2020). Tailoring activities to individual safety needs is important, particularly for children who have experienced maltreatment (Klorer, 2016). Assessment guides art interventionists to apply a variety of techniques, including directive, client-centered, symbolic, and relational interventions (Gil, 1991).

Assessment with Sandra and Harvey during the Safety Stage

When inviting Sandra and Harvey to engage in artmaking, it was important to clarify that there is no right or wrong in art expression and their art would not be judged. Asking the children's permission to look at and talk about the art product together communicated respect. The interventionalists also discussed ways to protect the art product from damage or criticism, especially important in cases of ongoing abuse or safety concerns in the home.

During the safety stage, examining the art product and the ways in which Sandra and Harvey engaged with art materials helped to understand how trauma impacted them. Sandra and Harvey's therapists considered their responses to trauma, individual strengths, developmental stage, relationships, and cultural and community resources. These considerations were important in selecting goals and interventions to maximize protective factors and minimalize risk.

The therapists viewed Sandra and Harvey's symptoms as a reflection of the ways the children were responding to and coping with trauma. Sandra was experiencing intrusive thoughts, anxiety, depressed mood, and loss of interest in her friends and her usual activities. Harvey worried that something bad would happen to his sister and mother, was having nightmares, difficulty concentrating in school, and longed to see his father again.

Art assessment also helped the therapists to identify individual strengths and potential sources of resilience (Wilkinson & Chilton, 2018). Sandra's therapist noticed how Sandra used a lot of words and symbols in her artwork and was comfortable with expressing her experiences cognitively and symbolically (Hinz, 2020). During the safety stage, youth may be invited to represent "what is important to me" or "my safe people" in a drawing, symbols crafted in clay, or a collage made with cut out magazine pictures and words. For example, Sandra's therapist noticed her strong connection to family when she described helping her grandmother plan for an upcoming family gathering. She invited Sandra to select from magazine pictures, words, scrapbook paper, and gems to create a collage showing her vision for the upcoming family celebration. Sandra described her admiration for her grandmother and mother because of their determination to make sure family traditions were passed down to the next generations (see Figure 4.1).

Understanding how trauma impacts child development helped Sandra and Harvey's therapists select goals and interventions. As a young adolescent, it was important to help Sandra develop a positive identity in the context of her peer

Figure 4.1   An Art Collage.

relationships. Goals of her treatment included reducing her trauma symptoms, identifying her strengths, and connecting her with a community of survivors.

Harvey's therapist considered that cognitive and verbal interventions may not be effective for a seven-year-old who is in a state of fear; rather, sensory, and non-verbal approaches are recommended (Gaskill & Perry, 2014). Goals for his therapy were to increase his sense of safety and reduce self-blame. His therapist noted that Harvey was comfortable sharing his feelings and enjoyed using clay, building with wood, and folding paper which provided a safe outlet to express himself. Harvey began by creating art about what makes him happy and what he enjoys doing, including outings to the park with his mom and sister. He was excited to make gifts for his family members, evidence of his positive relationships as a protective factor for his healing.

Sandra and Harvey's relationships were explored through family drawings. Using family drawings to assess attachment is supported by a study by Backos and Samuelson (2017) in which they examined drawings created by mothers and children who experienced domestic violence. In cases where the individuals tested positive for Post-Traumatic Stress Disorder (PTSD), family members were drawn more separated and isolated than in the artwork of women and children who were negative for PTSD. Sandra and Harvey's therapists also applied their understanding of normative stages of art development when viewing their family drawings (Lowenfeld & Brittain, 1987; Malchiodi, as cited in Steele & Malchiodi, 2012).

Sandra represented her family with shapes and symbols and described her mother and her grandmother as strong female role models. She added that her mother's protective and caring response when she told her about the sexual abuse made a huge impact on Sandra and helped her to feel comfortable starting therapy. Harvey's therapist established safety before he was invited to draw his family. Harvey drew himself standing between his mom and sister, all holding hands and smiling. His close and connected relationships with his family became clear. He stated that he could have protected his family from harm. Harvey's therapist knew it was important to help him understand that he was not responsible for the abuse.

Identifying familial, cultural, and community resources provided the basis for a respectful and strength-based approach with Pamela's family. Jackson (2020) points out that "Art is a representation of our experience or worldview" (p. 37). Provision of culturally responsive art materials is an important consideration when working with families (Jackson et al., 2018). The children's therapists selected art materials which included images of diverse people, religious symbols, and colorful fabrics and papers.

Pamela's therapist, who was from the dominant cultural group, engaged in ongoing self-reflection and consultation in the development of cultural humility (Jackson, 2020). The family's strong connections to their church, spirituality, and support persons were incorporated into their therapy goals. Pamela's therapist encouraged her to continue in her women's support group at her church. Following this initial assessment of strengths and needs, specific art interventions were used to establish safety as the children began to work on their trauma-focused goals.

Art Interventions Establish Safety with Sandra and Harvey

Observations of what Sandra and Harvey expressed in their art helped to determine when to approach direct discussion about the trauma and when to provide distance. Like many youths, Sandra avoided thinking or talking about her traumatic experiences and tried to push her feelings away. Sandra's therapist talked with her about how important it is to have a safe way to label and express her emotions in therapy. With this goal in mind, her therapist invited Sandra to create watercolor "feeling cards" to express her emotions. Sandra used colors and shapes to depict a feeling on each card and then used her own words to label each feeling. These cards were then used as Sandra and her therapist discussed feelings in response to sexual abuse (see Figure 4.2).

During the safety stage, Harvey's therapist gave him a choice of art materials and suggested a theme based on his therapy goals. He learned facts and dispelled myths about sexual abuse and family fighting. The feeling cards activity was adapted for Harvey's younger age by having him draw faces inside pre-drawn circles (Heegaard, 1991). Harvey showed his feelings of sadness about missing his father, anger toward his stepfather for sexually abusing his sister, and worry that

Figure 4.2   Watercolor Feeling Cards.

bad things would happen again. Harvey's mother had been hesitant to talk with him about his sister's sexual abuse for fear it would be too upsetting for him. His therapist talked with Pamela about how honest discussion in families is critical for breaking the cycle of abuse and helped her to talk to Harvey about the abuse.

A wide range of art interventions were available to Harvey and Sandra's therapists during the safety stage. Art interventions at this stage include a focus on representations of strengths and sources of comfort. The therapists also considered that some approaches that may be soothing for one child might cause distress for another child. One intervention used with Harvey was creating an image of a safe, calm, or happy place using guided imagery (Cohen, Mannarino, & Deblinger, 2006). Sandra made a list of soothing items and activities for each of the five senses, including pleasant items to view, smell, taste, hear, and touch.

Additional relaxing activities with Sandra and Harvey included painting images of sunsets with fluid paint, making comfort pillows using fabric markers on a pillowcase, creating a dream catcher to hang near the bed, and making worry dolls to tell their worries to and place under their pillow at night. Harvey also benefited from adding an image of his grandmother who makes him feel safe to a drawing of his bothersome dreams (Heegaard, 1991). Contained spaces, including using smaller paper or pre-drawn shapes, help some children to manage overwhelming feelings and aids in self-regulation. Sandra created a series of mandalas—a type of artwork created within a circle—which has been shown to decrease anxiety (Curry & Kasser, 2005). These activities helped prepare Sandra and Harvey for the remembrance and mourning stage, described in the following section.

Remembrance and Mourning Stage

Stage two trauma recovery involves remembrance and mourning (Herman, 1997). An evidence-based intervention, Trauma-Focused Cognitive Behavioral Therapy, involves the development of a trauma narrative in which the child tells the details of their traumatic experience (Cohen, Mannarino, & Deblinger, 2006). Interventionalists consider that for children who have experienced cumulative trauma, attachment problems, or cannot recall specific events, verbal trauma narratives are not always a good fit (Klorer (2016). Rather, these children may benefit from using art to express what they cannot express verbally.

Children may create a visual trauma narrative, including their experiences before, during, and after the traumatic events. They can choose to create a book to depict their journey, or select music, sculpture, sand tray figures, photographs, or other forms of creative expression (Cohen, Mannarino, & Deblinger, 2006). Representing the trauma in the form of a metaphor, such as a monster that can be transformed, can provide youth with emotional distance as they make meaning of their experiences (Kruger & Swanepoel, 2017).

Art imagery and the way children use art materials guides when to move forward by shifting materials and invitations to create art on a particular topic, and when to step back and let the process lead naturally (Hinz, 2020). Artwork is thought to bring the unconscious to awareness and access non-verbal trauma (Gantt & Tripp, 2016). Interventionalists pay attention to the timing of the child's insights, provide feedback, and wonder about the meanings contained in the artwork, rather than imposing resolution prematurely. It is important for children to have opportunities to express associated thoughts and feelings as they address their traumatic experiences (Gil, 1991).

In the process of expressing their stories, children can be helped to move beyond an identity as "victim" to an identity as a "survivor" and "thriver" (Chew, 1998). Re-looking at previously created images allows children to reflect on positive changes in identity (Harber, 2011). Each of these considerations were adapted to Sandra and Harvey's needs, described in the next section.

Sandra and Harvey Process Their Trauma

As Sandra and Harvey entered the remembrance and mourning stage, their therapists helped them to address their trauma. Art helped the children to express their thoughts and feelings, make meaning of the trauma, and implement coping strategies to manage distress. Sandra used art journaling to explore the impact of the sexual abuse on her identity, peer relationships, and self-esteem. She included the events before, during, and after the sexual abuse. At the start of each session, Sandra reviewed the previous pages of her journal before adding additional pages to her story to reduce avoidance of direct discussion about the sexual abuse and to help Sandra recognize her growing resilience.

For his trauma narrative, Harvey first drew pictures of his favorite memories with his mom and his sister. As he became more comfortable, his therapist invited Harvey to draw a picture of the day his father hurt his mother, which was expressed in a flurry of scribbles made on the page. Harvey shared his wish that he could have been able to protect his big sister. He began to understand he was not responsible for stopping the sexual abuse from happening. Next, his therapist encouraged Harvey to draw images of helpful activities, including riding his bike to the park with his family. Young children, like Harvey, can benefit from creating artworks representing their helpers which are then incorporated into their story, as in the following image (see Figure 4.3).[3]

An additional art intervention that helped Sandra during the remembrance and mourning stage is called the "let go and keep box." At the end of each session, she identified thoughts or feelings she wanted to symbolically "let go of" and leave with her therapist. She wrote each of these down on slips of paper which were folded and placed inside a decorated box kept in the therapist's office. Next, she wrote coping thoughts she wanted to "keep" or think about during the

Figure 4.3 Angels of Protection.

upcoming week. The activity offers an opportunity to debrief after talking about trauma, externalize traumatic thoughts, and practice coping skills between sessions, as in the following example (see Figure 4.4).

As Sandra and Harvey shared their traumatic experiences, their therapists validated common thoughts and feelings as natural in response to trauma, and corrected misinformation. Sandra and Harvey began to integrate their trauma experiences into their life story and to look forward to the future as they entered the third stage of trauma recovery, the reconnection stage.

Reconnection Stage

The last stage focuses on reconnection with the self, world, and relationships beyond the trauma experience. The reconnection stage involves making meaning of the trauma and developing a connection to one's identity as a survivor. Newly developed beliefs validate and instill hope for continued recovery. Many individuals gain a sense of connection to other survivors (Herman, 1997).

Distress due to past trauma may re-surface at different ages and stages or during important events in the child's life. Interventionists prepare children and

Figure 4.4   Let Go and Keep Box.

their caregivers to cope with future reminders of trauma. It is important to discuss options for re-entering therapy if it becomes necessary.

Sandra and Harvey and the Reconnection Stage

To help Sandra as she prepared for testifying in criminal proceedings, her therapist invited her to paint rocks with soothing colors and positive words to serve as a reminder of comfort she would take with her to court. Sandra's therapist also gave her an art journal and other art materials to use after therapy ended.

Toward the end of his therapy, Harvey created a "dream house" for his family out of sticks and paper, which he said would have indoor and outdoor pools, three large flat screen TVs, and a team of people to help his mother cook and clean so she could relax. Harvey and his therapist decorated a transitional box for him to take home as a reminder of his time in therapy.

Sandra and Harvey developed safety plans illustrated in art. Sandra represented signs of healthy and unhealthy relationships and friendships in a collage. Harvey created a poster demonstrating actions kids can take to protect themselves, including practicing asking for help in various situations. Additionally, Sandra wrote a letter to another survivor and Harvey made his own book of advice for other kids (Spinal-Robinson & Wickham, 1993).

A review of all their art made throughout treatment enabled Sandra and Harvey to talk about the struggles and growth that took place over time. They also made artwork expressing their hopes and dreams for their futures. Discussing options for continuing art and creative forms of expression helped Sandra and Harvey to establish ongoing avenues for coping (Lusebrink & Hinz, 2016).

Sandra's Survivors Art Therapy Group

Herman (1997) recommends group therapy for survivors during the reconnection stage. Powerful group art therapy interventions with child survivors of sexual abuse and group art therapy with adolescent survivors of sexual assault have been implemented (Pifalo, 2002; Backos & Pagan, 1999). Sandra's survivor's support group created a sense of belonging with a community of teen survivors. She created affirmation cards with images and words of inspiration to give to her fellow group members, solidifying her positive identity as a survivor and thriver. To address socio-political empowerment, Sandra and her fellow group members created "protest signs" with slogans (Crisci et al., 1998, p. 457).

Caregiver–Child Interventions with Pamela and Her Children

Attention to supporting healthy attachment between Pamela and her children continued during the reconnection stage. Art activities used with the family included making gifts for each other out of art materials, tracing each other's hands, drawing portraits of one another, and a "scribble chase" game in which the parent and child take turns "chasing" the other person's line as they draw on a shared piece of paper (Malchiodi, 2014, p. 58). These art interventions strengthened their family relationships.

During family sessions, Pamela talked with her children about the ways in which she is taking steps to protect them. Sandra shared her art journal with her mother. Harvey gave his sister and mother the gifts he made for them throughout therapy. Sandra continued to make plans for the upcoming family gathering and her brother was proud to make the decorations for the event.

Recommendations

Pursuing Additional Knowledge and Training

This chapter introduced a strength-based art approach to the journey from trauma to resiliency. Practitioners are advised to seek formalized training and education in the field of art therapy and try art activities themselves before offering them to families. The American Art Therapy Association provides a wealth of information about the profession, educational programs, and art therapy supervision (arttherapy.org).

Response Art

The interventionalist's view of the world can be deeply impacted by supporting families as they confront their most painful experiences. The making of response art following a session or in supervision provides a new perspective and mobilizes support among colleagues in group settings (Fish, 2012). Through applying a technique called *El Duende* process painting, in which the same canvas is painted on in multiple layers, the author of this chapter re-affirmed her commitment to trauma work (Abbenante, as cited in Sanders, 2018). The inspiration she gained from working with children and families is reflected in the layers of paint and musical notes. A key embedded on the canvas represents the courage and wisdom of survivors as expressed in the arts. The therapist is positively transformed through witnessing the resilience of each child and family (see Figure 4.5).

Creativity Transforms Trauma-Informed Practice

As we saw in this chapter, creative expression is a powerful intervention in the treatment of trauma. Art therapy embodies the core qualities of trauma-informed

Figure 4.5   Author's Response Art.

care that were central to Pamela, Sandra, and Harvey's recovery (National Center for Trauma-Informed Care as cited in Steele & Malchiodi, 2012, p. 17). Art made visible the ways in which Sandra and Harvey coped with their trauma and allowed Sandra and Harvey to reflect on positive changes in their family. Art promoted their sense of safety by providing choices about how and what to express. Goals were based on collaboration with Pamela and her children and incorporated familial and cultural forms of creative expression (Jackson, 2020). Healing from trauma happened in the context of their strong family and community bonds and art activities served to deepen these relational connections (Chapman, 2014). Sandra's art journal and Harvey's art projects helped to develop new perspectives on their experiences (Carolan & Stafford, 2018). Through sharing their thoughts and feelings with their mother and receiving her support, the family came to believe that recovery from trauma was possible.

Investment in the arts by trauma-informed systems is a crucial step to strengthen relationships, incorporate innovative approaches, and increase the capacity of providers to support the well-being of communities. The many pivotal contributions of the field of art therapy include arts-based research and supervision, studio arts experiences within organizations, and partnerships with community artists in the prevention of child maltreatment. It is critical that creativity is made accessible as a primary resource for all families like Pamela's on their journey from trauma to resiliency.

Notes

1. Reprinted with permission, Méndez-Negrete, J. (2013, p. 318). Expressive creativity: Narrative text and creative cultural expressions as a healing praxis. *Journal of Creativity in Mental Health, 8*, pp. 315–325. doi:10.1080/15401383.2013.821934
2. This fictitious case story is a compilation of presenting experiences commonly encountered in trauma therapy.
3. The artwork images in the chapter were not created by the individuals depicted in this fictional case story.

References

American Art Therapy Association. (2017, June). Definitions of the profession. Retrieved from https://www.arttherapy.org/upload/2017_DefinitionofProfession.pdf

Backos, A., & Pagon, B. E. (1999). Finding a voice: Art therapy with female adolescent sexual abuse survivors. *Art Therapy: Journal of the American Art Therapy Association, 16*(3), 162–132. https://doi.org/10.1080/07421656.1999.10129650

Backos, A., & Samuelson, K. W. (2017). Projective drawings of mothers and children exposed to intimate partner violence: A mixed methods analysis. *Art Therapy: Journal of the American Art Therapy Association, 34*(2), 58–67. https://doi.org/10.1080/07421656.2017.1312150

Carolan, R., & Stafford, K. (2018). Theory and art therapy. In R. Carolan & A. Backos (Eds.), *Emerging perspectives in art therapy: Trends, movements, and developments* (pp. 17–32). New York: Routledge.

Chapman, L. (2014). *Neurobiologically informed trauma therapy with children and adolescents: Understanding mechanisms of change.* New York: W.W. Norton.

Chew, J. (1998). *Women survivors of childhood sexual abuse: Healing through group work, beyond survival.* New York: Haworth.

Cohen, J. A., Mannarino, A. P., & Deblinger, E. (2006). *Treating trauma and traumatic grief in children and adolescents.* New York: Guilford.

Crisci, G., Lay, M., & Lowenstein, L. (1998). *Paper dolls and paper airplanes: Therapeutic exercises for sexually traumatized children.* Indianapolis, IN: Kidsrights.

Curry, N. A., & Kasser, T. (2005). Can coloring mandalas reduce anxiety? *Art Therapy: Journal of the American Art Therapy Association, 22*(2), 81–85. https://doi.org/10.1080/07421656.2005.10129441

Fish, B. J. (2012). Response art: The art of the art therapist. *Art Therapy: Journal of the American Art Therapy Association, 29*(3), 138–143. https://doi.org/10.1080/07421656.2012.701594

Gantt, L., & Tripp, T. (2016). The image comes first: Treating preverbal trauma with Art Therapy. In J. L. King (Ed.), *Art therapy, trauma, and neuroscience: Theoretical and practical perspectives* (pp. 67–99). New York: Routledge.

Gaskill, R. L., & Perry, B. (2014). The neurobiological power of play: Using the neurosequential model of therapeutics to guide play in the healing process. In C. A. Malchiodi & D. A. Crenshaw (Eds.), *Creative arts and play therapy for attachment problems* (pp. 178–194). New York: Guilford. https://doi.org/10.1080/07421656.2012.701594

Gil, E. (1991). *The healing power of play: Working with abused children.* New York: Guilford.

Harber, K. (2011). Creating a framework: Art therapy elicits the narrative. *Art Therapy: Journal of the American Art Therapy Association, 28*(1), 19–25. https://doi.org/10.1080/07421656.2011.557766

Hass-Cohen, N., Bokoch, R., Findlay, J. C., & Witting, A. B. (2018). A four-drawing art therapy trauma and resiliency protocol study. *Arts in Psychotherapy, 61*, 44–56. https://doi.org/10.1016/j.aip.2018.02.003

Heegaard, M. (1991). *When something terrible happens: Children can learn to cope with grief.* Minneapolis, MN: Woodland.

Herman, J. (1997). *Trauma and recovery: The aftermath of violence-from domestic abuse to political terror.* New York: Basic Books.

Hinz, L. D. (2020). *Expressive therapies continuum: A framework for using art therapy* (2nd ed.). New York: Taylor and Francis.

Jackson, L. C. (2020). *Cultural humility in art therapy: Applications for practice, research, social justice, self-care, and pedagogy.* London: Jessica Kingsley.

Jackson, L., Mezzera, C., & Satterberg, M. (2018). Wisdom through diversity in art therapy. In R. Carolan & A. Backos (Eds.), *Emerging perspectives in art therapy: Trends, movements, and developments* (pp. 105–122). New York: Routledge.

Kagan, S. L., & Lusebrink, V. B. (1978). The expressive therapies continuum. *Art Psychotherapy, 5*(4), 171–180. https://doi.org/10.1016/0090-9092(78)90031-5

Klorer, P. G. (2016). Neuroscience and art therapy with severely traumatized children: The art is the evidence. In J. L. King (Ed.), *Art therapy, trauma, and neuroscience: Theoretical and practical perspectives* (pp. 42–66). New York: Routledge.

Kruger, D., & Swanepoel, M. (2017). Gluing the pieces together: Female adolescents' construction of meaning through digital metaphoric imagery in trauma therapy. *Arts in Psychotherapy, 54,* 92–104. https://doi.org/10.1016/j.aip.2017.04.01

Lowenfield, V., & Brittain, W. (1987). *Creative and mental growth* (8th ed.). New York: MacMillan.

Lusebrink, V. B., & Hinz, L. D. (2016). The expressive therapies continuum as a framework in the treatment of trauma. In J. L. King (Ed.), *Art therapy, trauma, and neuroscience: Theoretical and practical perspectives* (pp. 42–66). New York: Routledge.

Malchiodi, C. (2012). Sensory based, trauma informed assessment. In W. Steele & C. A. Malchiodi (Eds.), *Trauma-informed practices with children and adolescents* (pp. 49–71). New York: Taylor & Francis.

Malchiodi, C. (2014). Art therapy, attachment, and parent-child dyads. In C. Malchiodi & D. A. Crenshaw (Eds.), *Creative arts and play therapy for attachment problems* (pp. 2–68). New York: Guilford.

Méndez-Negrete, J. (2013). Expressive creativity: Narrative text and creative cultural expressions as a healing praxis. *Journal of Creativity in Mental Health, 8*(3), 315–325. https://doi.org/10.1080/15401383.2013.821934

Metzl, E. S. (2009). The role of creative thinking in resilience after Hurricane Katrina. *Psychology of Aesthetics, Creativity, and the Arts, 3*(2), 112–123. https://doi.org/10.1037/a0013479

Mohr, E. (2014). Posttraumatic growth in youth survivors of a disaster: An arts-based research project. *Art Therapy: Journal of the American Art Therapy Association, 31*(4), 155–162. https://doi.org/10.1080/07421656.2015.963487

Pifalo, T. (2002). Pulling out the thorns: Art therapy with sexually abused children and adolescents. *Art Therapy: Journal of the American Art Therapy Association, 19*(1), 12–22. https://doi.org/10.1080/07421656.2002.10129724

Prescott, M. V., Sekunder, B., Bailey, B., & Hoshino, A. (2008). Art making as a component and facilitator of resiliency with homeless youth. *Art Therapy: Journal of the American Art Therapy Association, 25*(4), 156–163. https://doi.org/10.1080/07421656.2008.10129549

Sanders, G. (2018). Emerging paradigms in art therapy supervision: The use of response art. In R. Carolan & A. Backos (Eds.), *Emerging perspectives in art therapy: Trends, movements, and developments* (pp. 155–165). New York: Routledge.

Spinal-Robinson, P., & Wickham, R. E. (1993). *High tops: A workbook for teens who have been sexually abused.* Notre Dame, IN: Self-Esteem Janice Publishers.

Steele, W., & Malchiodi, C. A. (2012). *Trauma-informed practices with children and adolescents.* New York: Taylor & Francis.

Wilkinson, R. A., & Chilton, G. (2018). *Positive art therapy theory and practice: Integrating positive psychology with art therapy.* New York: Routledge.

Chapter 5

Refugees' Resettlement and Traumatic Experiences

Utilizing Trauma-Informed Practices with Refugee Women to Address War Trauma and Enhance Resilience

Shulamit N. Ritblatt and Audrey Hokoda

On the TV screen, we all saw the lifting of babies from their parents' arms by American soldiers trying to get them to safety. We all saw the pictures of thousands of Afghan people trying to flee their country, desperate to escape due to the departure of the American military and the regained control of the Taliban. In 2020, the United Nations High Commissioner for Refugees (UNHCR) reported that an estimated 26.4 million of the 82.4 million persons forcibly displaced worldwide were refugees. Since 1975, more than 3.7 million refugees have settled in the US (USA UNHCR, 2021). More than two-thirds of the refugees have originated from five countries in 2020: Syria, Venezuela, Afghanistan, South Sudan, and Myanmar. Among the refugees, there are 48% women and a quarter of them are aged 18 years and above (UNHCR, 2021). In 1980, the Refugee Act law was signed to provide a consistent, permanent formal system to address the incoming refugees and asylum seekers to the US and provide the support as outlined in the policies.

DOI: 10.4324/9781003046295-7

Who is a refugee? What are the effects of being a refugee on individuals, families, and children? How do women and children, the most vulnerable, fare as refugees? How can we use trauma-informed practices to support their resilience and address their needs? This chapter will present the traumatic experiences of refugees in their quest for resettlement and will focus specifically on women refugees, their vulnerable position and status, and ways to work and address their needs and parental role utilizing trauma-informed practices.

Refugees, Trauma, and Resettlement

Under the Immigration and Nationality Act (INA), "a refugee is an alien who, generally, has experienced past persecution or has a well-founded fear of persecution on account of race, religion, nationality, membership in a particular social group, or political opinion" (USRAP Report, 2021). Kunz's Kinetic Model of Refugee Theory (1973; 1981) offers two categories of refugees based on their departure and flight patterns: Anticipatory and acute. The anticipatory group has awareness of the danger early on and prepares for the departure and resettlement in a more orderly manner, whereas the acute group is forced to leave their homes with no warning or notice. This group of refugees face more traumatic experiences than the anticipatory refugees who are more in control of their destiny. Understanding refugees' experiences in the context of historical, social, and political forces is important to supporting their needs as they adjust to their new homes (George, 2010).

Refugees not only leave behind their homes, social support systems, and cultural understanding of their environments, they may have also experienced major traumas in the wake of war and terror such as forced migration, torture, rape, injury, starvation, and/or the witnessing of the death of friends and family members (Lambert & Alhassoon, 2015; Palic & Elklit, 2011). Upon their arrival in new countries, refugees are likely to experience in their resettlement an array of new stressors, including separation from family and friends, exposure to disease, refugee camps, problems assimilating in new cultures, difficulty obtaining asylum status, housing problems, and social isolation (Lambert & Alhassoon, 2015; Ostrander et al., 2017; Shannon et al., 2015).

To understand the resettlement experiences of refugees, Interiano-Shiverdecker, Kondili, and Parikh-Foxx (2020) adapted the concepts of cultural and social capital developed by Pierre Bourdieu (1986). Cultural capital includes the resources such as skills, educational qualifications, and cultural attitudes and practices that one has, and social capital is being a member of a group and having a social network that can provide support. According to their research findings, refugees lose both social and cultural capital when they resettle in a new country, and this increases the challenges they face. Ndofor-Tah et al. (2019) propose the Integration Framework that describe 14 indicators involved in the resettlement of the refugees: Work, education, housing, health and social care, leisure, social bonds, social bridges, social links, language and communication, culture, digital skills, safety, stability, and rights and responsibilities. Strang and Quinn (2021) indicated that trust must be added to the framework as it is the facilitator of the integration process. These indicators correspond to the social and cultural capital that refugees have lost when leaving their home country.

Physical and Mental Health Effects Associated with Trauma

The cumulative loss and trauma refugees have experienced puts them at risk for physical and mental health problems; they are ten times more likely than the general population to have Post-Traumatic Stress Disorder (PTSD), depression, and substance use (Delker & Freyd, 2014; Fazel et al., 2005; Salt et al., 2017; Steel et al., 2009). Various symptoms of PTSD and depression in trauma-exposed refugees include anxiety, poor concentration, disorientation, flashbacks, nightmares, hypervigilance, violent outbursts, crying, and suicide attempts (Shannon et al., 2015; Tay et al., 2015).

Chronic exposure to trauma can cause neurobiological disruptions that primarily affect the hypothalamic–pituitary–adrenal axis and relate to heightened fear and threat responses (Schore, 2001). This disruption affects one's ability to access the prefrontal cortex of the brain which impacts executive functioning skills such as emotional and behavioral regulation, language skills, memory, and problem-solving. Individuals repeatedly experiencing this heightened stress response system can exhibit physical illnesses (e.g., pain, gastrointestinal disorders, cardiovascular disease), mental pathologies (e.g., depression, PTSD, Post-Traumatic Embitterment Disorder [PTED], panic disorder, anxiety), as well as risky behaviors that includes drug and alcohol use, sexual promiscuity, and antisocial behaviors (Abajobir et al., 2017; Flores-Torres et al., 2020; Kleber, 2019; Linden & Arnold, 2021; Sowder et al., 2018).

Experiences of Women Refugees and Their Children

Women refugees face challenges as they adapt to a new country. In many of their home countries, women are marginalized and have limited power living in a patriarchal cultural structure, which may be linked to domestic violence comprising verbal, physical, and financial abuse (Fineran & Kohli, 2020).

Refugee women are especially vulnerable to violence (De Schrijver et al., 2018), with women refugees reporting higher levels of Intimate Partner Violence (IPV) than any other group of women (Sabri et al., 2018). Although US laws may be less tolerant of violence between married couples than the Middle East, lack of knowledge of such laws and cultural norms and expectations for Middle Eastern women may prevent them from seeking help. Because refugee women are expected to be the primary family caregivers, often isolated and financially dependent on their husbands, they may be forced to endure violence as their role is to keep their families together and they see few options. Cultural norms make it difficult for women to seek employment outside of the home; they may also lack the support from their family to acquire the necessary education needed for most jobs (Moghadam, 2003).

Refugee women who have experienced trauma and violence in their country are at risk for mental health problems such as depression and Post-Traumatic Stress Disorder, and they may show difficulties in regulating their emotions and behaviors, as well as display social information processing biases (Fazel et al., 2012; Heptinstall et al., 2004). Many of these women continue to live with fear that someone in their family who still lives back in their homeland will die. As they resettle in a new country, refugee women express unhappiness, distress, isolation, and loneliness (Ranck, 2011). They find it hard to locate a social network of support and report having a difficult time seeking help outside of the home and accessing mental health services (Ellis et al., 2010). Refugee mothers may face additional challenges as parent/child relationships might be negatively affected due to different acculturation processes experienced by their children. Children acquire the native language and socialize faster than their parents, and parents often need to rely on children for support when engaging with agencies (Frounfelker et al., 2017; Kohli & Fineran, 2020). The loss of supportive social structures supporting their parental status, roles, and beliefs can create more stress and conflict for refugee women (Kohli & Fineran, 2020).

The children are also at risk for experiencing trauma in the wake of fleeing persecution and facing resettlement with their families. Like their parents, many of them have been exposed to violence, deprivation in refugee camps, and loss of family, friends, and community. Even if they were spared exposure to direct violence and trauma, their well-being is influenced by their parents' responses to the traumas they experienced (Eruyar et al., 2018). This is called intergenerational trauma and refers to the interconnectivity among family members across generations—when one generation experiences trauma and the next generations suffer the ongoing impact on their health and well-being. Research on intergenerational effects of trauma has focused on family factors and parents' coping as the main mechanisms by which parents' trauma affects their children's well-being (Isobel et al., 2019; Lehrner & Yehuda, 2018; Sangalang & Vang, 2017). Refugee women exposed to violence and trauma exhibiting PTSD can struggle controlling their temper and regulating their emotions and are at risk for harsh, aggressive parenting with their children. Middle Eastern refugee women, due to their past violent experiences, might be conditioned to think and react aggressively (Reitmanova, 2009). Heightened fear, hypervigilance, and anxiety may be modeled as coping strategies when stressed, and children may learn their parents' beliefs that the world and people are dangerous (Janoff-Bulman, 1992). Studies report that immigrant survivors of torture and war have children who exhibit more anxiety, depression, and psychological problems (e.g., Daud et al., 2005). Symptoms of traumatic stress in children of refugees include increased anti-social and delinquent behaviors (Sangalang et al., 2017), as well as, temper tantrums, poor academic performance, erratic sleeping and eating habits, nightmares, somatic complaints, and impaired social skills (Park & Katsiaficas, 2019).

Resilience and Post-Traumatic Growth in Refugees

Despite risks for negative trauma effects, many refugees who are trauma survivors also have an ability to heal and grow (George, 2010). Survivors of trauma can show Post-Traumatic Growth (PTG) (Joseph, 2009; Tedeschi & Calhoun, 1996; Xiaoli et al., 2019) in which they feel they have positively grown or changed following adversity. For example, survivors may feel more appreciative of life and their own strengths, they may feel more spiritually connected, and they may see positive changes in their relationships (Tedeschi & Calhoun, 1996). Growth following trauma is facilitated by a strong social support system and spiritual foundation, as well as by an individual's capacity to positively reevaluate the situation and cognitively reflect (Henson et al., 2021). When individuals experience traumas, their core beliefs about their safety, people, and the world can be shattered (Janoff-Bulman, 1992). Rebuilding these core assumptions about their world requires cognitive effort—one must deliberately reflect on their experiences rather than be overwhelmed with intrusive memories of their traumas. This is a goal of therapies focused on coping with trauma—creating a safe place where one can recall and reflect on their experiences while managing the emotional distress. This can help survivors develop a better understanding of the impact of their experiences and produce a narrative of their traumas that has meaning and purpose (Triplett et al., 2012).

Research on refugees reveal protective factors associated with their resilience and PTG as they resettle into new countries. Strong social support systems have been highlighted as important for Middle Eastern refugees. For example, in Middle Eastern refugees resettling in Germany, social support and individual resilience is negatively related to psychological distress (Schlechter et al., 2021). A study on 626 Syrian refugees in Canada provides more evidence on the importance of building relationships with families and connecting with religious organizations to help them network and obtain support (UNHCR, RCPS, 2020). Further, Islamic religious coping is an important influence on the resilience and healing from trauma in adult Muslim refugees (Skalisky et al., 2020).

Women refugees emphasize not only the importance of external resources that provide ongoing support throughout the resettlement process, but also the importance of positive hopeful internal thinking and beliefs in helping them grow from the adversities they have experienced (Goodman et al., 2017). When mothers have memories of love and strong attachment to their own mothers and caregivers, these memories, called "Angel memories," can serve to protect against the transmission of negative trauma effects on their children (Lieberman et al., 2005; Narayan et al., 2017; 2019). Narratives shared by Burmese refugee women revealed how their stories of positive growth were intertwined with their stories of surviving experiences of trauma, loss, and hardship (Maung et al., 2021). Validation and affirmation of the past traumatic experiences are paramount to helping the survivors develop their narrative and their understanding that healing is a process. When parents share these narratives of survival and coping with their children, this can promote recovery (Miller et al., 2019) and be beneficial to the children as they also find meaning in what happened to their family. These shared narratives of endurance and courage can instill pride in their family and the cultural values and traditions that helped them survive, building resilience in future generations (Argenti & Schramm, 2009). Participating in cultural celebrations, expressing themselves through art and literature, and finding purpose by becoming an activist or helping others are ways descendants of survivors of trauma have shown resilience and positive growth (Malchiodi, 2020; Nagata & Patel, 2021; Whyte, 2020).

Trauma-Informed Interventions

Trauma-informed care (TIC) has been successful in helping survivors of trauma. Trauma-informed practices focus on safety and trusting relationships, while supporting survivors' choice and control when healing from adversities (Butler et al., 2011; Clervil et al., 2013). Despite the success of trauma-informed programs, there are unique barriers for refugees obtaining treatment that include, language, educational deficits, fear of stigma associated with mental health issues, and lack of trust in the new country's systems of care (Hinton et al., 2012; Shannon et al., 2015). It is critical when providing trauma-informed services that we understand these social and cultural barriers and alter medical/ traditional service modes for people resistant to mental health services, offering therapeutic activities aligned with their social cultural beliefs. Partnering with community leaders/brokers, providing for basic needs first while building trust, and offering different modes of psychoeducational therapies highlighting their strengths and resilience are strategies for successfully working with refugee families (Pejic et al., 2017).

Refugees who have experienced trauma may have difficulty talking about their experiences and symptoms in traditional clinical therapies, and they may need non-traditional interventions that provide opportunities to develop trust and feel safe (Ely et al., 2017). Non-verbal, expressive, and body-oriented activities can help connect trauma survivors with their feelings, memories, and physical being (Clervil et al., 2013). Survivors of war and violence can use art to provide a restorative expression of the traumatic events they have experienced (Denov & Shevell, 2019). Goodman and Dent (2019) implemented a two-generation intervention to parents with young children offering yoga to the parents, and storytelling and acting of the story for the young children. Other modifications that can be helpful for working with refugee populations include providing trauma focused services in spaces that are perceived as natural environments as refugees may be resistant to entering mental health clinics. For example, children of refugee families who have trauma-related mental health problems can receive the treatment via a child psychiatric consultation in the schools, primary care medical clinics, or at community organizations. This offers culturally appropriate services in familiar, safe community spaces (Rousseau et al., 2012).

Research has described the benefits of using cultural brokers in providing social services to refugee and immigrant populations (Lin et al., 2018; Salami et al., 2018). Cultural brokers focus on bridging individuals of different cultural backgrounds, as they understand the group's traditions and beliefs, communication styles, and practices (Jezewski, 1990). For example, cultural brokers develop an emotional connection that increases the engagement of families, and cultural brokers can serve as role models as the parents and their children adjust to the new culture (Lin et al., 2018; Yohani et al., 2019). Use of cultural brokers are highlighted in trauma systems therapies addressing the needs of refugee youth and families as they connect with school and community (Kaplin et al., 2019). Reflective practices are also successful in trauma-informed interventions. Using the reflective process helps service providers tailor the course of interventions to the clients' preferences (Butler et al., 2011), and thus, follows trauma-informed principles of empowering individuals to collaborate and share power in the planning of sessions. Creating a therapeutic environment that supports the participants' choices and sense of control builds their self-efficacy and contributes to the building of trusting relationships (Butler et al., 2011). Reflective practices help participants cope with traumatic stress and allows one to express emotions in a safe place (Sprang et al., 2011). It can encourage individuals to reflect on past experiences without judgment, to slow down and choose their actions and next steps (Heffron & Murch, 2010).

Showcase: Utilizing Trauma-Informed Practices Working with Middle Eastern Refugee Women

The current pilot intervention was developed for Middle Eastern refugee women with young children settling into the US. Guided by trauma-informed principles, the program focused on safety and trusting relationships, and supporting choice, shared power, and strengths (Butler et al., 2011; Clervil et al., 2013). The group facilitator of the pilot program was an immigrant from Jordan who understood the cultural norms and values held by the Middle Eastern refugee women participants. The participants were 5 women (from Jordan, Iran, Iraq, Morocco, and Syria), ages 29–50, with 3–5 children each; they were recruited from schools, faith-based organizations, and community agencies serving Middle Eastern refugee families. The sessions took place at the group facilitator's home, were conducted in Arabic, and food (e.g., fruits, nuts) was offered. Each session was scheduled based on the availability of the women, as opposed to more typical weekly sessions at a community agency or school. Having a cultural broker and making these adjustments in location and scheduling of the sessions addressed some of the barriers in language and service access that refugee women face. The pilot program also used a group intervention format as this can help decrease isolation, empower one to examine issues of trauma (Elliot et al., 2005), and can enhance individual and family resiliency (Cohen, 2011). Providing a private and safe setting where the women could take off their head-covers and share intimate memories and feelings without fear of stigma were adjustments made for these Middle Eastern refugee women to follow trauma-informed principles of safety, trust, and empowerment (Al-sennawi, 2014).

All sessions shared the same general structure and sequencing following trauma-informed principles to promote safety and predictability (Herman, 1992; Osofsky, 2009). Each session started with "checking in" with each woman allowing each one to share how she was doing, and this was followed by an "ice breaker" activity to strengthen and build the relationships among the women. A song was then played, with the facilitator translating the lyrics, the women shared how they felt listening to the song, and after summarizing what they had said, the facilitator introduced the topic of the session and the activity for the day. The lessons incorporated expressive arts (e.g., music, movement, drawing) that can help survivors of trauma who have difficulty accessing the prefrontal cortex part of the brain that governs language and verbal skills and who may not benefit from talk-based therapies (Faulkner, 2017; Malchiodi, 2020; van der Kolk, 2014). These non-traditional, non-verbal, body-oriented activities that can help connect trauma survivors with their feelings, memories, and physical being (Clervil et al., 2013) were used in every session. Another feature of this intervention was the incorporation of reflective practice in every session. Reflective expressive activities and group discussion were centered on their learning from their traumas, reflecting on how their past experiences have affected their parenting, relationships, and self-esteem. In the therapeutic environment that the group facilitator created in her home, the women could reflect on their responses to trauma and express their emotions in a safe place without judgment (Al-sennawi, 2014).

Description of Trauma-Informed Lessons

Ten lessons were developed based on research on refugees and trauma-informed practices, with each session utilizing multi-sensory-based activities that included music, movement, animation, art, photos, reflection, and relaxation techniques. The music and lessons were adapted from an early childhood program, Circle of Education® (Ritblatt, 2013), that focuses on social emotional wellness.

The first lessons addressed self-esteem and the recognition of the women's strengths as survivors of trauma and migration. Three themes within these lessons, "My culture of origin," the "Culture of women," and "Past-trauma—war, arranged marriage," focused on addressing the women's pre-migration, migration, and post-migration traumas (DeCandia et al., 2013; George, 2012), and on helping them develop a coherent narrative of their past (Butler et al., 2011). These first lessons aimed to build self and cultural awareness and to promote bonding between the women as they share histories, challenges, and cultural values. They participated in interactive pair-share, drawing, and photo art activities as they talked about their lives and families. Songs from the Circle of Education (CoE, Ritblatt, 2013) such as, *We are All Special**, *Languages all around us**, *I Love Story Time**, and *Memories** helped elicit reflection about their strengths and challenges, "Angel memories" and loved ones, and experiences with war, family loss, arranged marriage, and adjustment to the US.

The next set of lessons centered on identifying the effects of trauma and on promoting positive coping strategies. Songs such as *Things are Changing** and *It's OK to Say Good Bye** focus on dealing with change and loss, and sample follow-up reflective questions were: What changes and goodbyes come to your mind when listening to these songs? Which relationships do you think about? Can change be good? Other lessons taught about depression, feeling a loss of control, and an inability to express emotions. Songs such as *Getting Mad is Not the*

Way*, *Keep Your Hands to Yourself**, and *Words Can Help and Words Can Hurt** prompted a discussion about dealing with strong emotions, problems with corporal punishment, and the harm these interactions can cause to the relationships with their children and others. After they shared positive strategies to cope with stress and negative emotions, they were encouraged to dance and create music as they were provided with instruments (e.g., drums, maracas, jingling bells), as well as scarves to have fun and express themselves through music and movement. They practiced breathing exercises, engaged in meditation, and learned the importance of prioritizing self-care.

The next sessions continued to focus on trauma and how it affects the women's relationships, particularly with their children. The songs, *I like you when** and *Routines I do each day**, encourage the women to reflect on positive memories and family routines that include sharing a family meal and reading a favorite book together. The sessions reviewed the importance of positive parenting and included lessons on anger management and positive communication. Another activity using children's books prompted a discussion on the challenges of raising their children and navigating the community as they struggle with English language skills. A song, *Every Night I Dream**, instills hope, positive thinking, and courage as they conquer fears and go off on adventures, and an activity in which the women made a collage of pictures from magazines elicited conversations highlighting their interests and personal strengths.

The last sessions end the program, emphasizing the importance of self-care and love of self and others.

The women began to create a family photo album that included past photos if they had any, as well as recent photos. A writing activity instructed women to think about the name of a special person who changed their life. The women discussed strengths in themselves and the narrative of resilience that they want to share with their children. The songs, *Let's do Aerobics**, *Stretching**; and *It's Time for a Checkup** were played which prompted dancing and exercising, as well as attention to other forms of self-care (e.g., doctor's visits, nutrition). In addition to encouraging physical self-care, the women engaged in a positive affirmation activity in which they shared what they like about themselves with the group.

Discussion and Future Directions

This chapter reviewed the unique challenges refugee women with children face as they resettle into the US. Despite their risk for PTSD and depression, refugees' mental health problems are often not addressed due to language barriers, stigma, inability to navigate healthcare systems and services, and lack of available screenings focusing on past trauma and mental health (Pace et al., 2015). Western models of pathology and therapy do not match refugees' cultural and linguistic sensitivities and therefore can create distrust, stigma, and shame (Im et al., 2020). Thus, it is recommended to replace individual pathological models of mental health services with psychosocial holistic approaches that are strength-based and promote resiliency (Im et al., 2020). Culturally appropriate education and health promotion services include non-traditional modes of interventions, such as music, arts, yoga, and guided imaginary techniques (Ely et al., 2017; Pace et al., 2015).

A pilot intervention was developed for Middle Eastern women with young children that addressed many of these barriers through trauma-informed practices. A cultural broker who understood the women's beliefs, spoke Arabic and held the sessions in her home, created an environment that promoted their feelings of safety and trust. Being in a group with other women who shared similar traumatic experiences helped them form relationships with each other, and receive and give peer support, as their self-awareness and sensitivity to their children's needs increased. Non-verbal, expressive arts were used to help the women connect with their feelings and memories, and the activities were engaging and helped the women bond. Reflective practices were also used in every session as the women learned to slow down and reflect on their past traumas and the strengths and coping strategies that helped them survive.

Research points to the importance of providing women refugees with culturally responsive counseling and psychoeducational programs to help support their parenting and child-rearing practices, as well as receive information that can protect them from violence (Fineran & Kohli, 2020). To address the social and emotional needs of young children in refugee families we need to: (a) integrate trauma-informed practices into the early educational programs; have well-trained professionals who are well versed in mental health; (b) implement home visitation programs to assess the needs and the severity of the trauma and its effects on the family and parent/child relationship; (c) connect families to services; and (d) use screenings tools to identify mental health needs early and provide the needed intervention (Park & Katsiaficas, 2019). It is important to support women refugees who are most vulnerable, who are interconnected to the whole family system (Ostrander et al., 2017), and as primary caregivers of their children, may be best able to promote resilience and to prevent the transmission of negative trauma effects on future generations.

References

Abajobir, A. A., Kisely, S., Maravilla, J. G., Williams, G., & Najman, J. M. (2017). Gender differences in the association between childhood sexual abuse and risky sexual behaviours: A systematic review and meta-analysis. *Child Abuse and Neglect*, *63*, 249–260.

Al-Sennawi, D. (2014). *Reflective practice using music-based program to support self-awareness and mental health with women from Middle-East.* Thesis project for completion of Master degree in Child Development, SDSU.

Argenti, N., & Schramm, K. (2009). *Remembering violence: Anthropological perspectives on intergenerational Transmission.* New York: Berghahn Books.

Bourdieu, P. (1986). The forms of capital. In J. G. Richardson (Ed.), *Handbook of theory and research for the sociology of education* (pp. 241–258). New York: Greenwood.

Butler, L. D., Critelli, F. M., & Rinfrette, E. S. (2011). Trauma-informed care and mental health. *Directions in Psychiatry, 31,* 197–210.

Clervil, R., Guarino, K., DeCandia, C. J., & Beach, C. A. (2013). *Trauma-informed care for displaced populations: A guide for community-based service providers.* Waltham, MA: The National Center on Family Homelessness, A Practice Area of American Institutes for Research Health and Social Development Program.

Cohen, R. (2011). *The impacts of affordable housing on health: A research summary.* Washington, DC: Center for Housing Policy and Enterprise Community Partners.

Daud, A., Skoglund, E., & Rydelius, P. A. (2005). Children in families of torture victims: Transgenerational transmission of parents' traumatic experiences to their children. *International Journal of Social Welfare, 14*(1), 23–32. Retrieved from https://doi-org .libproxy.sdsu.edu/10.1111/j.1468-2397.2005.00336.x

DeCandia, C. J., Murphy, C. M., & Coupe, N. (2013). Needs of special populations of families without homes. In M. Haskett, S. Perlman, & B. Cowan (Eds.), *Supporting families experiencing homelessness: Current practices and future directions* (pp. 79–201). New York: Springer Science + Business Media. doi:10.1007/978-1-4614-8718-0_5

Delker, B. C., & Freyd, J. (2014). From Betrayal to the bottle: Investigating possible pathways from trauma to problematic substance use. *Journal of Traumatic Stress, 27*(5), 576–584.

Denov, M., & Shevell, M. C. (2019). Social work practice with war-affected children and families: The importance of family, culture, arts, and participatory approaches. *Journal of Family Social Work, 22*(1), 1–16. https://doi.org/10.1080/10522158.2019 .1546809

De Schrijver, L., Vander Beken, T., Krahé, B., & Keygnaert, I. (2018). Prevalence of sexual violence in migrants, applicants for international protection, and refugees in Europe: A critical interpretive synthesis of the evidence. *International Journal of Environmental Research and Public Health, 15*(9), 1979. https://doi.org/10.3390 /ijerph15091979

Elliott, D. E., Bjelajac, P., Fallot, R. D., Markoff, L. S., & Reed, B. G. (2005). Trauma-informed or trauma-denied: Principles and implementation of trauma-informed services for women. *Journal of Community Psychology, 33*(4), 461–477. https://doi .org/10.1002/jcop.20063

Ellis, B. H., Lincoln, K. A., Charney, E. M., Ford-Paz, R., Benson, M., & Strunin, L. (2010). Mental health service utilization of Somali adolescents: Religion, community, and school as gateways to healing. *Transcultural Psychiatry, 47*(5), 789–811.

Ely, E. G., Koury, S., Bennett, K., Hartinger, C., Green, S., & Nochajski, T. (2017). "I Feel Like I Am Finding Peace": Exploring the use of a combined art therapy and adapted seeking safety program with refugee support groups. *Advances in Social Work, 18*(1), 103–115. https://doi.org/10.18060/21130

Eruyar, S., Maltby, J., & Vostanis, P. (2018). Mental health problems of Syrian refugee children: The role of parental factors. *European Child and Adolescent Psychiatry*, *27*(4), 401–409.

Faulkner, S. (2017). Rhythm2Recovery: A model of practice combining rhythmic music with cognitive reflection for social and emotional health within trauma recovery. *Australian and New Zealand Journal of Family Therapy*, *38*(4), 627–636. https://doi.org/10.1002/anzf.1268

Fazel, M., Reed, R. V., Panter-Brick, C., & Stein, A. (2012). Mental health of displaced and refugee children resettled in high-income countries: Risk and protective factors. *Lancet*, *379*(9812), 266–282.

Fazel, M., Wheeler, J., & Danesh, J. (2005). Prevalence of serious mental disorder in 7000 refugees resettled in western countries: A systematic review. *Lancet*, *365*(9467), 1309–1314.

Fineran, S., & Kohli, H. (2020). Muslim refugee women's perspectives on intimate partner violence. *Journal of Family Social Work*, *23*(3), 199–213.

Flores-Torres, M. H., Comerford, E., Signorello, L., Francine Grodstein, F., Lopez-Ridaura, R., de Castro, F., … Martín Lajous, M. (2020). Impact of adverse childhood experiences on cardiovascular disease risk factors in adulthood among Mexican women. *Child Abuse and Neglect*, *99*, 104175.

Frounfelker, R., Assefa, M., Smith, E., Hussein, A., & Betancourt, T. (2017). 'We would never forget who we are': Resettlement, cultural negotiation, and family relationships among Somali Bantu refugees. *European Child and Adolescent Psychiatry*, *26*(11), 1387–1400. https://doi.org/10. 1007/s00787-017-0991-1

George, M. (2010). A theoretical understanding of refugee trauma. *Clinical Social Work Journal*, *38*(4), 379–387. https://doi.org/10.1007/s10615-009-0252-y

George, M. (2012). Migration traumatic experience and refugee distress: Implications for social work practice. *Clinical Social Work Journal*, *40*(4), 429–437. https://doi.org/10.1007/s10615-012-0397-y

Goodman, D. R., Vesely, C. K., Letiecq, B., & Cleaveland, C. L. (2017). Trauma and resilience among refugee and undocumented immigrant women. *Journal of Counseling and Development*, *95*(3), 309–321.

Goodman, G., & Dent, V. F. (2019). When I became a refugee, this became my refuge: A proposal for implementing a two-generation intervention using yoga and narrative to promote mental health in Syrian refugee caregivers and school readiness in their preschool children. *Journal of Infant, Child, and Adolescent Psychotherapy*, *18*(4), 367–375. https://doi.org/10.1080/15289168.2019.1680939

Heffron, M. C., & Murch, T. (2010). *Reflective supervision and leadership: In infant and early childhood programs*. Washington, DC: Zero to Three.

Henson, C., Truchot, D., & Canevello, A. (2021). What promotes post traumatic growth? A systematic review. *European Journal of Trauma and Dissociation*, *5*(4), 100195.

Heptinstall, E., Sethna, V., & Taylor, E. (2004). PTSD and depression in refugee children: Associations with pre-migration trauma and post-migration stress. *European Child and Adolescent Psychiatry*, *13*(6), 373–380. https://doi.org/10.1007/s00787-004-0422-y

Herman, J. L. (1992). *Trauma and recovery: The aftermath of violence—From domestic abuse to political terror*. New York: Basic Books.

Hinton, D. E., Rivera, E. L., Hofmann, S. G., Barlow, D. H., & Otto, M. W. (2012). Adapting CBT for traumatized refugees and ethnic minority patients: Examples from culturally adapted CBT (CA-CBT). *Transcultural Psychiatry, 49*(2), 340–365. https://doi.org/10.1177/1363461512441595

Im, H., Rodriguez, C., & Grumbine, J. M. (2020). A MultiTier model of refugee mental health and psychosocial support in resettlement: Toward trauma-informed and culture-informed systems of care. *Psychological Services*. Advance online publication. http://doi.org/10.1037/ser0000412

Interiano-Shiverdecker, C. G., Kondili, E., & Parikh-Foxx, S. (2020). Refugees and the system: Social and cultural capital during U.S. resettlement. *International Journal for the Advancement of Counselling, 42*(1), 48–64. https://doi.org/10.1007/s10447-019-09383-9

Isobel, S., Goodyear, M., Furness, T., & Foster, K. (2019). Preventing intergenerational trauma transmission: A critical interpretive synthesis. *Journal of Clinical Nursing, 28*(7–8), 1100–1113. https://doi-org.libproxy.sdsu.edu/10.1111/jocn.14735

Janoff-Bulman, R. (1992). *Shattered assumptions: Towards a new psychology of trauma*. New York, NY: Free Press.

Jezewski, M. A. (1990, August). Culture brokering in migrant farm worker health care. *Western Journal of Nursing Research, 12*(4), 497–513.

Joseph, S. (2009). Growth following adversity: Positive psychological perspectives on posttraumatic stress. *Psychological Topics, 18*(2), 335–343.

Kaplin, D., Parente, K., & Santacroce, F. A. (2019). A review of the use of trauma systems therapy to treat refugee children, adolescents, and families. *Journal of Infant, Child, and Adolescent Psychotherapy, 18*(4), 417–431. https://doi.org/10.1080/15289168.2019.1687220

Kleber, R. J. (2019). Trauma and public mental health: A focused review. *Frontiers in Psychiatry, 10*, Article 451. 10.3389/fpsyt.2019.00451

Kohli, H. K., & Fineran, S. (2020). If they misbehaved, we took a stick to discipline them: Refugee mothers' struggles raising children in the United States. *Child and Family Social Work, 25*(2), 488–495.

Kunz, E. (1973). The refugee in flight: Kinetic models and forms of displacement. *International Migration Review, 7*(2), 125–146.

Kunz, E. (1981). Exile and resettlement: Refugee theory. *International Migration Review, 15*, 42–51.

Lambert, J. E., & Alhassoon, O. M. (2015). Trauma-focused therapy for refugees: Meta-analytic findings. *Journal of Counseling Psychology, 62*(1), 28–37.

Lehrner, A., & Yehuda, R. (2018). Trauma across generations and paths to adaptation and resilience. *Psychological Trauma: Theory, Research, Practice and Policy, 10*(1), 22–29. https://doi.org/10.1037/tra0000302

Lieberman, A. F., Padrón, E., Van Horn, P., & Harris, W. W. (2005). Angels in the nursery: The intergenerational transmission of benevolent parental influences. *Infant Mental Health Journal, 26*(6), 504–520. https://doi.org/10.1002/imhj.20071

Lin, C.-H., Chiang, P. P., Lux, E. A., & Lin, H. F. (2018). Immigrant social worker practice: An ecological perspective on strengths and challenges. *Children and Youth Services Review, 87*(C), 103–113.

Linden, M., & Arnold, C. P. (2021). Embitterment and posttraumatic embitterment disorder (PTED): An old, frequent, and still underrecognized problem. *Psychotherapy and Psychosomatics, 90*(2), 73–80. https://doi.org/10.1159/000511468

Malchiodi, C. A. (2020). *Trauma and expressive arts therapy: Brain, body, and imagination in the healing process*. New York: The Guilford Press.

Maung, J., Nilsson, J. E., Jeevanba, S. B., Molitoris, A., Raziuddin, A., & Soheilian, S. S. (2021). Burmese refugee women in the Midwest: Narratives of resilience and Posttraumatic Growth. *Counseling Psychologist, 49*(2), 269–304.

Miller, K. K., Brown, C. R., Shramko, M., & Svetaz, M. V. (2019). Applying trauma-informed practices to the care of refugee and immigrant youth: 10 Clinical pearls. *Children, 6*(8), 94. https://doi.org/10.3390/children6080094

Moghadam, V. M. (2003). *Modernizing women: Gender and social change in the Middle East*. Boulder, CO: Lynne Rienner Publishers.

Nagata, D. K., & Patel, R. A. (2021). "Forever foreigners": Intergenerational impacts of historical trauma from the World War II Japanese American incarceration. In P. Tummala-Narra (Ed.), *Trauma and racial minority immigrants: Turmoil, uncertainty, and resistance* (pp. 105–126). American Psychological Association. https://doi.org/10.1037/0000214-00

Narayan, A. J., Ghosh Ippen, C., Harris, W. W., & Lieberman, A. F. (2017). Assessing angels in the nursery: A pilot study of childhood memories of benevolent caregiving as protective influences. *Infant Mental Health Journal, 38*(4), 461–474. https://doi.org/10.1002/imhj.21653

Narayan, A. J., Ippen, G. C., Harris, W. W., & Lieberman, A. F. (2019). Protective factors that buffer against the intergenerational transmission of trauma from mothers to young children: A replication study of angels in the nursery. *Development and Psychopathology, 31*(1), 173–187. https://doi.org/10.1017/s0954579418001530

Ndofor-Tah, C., Strang, A., Phillimore, J., Morrice, L., Michael, L., Wood, P., & Simmons, J. (2019). *Home Office indicators of integration framework 2019*. Home Office Research Report 109. London: Home Office.

Osofsky, J. D. (2009). Perspectives on helping traumatized infants, young children, and their families. *Infant Mental Health Journal, 30*(6), 673–677.

Ostrander, J., Melville, A., & Berthold, S. M. (2017). Working with refugees in the U.S.: Trauma-informed and structurally competent social work approaches. *Advances in Social Work, 18*(1), 66–79. https://doi.org/10.18060/21282

Pace, M., Al-Obaydi, S., Nourian, M. M., & Kamimura, A. (2015). Health services for refugees in the United States: Policies and recommendations. *Public Policy and Administration Research, 5*(8), 63–68.

Palic, S., & Elklit, A. (2011). Psychosocial treatment of posttraumatic stress disorder in adult refugees: A systematic review of prospective treatment outcome studies and a critique. *Journal of Affective Disorders, 131*(1–3), 8–23.

Park, M., Katsiaficas, C., & Migration Policy Institute (MPI). (2019). Leveraging the potential of home visiting programs to serve immigrant and dual language learner families. Policy brief. In *Migration Policy Institute*, Migration Policy Institute.

Pejic, V., Alvarado, A. E., Hess, R. S., & Groark, S. (2017). Community-based interventions with refugee families using a family systems approach. *Family Journal: Counseling and Therapy for Couples and Families, 25*(1), 101–108.

Ranck, E. R. (2011). Judith A. Colbert: Welcoming newcomer children: The settlement of young immigrants and refugees: A resource for teachers and others with an interest in supporting the settlement of young children from birth through age eight. *International Journal of Early Childhood, 43*(3), 305–307.

Reitmanova, S. (2009). Review of 'Working with immigrant women. Issues and strategies for mental health professionals'. *Journal of Mental Health, 18*(2), 186–187. https://doi.org/10.1080/09638230802523062

Resettlement and Complementary Pathways Service (RCPS). (2020). *The impact of government-sponsored refugee resettlement: A meta study of findings from six countries.* Geneva: Office of the United Nations High Commissioner for Refugees (UNHCR).

Ritblatt, S. N. (2013). *Circle of Education program.* San Diego, CA: Delibrainy.

Rousseau, C., Measham, T., & Nadeau, L. (2012). Addressing trauma in collaborative mental health care for refugee children. *Clinical Child Psychology and Psychiatry, 18*(1), 121–136.

Sabri, B., Nnawulezi, N., NjieCarr, V. P. S., Messing, J., Ward-Lasher, A., Alvarez, C., & Campbell, J. C. (2018). Multilevel risk and protective factors for intimate partner violence among African, Asian, and Latina immigrant and refugee women: Perceptions of effective safety planning interventions. *Race and Social Problems, 10*(4), 348–365. https://doi.org/10.1007/s12552-018-9247-z

Salami, B., Salma, J., & Hegadoren, K. (2018). Access and utilization of mental health services for immigrants and refugees: Perspectives of immigrant service providers. *International Journal of Mental Health Nursing,* July 2018. Retrieved from https://doi.org/10.1111/inm.12512

Salt, R. J., Costantino, M. E., Dotson, E. L., & Paper, B. M. (2017). "You are not alone" strategies for addressing mental health promotion with a refugee women's sewing group. *Issues in Mental Health, 38*(4), 337–343.

Sangalang, C., & Vang, C. (2017). Intergenerational trauma in refugee families: A systematic review. *Journal of Immigrant and Minority Health, 19*(3), 745–754. Retrieved from https://doi-org.libproxy.sdsu.edu/10.1007/s10903-016-0499-7

Sangalang, C. C., Jager, J., & Harachi, T. W. (2017). Effects of maternal traumatic distress on family functioning and child mental health: An examination of Southeast Asian refugee families in the U.S. *Social Science and Medicine, 184*, 178–186.

Schlechter, P., Wilkinson, P. O., Knausenberger, J., Wanninger, K., Kamp, S., Morina, N., & Hellmann, J. H. (2021). Depressive and anxiety symptoms in refugees: Insights from classical test theory, item response theory and network analysis. *Clinical Psychology and Psychotherapy, 28*(1), 169–181.

Schore, A. N. (2001). The effects of early relational trauma on right brain development, affect regulation, and infant mental health. *Infant Mental Health Journal, 22*(1/2), 201–269.

Shannon, P. J., Wieling, E., Simmelink-McCleary, J., & Becher, E. (2015). Beyond stigma: Barriers to discussing mental health in refugee populations. *Journal of Loss and Trauma: International Perspectives on Stress & Coping, 20*(3), 281–296. https://doi.org/10.1080/15325024.2014.934629

Skalisky, J., Wanner, S., Howe, B., & Mauseth, K. (2020). Religious coping, resilience, and involuntary displacement: A mixed-methods analysis of the experience of Syrian and Palestinian refugees in Jordan. *Psychology of Religion and Spirituality.* Advance online publication. https://doi.org/10.1037/rel0000390

Sowder, K. L., Knight, L. A., & Fishalow, J. (2018). Trauma exposure and health: A review of outcomes and pathways. *Journal of Aggression, Maltreatment and Trauma, 27*(10), 1041–1059. https://doi.org/10.1080/10926771.2017.1422841

Sprang, G., Craig, C., & Clark, J. (2011). Secondary traumatic stress and burnout in child welfare workers: A comparative analysis of occupational distress across professional groups. *Child Welfare*, *90*(6), 149–168.

Steel, Z., Chey, T., Silove, D., Marnane, C., Bryant, R. A., & Van Ommeren, M. (2009). Association of torture and other potentially traumatic events with mental health outcomes among populations exposed to mass conflict and displacement: A systematic review and meta-analysis. *JAMA: Journal of the American Medical Association*, *302*(5), 537–549.

Strang, A. B., & Quinn, N. (2021). Integration or isolation? Refugees' social connections and wellbeing. *Journal of Refugee Studies*, *34*(1). https://doi.org/10.1093/jrs/fez040

Tay, A. K., Rees, S., Chen, J., Kareth, M., & Silove, D. (2015). Examining the broader psychosocial effects of mass conflict on PTSD symptoms and functional impairment amongst West Papuan refugees resettled in Papua New Guinea (PNG). *Social Science and Medicine*, *132*, 70–78. https://doi.org/10.1016/j.socscimed.2015.03.020

Tedeschi, R. G., & Calhoun, L. G. (1996). The posttraumatic growth inventory: Measuring the positive legacy of trauma. *Journal of Traumatic Stress*, *9*(3), 455–472. https://doi.org/10.1002/jts.2490090305

Triplett, K. N., Tedeschi, R. G., Cann, A., Calhoun, L. G., & Reeve, C. L. (2012). Post-traumatic growth, meaning in life, and life satisfaction in response to trauma. *Psychological Trauma: Theory, Research, Practice, and Policy*, *4*(4), 400–410.

USRAP Report (UNHCR). (2021). Retrieved from https://www.unrefugees.org/refugee-facts/usa/

van der Kolk, B. (2014). *The body keeps the score: Mind, brain and body in the transformation of trauma*. London: Allen Lane.

Whyte, L. (2020). Reliving the past to release the present: Traumatic memories and letters to my younger self. Motive8.Me Press.

World Health Organization. (2018). *Displaced or refugee women are at increased risk of violence. What can WHO do?* Geneva, Switzerland: World Health Organization.

Xiaoli, W., Kaminga, A. C., Wenjie, D., Jing, D., Zhipeng, W., Xiongfeng, P., & Aizhong, L. (2019). The prevalence of moderate-to-high posttraumatic growth: A systematic review and meta-analysis. *Journal of Affective Disorders*, *q243*, 408–415.

Yohani, S., Brosinsky, L., & Kirova, A. (2019). Syrian refugee families with young children: An examination of strengths and challenges during early resettlement. *Journal of Contemporary Issues in Education*, *14*(1), 13–32.

Chapter 6

Creciendo Juntos (Growing Together)

Building Leadership in Latino Parents in a Trauma-Informed Elementary School

Audrey Hokoda, Maria del Carmen Rodriguez, Shulamit N. Ritblatt, Shannon Schiele, and Colette L. Ingraham

> *Being in the Trauma-Informed Community Schools (TICS) group has changed my way of thinking and looking at life, particularly with my family. It allows me to understand events in my past (trauma), helped me to heal, to forgive, to know myself, my strengths and weaknesses and thus to make the best of me to offer it to my husband and children. I have learned that I must be an example for those around me, that change starts with me. I found a group of friends and allies whom I trust and I love deeply, that in difficult days have been supporting and understanding. They are my place of refuge. That and more is TICS for me.[1]*

> —*Maria Alvarado*

Maria and Mateo Alvarado immigrated to the US, leaving family in Mexico, striving for the American dream. They faced challenges as they learned to adapt, find work, learn English, and raise three American children. Living in a poor

DOI: 10.4324/9781003046295-8

urban area with high levels of gun and gang violence, their multiethnic neighborhood is also rich with churches, restaurants, businesses, and organizations that support the community. Maria and Mateo's children were also attending a trauma-informed elementary school (Ingraham et al., 2016), which included a parent leadership program, *Creciendo Juntos* (Growing Together). This chapter describes the process of building and sustaining this trauma-informed parent leadership program and its impact on the primarily Spanish-speaking Latino parents and families that live in this neighborhood with Maria, Mateo, and their children.

Challenges Facing Many Latino Immigrant Families in the US

Exposure to trauma is prevalent among children in the US. Roughly 45% of school-aged children have experienced trauma and adverse childhood experiences—ACEs (Sacks & Murphey, 2018). Many immigrant families, such as those living in Maria and Mateo's neighborhood, have experienced multiple traumas and stressors in their country of origin, during migration, and post-migration (Cleary et al., 2018; Comas-Díaz, 2021; McDermott & Ainslie, 2021). Children living in low-income households are twice as likely to have experienced two or more ACEs compared to children from affluent families (Ramirez et al., 2017). Low-income minority children and families are at greater risk for trauma and stressors that include food insecurity, and lack of health insurance, childcare, and affordable housing (Wight et al., 2011). Low-income Latino children, across immigration generation status, experience parental divorce/separation, and exposure to substance abuse in the home, domestic and community violence, and discrimination (Loria & Caughy, 2017). Experiencing or witnessing increased racism and xenophobia in the US (Armenta et al., 2021), acculturative stressors, and family separations or fears of deportation for families with members who are undocumented (Suárez-Orozco et al., 2021) are additional traumas and stressors experienced by Latino immigrant families.

Childhood trauma has a long-term effect on one's physical and mental health (Felitti et al., 1998; van der Kolk, 2014). Chronic exposure to trauma can cause a person to respond neurobiologically with hyperarousal, heightened fear and threat responses, and this can influence their ability to learn, remember, and regulate emotions and behaviors (National Child Traumatic Stress Network—NCTSN Schools Committee, 2017). In the classroom, heightened fear responses may lead traumatized children to be highly anxious, hypervigilant, and inattentive. They may show dissociative responses and depressed affect, and they may withdraw from interacting with others. Hyperarousal and decreased ability to regulate one's emotions may lead to disruptive outbursts in class, irritability and aggression, and self-destruction or recklessness—behaviors that get them labeled as problems. Traumatized children may be more at risk for needing special education services, having lower achievement scores (Perfect et al., 2016), as well as having teachers report behavioral concerns (Blodgett & Lanigan, 2018).

Promoting Intergenerational Resilience in Response to Trauma

Research on many populations experiencing various historical, racial, and other traumas shows that it can have an intergenerational influence on families (Cerdeña et al., 2021; Sangalang & Vang, 2017). For example, some studies report that immigrant survivors of torture and war have children who exhibit more anxiety, depression, and psychological problems (e.g., Daud et al., 2005; Field et al., 2013). Studies examining the mechanisms explaining how trauma affects future generations consistently highlight the importance of parents' responses and adaptation after trauma that can positively and negatively influence their children's well-being (e.g., Isobel et al., 2019; Lehrner & Yehuda, 2018). Trauma impacts parents' beliefs about their safety and the world (Janoff-Bulman, 1992) and children may learn to perceive that the world is unpredictable and unsafe. Heightened fear and dissociative responses associated with trauma may disrupt parents' ability to be emotionally attuned and responsive to their children, and parents' arousal and reactivity may lead to more irritable and aggressive interactions with their children during stressful times. These early relational parental behaviors are particularly risky for young children given the plasticity of their brains and the importance of secure attachments in determining their views of themselves, how well they form relationships with others, and how well they can regulate their emotions (Schore, 2001).

Parents also show resilience, positive coping, and post-traumatic growth after exposure to trauma; for example, trauma survivors report benefits that include greater awareness of their personal strengths, closer relationships with others, and renewed spirituality and appreciation for life (e.g., Triplett et al., 2011). Parents' resilient coping can lead to their children being proud of how their family survived and coped with adversity. Families surviving communal trauma, who share experiences of historical, racial, and community traumas, can build resilience in future generations by helping their children find meaning and develop a narrative of what happened and by sharing cultural beliefs, values, and celebrations (Argenti & Schramm, 2009). Although acknowledging trauma is difficult and painful, Lehrner and Yehuda (2018) argue that there are benefits to recognizing communal endurance and strengths, and standing together to fight communal injustice. Resilience is seen in descendants of trauma survivors who make efforts to research family history, partake in cultural celebrations, express their views through art and literature, and become politically active (e.g., Malchiodi, 2020; Nagata & Patel, 2021; Whyte, 2020). In Latino immigrant families, such as those living in Maria and Mateo's neighborhood, cultural values such as family loyalty and solidarity (*familismo*), respect for elder community members (*respeto*), interpersonal harmony (*simpatía*), and faith may serve as protective factors and contribute to resilience and positive health outcomes across generations (Cardoso & Thompson, 2010; Lusk et al., 2021; Ruiz et al., 2016).

Trauma-Informed School-Based Programs

Programs incorporating core features of trauma-informed schools emphasize safety, educate school staff on identifying the effects of trauma, and teach ways to reduce traumatic stress (Blodgett, 2018; NCTSN, 2017; Rossen, 2020; Wolpow et al., 2016). Teaching staff to understand that children's impulsive, inattentive, or aggressive behaviors may be related to trauma versus disrespect, incompetence, and defiance can lead to more compassionate responses, and teachers learn to deescalate, calm, and create psychological safety for the children. Understanding that traumatized students have heightened threat and fear responses, schools with trauma-informed policies also enhance safety by paying attention to transitions, providing predictable schedules, consistency in teachers and staff, and quiet places for students to calm and self-regulate. Lessons on mindfulness, breathing, movement, and other strategies are provided to address hyperarousal and emotional dysregulation (e.g., Craig, 2016; Forbes, 2012; Mancini, 2020; Mendelson et al., 2015).

Programs of trauma-informed schools are also strength-based and focus on building protective factors in traumatized students and their families (Craig, 2016; NCTSN, 2017; Wolpow et al., 2016). They focus on being culturally responsive and on building partnerships and trusting relationships with families (e.g., Knotek & Sánchez, 2016). Understanding that cultural values, beliefs, and practices affect how one expresses and copes with trauma (de Arellano & Danielson, 2008), culturally responsive staff are humble, seek to understand their students' perspectives, and are flexible and non-judgmental. They aim to honor students' and their families' ethnic and cultural identities and instill pride in one's family history and resilience that helped when facing trauma and stressors (Pickens, 2020).

Evidence-based, trauma-informed, school-based programs such as the Cognitive-Behavioral Intervention for Trauma in Schools—CBITS, and Healthy Environments and Response to Trauma in Schools—HEARTS, have helped reduce trauma symptoms in students and improve their engagement in school (e.g., Dorado et al., 2016; Jaycox et al., 2012; Stein, Jaycox et al., 2003). The multi-tiered programs include individual and group sessions using cognitive-behavioral techniques to address trauma and associated mental health symptoms. Relaxation training is taught to address hyperarousal, anxiety, and fears. Cognitive therapeutic techniques include trauma exposure and processing of traumatic memories, strategies that teach social problem-solving, and ways to challenge depressive thoughts.

School-based mental health programs have been adapted to address trauma in Latino immigrant children (Kataoka et al., 2003; Stein, Kataoka et al., 2003). Recognizing the importance of family and relationship building, the CBITs program modified for immigrant families (Mental Health for Immigrants Program—MHIP) included more psychoeducation sessions (four two-hour multigroup sessions) for parents and family members (Stein et al., 2002). These sessions taught about trauma effects on children and ways to reduce traumatic stress symptoms, as well as positive parenting techniques. In these sessions, parents also shared experiences of trauma and loss they had experienced during immigration and during their own upbringing.

Engagement and Leadership in Latino Parents

Despite research supporting the importance of parent engagement in interventions for trauma (e.g., Lieberman et al., 2005), engaging parents in schools is challenging (Santiago et al., 2013) and unfortunately many schools have not been successful engaging Latino immigrant parents (Durán et al., 2020; Jasis & Ordoñez-Jasis, 2012). Low-income Latino parents may face logistical barriers to being involved in their children's school, such as lack of childcare, transportation, or flexible work hours (Durand, 2010). Hoover-Dempsey and Sandler (1995; 1997) proposed factors that influence parent involvement that are important for schools to consider when recruiting and supporting parents' engagement. These factors include parents' motivational beliefs, such as their perceptions of their role and self-efficacy, their perceptions of the invitations to engage, and perceptions of other life-contextual factors (e.g., time). These are factors influenced by culture and life circumstances that present barriers to immigrant Latino parents' engagement in their children's education (Durand, 2011; Tang, 2015). For example, some low-income parents of color may perceive their role as providing moral education at home, whereas teachers are responsible for teaching academic skills (Smrekar & Cohen-Vogel, 2001; Tang, 2015). In the US, schools are supposed to promote parents as collaborative partners with teachers, however in Mexican or Central American school institutions, this type of parent involvement is not expected or encouraged. The cultural value of *respeto* may also prevent Latino immigrant parents from engaging with their children's teachers as they may feel they are overstepping and disrespecting the teacher's authority (Delgado-Gaitan, 1992; Tang, 2015). Fear of being judged for their ethnicity or social class (Grace & Gerdes, 2019) and limited schooling and English skills (Smrekar & Cohen-Vogel, 2001; Turney & Kao, 2009) may be additional barriers affecting parents' self-efficacy for helping and their perceptions of the school's invitation to engage.

Traditionally, parents' engagement in their children's education has been narrowly defined as involvement at the school (e.g., classroom volunteering, parent conferences, PTA fundraising) leading to mistaken conclusions that low-income parents of color are less interested in promoting their children's academic success. Increasingly different types of parent involvement have been defined including home-based activities (e.g., Epstein et al., 2009). Epstein's model also puts responsibility on schools to increase parent involvement by promoting communication, shared decision-making, and community partnerships. As educators and researchers continue to expand the definition of parent engagement, there is recognition that in addition to parents' support, schools need to focus on building parents as advocates and decision-makers (Warren et al., 2016). The Dual Capacity-Building Framework for Family–School Partnerships Version 2 (Mapp & Bergman, 2019) describes how schools provide meaningful engagement opportunities by building strong relationships with families and by encouraging interaction and collaboration. Effective family–school partnerships build the capacity of both school staff and families by providing a welcoming environment, education, and social networking opportunities (Ingraham et al., 2016). By honoring strengths and connecting family engagement to student learning, schools can encourage parents' involvement in roles they are comfortable with (e.g., supporters, monitors, advocates). Similarly, others propose that building meaningful parent engagement in Latino immigrant parents involves creating opportunities for them to become activists as they advocate for their children and voice their concerns and recommendations for school and district policies (Carruba-Rogel et al., 2019; Durán et al., 2020).

Building the Trauma-Informed Community School (TICS) Program

Background on School-Community and Building Healthy Communities (BHC)

The Trauma-Informed Community School (TICS) program was funded by the Building Healthy Communities (BHC) Initiative (California Endowment) in their efforts to make transformative community change by supporting active engagement of residents. TICS was implemented at an elementary school in an urban area, east of downtown San Diego. The neighborhood has about 100,000 residents, almost 60% identify as Latino/Hispanic, and about 30% identify as Black, Asian, or another person of color (e.g., American Indian, multiple races). In addition to many Vietnamese, Somali, Cambodian, and Laotian refugees, its residents include a large percentage (10%) of undocumented immigrants; it is estimated that over half of the children living in the area have at least one undocumented parent. It is one of the poorest neighborhoods in the county with over 25% of the residents living below the poverty level; the neighborhood is densely populated, with high rates of crime and violence. However, the community has also benefited from over 30 years of investment from philanthropic and non-profit funding focused on redeveloping the area as an "urban village." Over the years, a police station, library, community center, and skate park, as well as numerous public–private partnerships supporting the health and safety of its residents have been added.

The TICS program supported the development of an elementary school as a welcoming neighborhood learning center, a place where residents feel a sense of belonging and emotional connection to the school and community, and a place where they feel they can make a difference and where everyone is able to help each other. These four components (membership, emotional connection, influence, and needs' fulfillment) are needed to build a "sense of community" (McMillan & Chavis, 1986). The elementary school chosen to participate in this ten-year project has over 80% of the families describing themselves as Latino and they are predominantly monolingual Spanish speakers or English language learners (ELLs); 98% are families of color identifying as Latino/Hispanic, Black, Asian, or multiple races, and 96% are economically disadvantaged. The school had been recognized by the school district as providing a safe environment, and the Principal recognized the importance of trusting relationships, community collaboration, and serving the whole child and their families. Monthly Principal's Chats were held in the school auditorium in which dozens of parents attended to socialize and to hear professionals from the community (e.g., lawyers, police officers) give Spanish and English presentations addressing resident concerns (e.g., immigration rights, community safety). The school had also built many partnerships with agencies and businesses to help with basic needs (e.g., food pantry, clothing donations).

Building the Trauma-Informed Program

Continuing the focus on relationship building, the TICS program began with nine months of resident community meetings where residents met with community and university organizers. Dinner and childcare were provided, fun, interactive activities and focus groups were implemented, and parents provided feedback on their priorities for their children, families, and community. The parents identified needs that included: How they can help their children succeed in school, relaxation/health promotion activities for parents, positive discipline/

parenting tips, and coping with domestic/community violence. A Resident Advisory Committee was formed with about ten parents volunteering to meet regularly to continue to share their views and guide the plans for how to address their concerns. As the parents voiced their needs, workshops were offered by faculty and students from the university and community organizations (e.g., law enforcement, county health providers, agencies addressing violence and conflict resolution). University courses were restructured with service-learning, community-based internships enabling dozens of undergraduate and graduate students studying child development, school psychology, counseling, conflict resolution, and violence prevention to support the school and families. With this school–university partnership, bilingual and bicultural college students served as parental liaison or cultural brokers (Howland et al., 2006; López et al., 2018), helping to teach English, computer skills, and other classes as the parents requested more skills to help their children learn.

University faculty also led workshops with teachers on recognizing trauma symptoms in children, and worked with teams of teachers who shared trauma-informed, restorative strategies they use in their classrooms (Ingraham et al., 2016). University undergraduate students, interested in becoming teachers and counselors, shadowed and assisted teachers, the counselor, and office staff, and received hands-on experiences working in an underserved, marginalized school-community. Focusing on the importance of early childhood and school readiness skills (e.g., Blair & Raver, 2015; National Association for the Education of Young Children- NAEYC, 2009), university faculty and students, in collaboration with a community healthcare center, provided parents of pre-K children with over 30 sessions of a First Five program (Pathways to Competence) that focuses on strengthening attachment relationships and building socio-emotional school readiness skills (Landy, 2009). University faculty and graduate students also led bilingual workshops on trauma-informed care in schools (e.g., Wolpow et al., 2016), how to resolve conflicts (e.g., Claassen & Claassen, 2008), how to help children with homework, and how to help their children succeed in school (see Ingraham et al., 2016).

Creciendo Juntos: A Trauma-Informed Parent Leadership Program

The TICS program helped support the continued development of a welcoming neighborhood learning center, where parents dropped their children at school, and then spent several mornings a week in the Parent Room (The Gathering Place), where they attended English and computer classes, drank coffee and ate pan dulce, and socialized with other parents. Opportunities to attend workshops were offered by community and university organizers addressing topics they requested on community and domestic violence, health, fitness, and nutrition.

By the end of the second year, the goal was to expand beyond providing services, education, and resources to families, and move toward providing increased opportunities for meaningful parent engagement and leadership.

Increasing Opportunities for Parent Leadership

University faculty and students worked with Parent Leaders who wanted to help facilitate workshops. In collaboration with faculty and graduate students in school psychology, Parent Leaders helped lead a workshop on positive communication in the family; they developed scenarios using stories from their interactions with their children, and then enacted the scenes showing restorative, positive communication strategies that parents could use. Another early workshop that Parent Leaders helped facilitate focused on educating about differences in schools in the US versus in Mexico, helping them redefine their role at the school as they learned that, in the US and at their school, they are encouraged to be collaborative partners and active in advocating for their children.

In partnership with community organizers and university staff specializing in parent involvement, about 40 parents participated in parent leadership workshops, learning more about different roles they can take at school that includes volunteering, mobilizing, and advocating (e.g., Warren et al., 2016). Parent leaders were supported as they increasingly helped plan and present at Principal's Chats, and they helped coordinate/recruit other parents to volunteer at Principal-led community-building and fundraising activities (e.g., food distribution, school clean-up, bookfairs). Teachers began dropping off materials that they needed help with (cutting letters and numbers for lessons, preparing home packets with announcements and homework), and as parents were gathering for coffee and socializing, many volunteered to help. Babies and toddlers were welcomed and over time, the Gathering Room had toys for pretend play, Spanish- and English-language music and books, and art supplies. Parents without childcare could participate, play with their little ones, connect with other parents, and help the school-community.

Artistic, creative parents helped make posters, bulletin boards, and newsletters for the school, with university students sometimes helping to translate their work into English and teach computer skills. On celebrations, such as Valentine's Day and *Día de las Madres* (Mother's day in Mexico—May 10), parents designed gift baskets for fundraising, and there were numerous informal potlucks with mole poblano, pozole, and gelatina de mosaico, as well as music to celebrate birthdays, baby showers, and other holidays. For *Cinco de Mayo*, teachers taught their students traditional dances (e.g., Jarana Yucateca, Jarabe Tapatío) from various regions in Mexico for an assembly attended by hundreds of family members. The whole school-community was involved, with school staff celebrating with their students and families; some years mariachi bands and folklorico dancers entertained, and always Parent Leaders, older siblings, and other family members helped to cook and serve carne asada tacos, elote, and tostilocos, while families picnicked, danced, played games, or did art activities created by the Parent Leaders. A sense of community was developing as families felt a sense of belonging and emotional connection with other families, as well as appreciation by their school and peers for their strengths and contributions.

Parent Leadership Guided by Research on Trauma-Informed Practices and Early Childhood

Impact of Addressing Trauma and Depressive Symptoms in Parents

The *Creciendo Juntos* parent leadership program, recognizing the importance of parents' adaptation following trauma and following guidelines for trauma-informed schools (NCTSN, 2017), included curriculum teaching parents to identify the effects of trauma and ways to reduce traumatic stress in their children and themselves. As parents learned to identify that their own and their children's intense emotions, aggression, inattention, and depression may be related to trauma, they became more forgiving and compassionate toward themselves and their children, and more hopeful about their future.

A Parent Leader describes the powerful impact that learning about trauma has had on her beliefs about herself and her family's future:

> *So, with my two children, before I started learning about trauma in the workshops, how trauma affects them in their daily life and in their education. Before learning that, every day in my house there were problems, fights, screams, and insults. Well, those were the attitudes that I learned as a child, because that's how I was treated. It has given me great joy to recognize that my problems of violence and bad attitude were due to trauma. I thought it was because that was my character and that it was the way I was, that I couldn't change. But I have learned, and it gives me great joy to be able to discover it because I know that my life and that of my children will change.*

Parent leaders describe how knowledge about trauma helped their relationships with their children and impacted their views about their family and the difficulties they have faced:

> *It has helped to be informed because I can understand better my children and I have a better relationship with them, compared to before I knew about the program. It has helped me be more involved here at school … It has changed*

my life totally, mine and my family. It is a very remarkable experience to learn about trauma, to see things we see as normal, that are not so normal, there are difficult things, that children go through and we as a family also.

It has helped me a lot, because I can identify the traumas we as parents sometimes expose our children to. Sometimes we give preference to one child or like in my case my middle child was used to being alone, and when the other children were born we didn't pay much attention ... So that's what we found in him. It was a trauma for him. Thanks to these classes I could identify that he suffered a trauma with the birth of his younger siblings ... I was able to help my child, spend time alone with him, and this was very nice for me.

The information is quite a lot, things that sometimes we don't know, how the brain functions, where our emotions are kept and understanding more about trauma, about how our head functions we get to know in reality that sometimes we are carrying many things.

After months of learning about trauma, processing its impact on their families with each other, and learning positive ways to reduce stress, the Parent Leaders began creating a series of workshops they would lead with other parents over the next couple of years. As they developed lessons teaching about trauma symptoms, they incorporated examples from their own children and described ways trauma symptoms can be expressed in parents' interactions with their children. They created several workshops on positive communication and healthy relationships, as they understood that strong attachments and family relationships are the best protective factors they can provide for their children. They created interactive small group activities tailored for the families they know, with some Parent Leaders prepared to lead the small groups and others prepared to speak more formally to the whole group with a slide presentation. They taught parents to identify trauma symptoms in their children and ways to reduce hyperarousal with relaxation, breathing, and mindfulness exercises. They also encouraged parents to have fun and play with their children, and incorporated Zumba dance, music, and skits into their workshops. They taught ways to deescalate conflicts and positive parenting techniques that create safety and do not trigger trauma symptoms in their children. They created worksheets for parents to take home to reinforce the importance of self-care and they taught parents ways to challenge negative, depressive thoughts associated with trauma.

Below are some statements written by parents who attended the Parent Leader-led workshops describing what they learned about prioritizing self-care and coping with depression:

I believe that what I have learned the most, for me is self-care, personal care. As a mother first we take care of our husband, the children, everything else and you leave yourself last. So, for me personally I have learned to make time for myself first and also to understand my children.

I've learned that we all have to be positive even when facing negative issues and we can always see life in a more positive way.

Well really is everything in general, because before my life was only being at home, trapped, that I fell into a depression and now my life is different. Now I came to school, share with more parents. I am aware of what is happening at school with my children, how much things we are carrying affect them and for me there are no words, like I always say, is something new that we can learn from other parents, you become aware, that there are many things, things that sometimes we don't imagine and for this, this program is good.

Impact of the Workshops on Relationships with Their Children and Families

Knowing the importance of building strong relationships to provide safety and resilience in their children, Parent Leaders emphasized positive parenting and communication skills, and had giveaways of games and toys (e.g., bubbles, Frisbees) for parents to take home after workshops to encourage relaxation and fun with their children.

After attending the Parent Leader-led workshops, parents report they learned to prioritize positive communication and quality time with their children and families.

Well, it has helped me in many ways, mainly to understand my children's behaviors and be more understanding with them. In general to be a better parent by spending more quality time with them, listening to them, having a warmer atmosphere at home and a better relationship with them. All of these have helped me be a better mother.

It has helped me more with the communication with my husband. Since we as Latinos come from a tradition where the parents do not play with their children. My husband grew up alone, so he didn't have that experience to share with his children. So, as he says, his father never played with him, never. We tried to talk and make an agreement that we need to spend time with our children ... You have to give them time for them to see that they are important to you and it is a beautiful experience.

I learned that spending time with children is important. The time could be even 10 or 20 minutes, giving them my full attention. This is something I didn't do before and now it makes me happy and motivates me to continue growing.

Focus on Early Childhood and Building
Family–School Partnerships

Guided by research on the effects of trauma on the developing brain, the *Creciendo Juntos* program focused on early childhood, fostering social emotional skills and strong attachments, and building family–school relationships as soon as they entered the elementary school. Parent leaders, who had been regularly attending First Five Pathways to Competence parenting classes, were introduced to the Circle of Education (CoE), a music and literacy-based program aimed at developing socio-emotional and school readiness skills (Ritblatt, 2013). The program uses a variety of teaching strategies that include the use of books, discussions, art, music, movement, and videos, and the lessons have learning outcomes aligned with the California Preschool Learning Foundations (California Department of Education, 2008). Offered in English and Spanish for teachers and parents, this enabled parents who were primarily monolingual, Spanish-speaking Mexican immigrants to know more about what their children were learning and become more engaged in their children's education as they reinforced lessons at home that their children's teachers were addressing in class.

As part of the *Creciendo Juntos* program, university students trained in CA Preschool Learning Foundations and National Association for the Education of Young Children (NAEYC) guidelines, led twenty CoE lessons in seven preschool and kindergarten classes addressing socio-emotional and school readiness skills affected by trauma (Schiele, 2015). For example, lessons using books, music, and art were led in classes to increase self-esteem (e.g., "It's Great to Be Me"), and teach friendship and cooperation (e.g., "Let's Use the Magic Words"), emotional regulation (e.g., "The Wild Me"), and self-care (e.g., "My Amazing Body," "Aerobic Streamers"). At the same time, Parent Leaders chose 16 CoE lessons that they taught in weekly 1-½-hour sessions with groups of 10–12 other parents.

The Parent Leaders said they wanted to build their children's self-esteem and encourage polite manners, and therefore they selected lessons and songs for their parent workshops that corresponded to those taught in their children's classrooms. For example, parents learned the song "It's Great to be Me" and read the books (e.g., Chrysanthemum, Emily's Magic Words) introduced in their children's classes. Parents then reinforced the goal of building self-esteem by completing home activities with their children (e.g., personalized placemats) and selecting activities that encouraged pride in their family history and ethnic and cultural identity (e.g., "The Story about My Name," "Special People in My Life," "Languages All Around Us"). Parent leaders also voiced that they wanted their children to learn to count and use numbers, and they wanted their children to like learning and do well in school, so they selected lessons that made daily routines more fun and educational. For example, as parents and children prepared healthy foods together in the activity "I am a Pizza Chef," they also talked about the shapes, colors, and textures of each ingredient. Additionally, they discovered the learning opportunities available on trips to the grocery store and to the park with different fun activities (e.g., "A Shape Treasure Hunt").

Three Parent Leaders carefully planned the parent workshops, first learning the CoE curriculum, selecting lessons that prioritized their goals for their children, creating prototypes of finished art projects, and then making packets of music and art materials for parents to take home after workshops to complete with their children. Other Parent Leaders also supported the workshops by taking different roles, such as helping prepare lesson materials and announcements, and distributing handouts and serving coffee to attendees. The atmosphere was welcoming as the parents socialized with each other, played with each other's babies and toddlers, and stayed afterwards to share ideas of how they address challenges and have fun with their children. A parent attendee reported, "The class has helped me understand that I can involve my children more in house chores. Before I didn't bother to teach them, but now they are more active at home." Another parent said, "I have done the craft activities with my children. This has given them something to do, and also gives us time to bond."

Highlights of the *Creciendo Juntos* Parent Leadership Program

The *Creciendo Juntos* program has met many of its goals in helping the school build a trauma-informed neighborhood learning center—a place where parents build strong relationships with others and feel a sense of community. Despite hesitation because of limited schooling or English skills, parents discovered multiple ways they could contribute to their children's learning and the school-community. They felt valued for their strengths and involvement, and as they participated more, their self-efficacy and beliefs about their ability to help increased.

Statements from parents indicated that the school has been successful in creating a safe place where they feel emotionally connected and a sense of belonging:

> *Something different is the warmth you feel when you come in the room which you don't find everywhere.*
>
> *The time I spend here is like spending it with my family.*

Parent leaders also reported that they have more confidence and were proud of their impact on others.

> *I have more confidence to talk to parents, because I remember at the beginning when I started coming to the program I was afraid to talk to anyone. Right now, I can give out information to parents. I can stand*

in front in of a group and express my opinions. I even can raise my hand, something I never did before. The more one comes here, the more confidence you gain and the more one learns to talk to other parents and invite them to come to the workshops here at school.

It has helped me be a part of my children's schools' life by giving me more confidence to talk to their teachers. It is giving me lots of courage.

The more we know the parents, the more we realize that all the tools we provide them at the workshops have helped them. For example, the advice we give, or our guidance on the best ways to listen to our children and understand them better.

Over the years, the Parent Leaders have expanded their roles, building relationships with staff from various agencies and helping to set up services for families at the school. Parent Leaders helped support other classes (e.g., parenting, nutrition, immigration rights) at the school, and participated in community health walks and events held by local police. They began broadening their influence beyond the neighborhood as they were asked to present at other schools, community events, and to professionals visiting from around the US (e.g., Harvard University, Johns Hopkins University, educators from Hawaii and Oregon) (see www.pacesconnection.com). As their confidence grew, they became activists, voicing their perspectives and recommendations at city-sponsored events (e.g., a violence-prevention summit sponsored by the Commission on Gang Prevention and Intervention, Human Relation Commission meeting). At a Local Control and Accountability Plan (LCAP) meeting, Parent Leaders shared their perspectives on equitable school funding and the educational needs of their children, and they traveled to Sacramento, meeting with legislators and advocating for trauma-informed, restorative justice policies.

The *Creciendo Juntos* program has been sustained over ten years with the help of a school–university collaboration in which dozens of undergraduate students continue to help volunteer at the school as part of their practicum course requirements. Similar to other trauma-informed and public health programs run in the community (e.g., Blitz et al., 2016), university field placements helped support and sustain the school and parent leadership program with minimal funding, and there are numerous benefits for the university students as they prepare to enter the workforce as educators, public health and social service providers. University field placements benefit both the schools and communities as well as the students (Norman & Siller, 2018) as they develop empathy and learn professional skills that help them become effective in working with and advocating for the populations most in need (e.g., Hernandez et al., 2014; Marquez et al., 2017).

The pandemic has exacerbated existing inequities in social health determinants and has particularly impacted low-income communities of color with increased loss of life, unemployment, food insecurity (Artiga et al., 2020; Fortuna et al., 2020; Krogstad & Lopez, 2020; Morales et al., 2020), as well as negative effects on mental health (Hibel et al., 2021; Villatoro et al., 2021). Leveraging of existing resources by university and other agencies can provide needed support to help underserved marginalized schools and communities (Ijadi-Maghsoodi et al., 2020). During the pandemic, Parent Leaders continued to work with university faculty and students, helping families get access and trained on distance learning. They continued to invite parents to weekly zoom coffee gatherings, as if they were in-person at the Gathering Place, leading discussions on topics such as stress and the pandemic, positive affirmations, educational resources for Latinx families, and recipe exchanges. They helped parents understand new California and Federal Summative English Language Proficiency Assessment (ELPAC) reclassification criteria and navigate school district websites in special education and family engagement, while providing ways for the families to feel connected to each other and the school.

In conclusion, culturally relevant resilience promotion and trauma-informed strategies were integral to building parent engagement, a school–community partnership, and a strong cadre of Parent Leaders. In many cases, parents learned approaches for strengthening their children and families, as well as contributing to their own healing and growth. The emerging sense of hope, transformation, and empowerment are reflected in the words of two of the Parent Leaders:

> *These are things you couldn't imagine you could ever do. So when you say a leader, the word says it … that you are a leader: a person that can change, who can help.*
>
> *Maria*

> *I believe that many people need this information, and they will be able to change their lives by learning they can have a better future and make their children good people and good citizens. If this good continues bringing a change in the community, there can be a change in the country.*
>
> *Eva*

Note

1. All quotations were originally delivered in Spanish, written or recorded, transcribed, and then translated to English.

References

Argenti, N., & Schramm, K. (Eds.). (2009). *Remembering violence: Anthropological perspectives on intergenerational transmission*. New York: Berghahn Books.

Armenta, A. D., Alvarez, M. J., & Zárate, M. A. (2021). Wounds that never heal: The proliferation of prejudice toward immigrants in the United States. In P. Tummala-Narra (Ed.), *Trauma and racial minority immigrants: Turmoil, uncertainty, and resistance (cultural, racial, and ethnic psychology)* (1st ed., pp. 15–30). Washington, D.C.: American Psychological Association.

Artiga, S., Orgera, K., Pham, O., & Corallo, B. (2020). *Growing data underscore that communities of color are being harder hit by COVID-19* [Internet]. Kaiser Fam. Found. Retrieved from https://www.kff.org/coronavirus-policy-watch/growing-data-underscore-com

Blair, C., & Raver, C. C. (2015). School readiness and self-regulation: A developmental psychobiological approach. *Annual Review of Psychology, 66*, 711–731. Retrieved from https://doi-org.libproxy.sdsu.edu/10.1146/annurev-psych-010814-015221

Blitz, L. V., Anderson, E. M., & Saastamoinen, M. (2016). Assessing perceptions of culture and trauma in an elementary school: Informing a model for culturally responsive trauma-informed schools. *Urban Review, 48*(4), 520–542. https://doi.org/10.1007/s11256-016-0366-9

Blodgett, C. (2018). Trauma-informed schools and a framework for action. In J. D. Osofsky & B. McAlister Groves (Eds.), *Violence and trauma in the lives of children*. Santa Barbara, CA: Praeger.

Blodgett, C., & Lanigan, J. D. (2018). The association between adverse childhood experience (ACE) and school success in elementary school children. *School Psychology Quarterly, 33*(1), 137–146. https://doi.org/10.1037/spq0000256

California Department of Education. (2008). *California preschool learning foundation* (1), 103–106. Retrieved from http://www.cde.ca

Cardoso, J. B., & Thompson, S. J. (2010). Common themes of resilience among Latino immigrant families: A systematic review of the literature. *Families in Society, 91*(3), 257–265.

Carruba-Rogel, Z., Durán, R. P., & Solis, B. (2019). Latinx parents' literacy practices and concientización in petitioning their local school board regarding funding priorities. *Peabody Journal of Education, 94*(2), 240–254. https://doi.org/10.1080/0161956x.2019.1598131

Cerdeña, J. P., Rivera, L. M., & Spak, J. M. (2021). Intergenerational trauma in Latinxs: A scoping review. *Social Science and Medicine, 270*, 113662. https://doi.org/10.1016/j.socscimed.2020.113662

Claassen, R., & Claassen, R. (2008). *Discipline that restores: Strategies to create respect, cooperation, and responsibility in the classroom*. Charleston, SC: Booksurge.

Cleary, S. D., Snead, R., DietzChavez, D., Rivera, I., & Edberg, M. C. (2018). Immigrant trauma and mental health outcomes among Latino youth. *Journal of Immigrant and Minority Health, 20*(5), 1053–1059.

Comas-Díaz, L. (2021). Sociopolitical trauma: Ethnicity, race, and migration. In P. Tummala-Narra (Ed.), *Trauma and racial minority immigrants: Turmoil, uncertainty, and resistance (cultural, racial, and ethnic psychology)* (1st ed., pp. 127–146). Washington, D.C.: American Psychological Association.

Craig, S. E. (2016). *Trauma-sensitive school: Learning communities transforming children's lives, K-5*. New York: Teachers College Press.

Daud, A., Skoglund, E., & Rydelius, P. A. (2005). Children in families of torture victims: Transgenerational transmission of parents' traumatic experiences to their children. *International Journal of Social Welfare, 14*(1), 23–32. Retrieved from https://doi-org.libproxy.sdsu.edu/10.1111/j.1468-2397.2005.00336.x

de Arellano, M., & Danielson, C. (2008). Assessment of trauma history and trauma-related problems in ethnic minority child populations: An informed approach. *Cognitive and Behavioral Practice*, *15*(1), 53–66. https://doi.org/10.1016/j.cbpra.2006.09.008

Delgado-Gaitan, C. (1992). School matters in the Mexican-American home: Socializing children to education. *American Educational Research Journal*, *29*(3), 495–513. https://doi.org/10.2307/1163255

Dorado, J. S., Martinez, M., McArthur, L. E., & Leibovitz, T. (2016). Healthy environments and response to trauma in schools (HEARTS): A whole-school, multi-level, prevention and intervention program for creating trauma-informed, safe and supportive schools. *School Mental Health: A Multidisciplinary Research and Practice Journal*, *8*(1), 163–176. Retrieved from https://doi-org.libproxy.sdsu.edu /10.1007/s12310-016-9177-0

Durán, R. P., Carruba-Rogel, Z., & Solis, B. (2020). Latinx immigrant parents' cultural communicative resources: Bridging the worlds of home, community, and school policy. *Equity and Excellence in Education*, *53*(1–2), 89–104. Retrieved from https://doi-org.libproxy.sdsu.edu/10.1080/10665684.2020.1756535

Durand, T. (2010). Latina mothers' school preparation activities and their relation to children's literacy skills. *Journal of Latinos and Education*, *9*(3), 207–222. Retrieved from https://doi-org.libproxy.sdsu.edu/10.1080/15348431003761182

Durand, T. M. (2011). Latino parental involvement in kindergarten: Findings from the early childhood longitudinal study. *Hispanic Journal of Behavioral Sciences*, *33*(4), 469–489.

Epstein, J. L., Sanders, M. G., Salinas, K. C., Jansorn, N. R., Van Voorhis, F. L., Martin, C. S., … Williams, K. J. (2009). *School, family, and community partnerships: Your handbook for action* (3rd ed.). Thousand Oaks, CA: Corwin Press.

Felitti, V. J., Anda, R. F., Nordenberg, D., Williamson, D. F., Spitz, A. M., Edwards, V., … Marks, J. S. (1998). Relationship of childhood abuse and household dysfunction to many of the leading causes of death in adults: The adverse childhood experiences (ACE) study. *American Journal of Preventive Medicine*, *14*(4), 245–258. Https://doi.org/10.1016/S0749-3797(98)00017-8

Field, N. P., Muong, S., & Sochanvimean, V. (2013). Parental styles in the intergenerational transmission of trauma stemming from the Khmer Rouge regime in Cambodia. *American Journal of Orthopsychiatry*, *83*(4), 483–494. https://doi.org /10.1111/ajop.12057

Forbes, H. T. (2012). *Help for Billy: A beyond consequences approach to helping challenging children in the classroom*. Boulder, CO: Beyond Consequences Institute, LLC.

Fortuna, L. R., Tolou-Shams, M., Robles-Ramamurthy, B., & Porche, M. V. (2020). Inequity and the disproportionate impact of COVID-19 on communities of color in the United States: The need for a trauma-informed social justice response. *Psychological Trauma: Theory, Research, Practice, and Policy*, *12*(5), 443–445. Retrieved from https://doi-org.libproxy.sdsu.edu/10.1037/tra0000889

Grace, M., & Gerdes, A. C. (2019). Parent-teacher relationships and parental involvement in education in Latino families. *Contemporary School Psychology*, *23*(4), 444–454. https://doi.org/10.1007/s40688-018-00218-9

Hernandez, K. E., Bejarano, S., Reyes, F. J., Chavez, M., & Mata, H. (2014). Experience preferred: Insights from our newest public health professionals on how internships/ practicums promote career development. *Health Promotion Practice*, *15*(1), 95–99. Retrieved from https://doi-org.libproxy.sdsu.edu/10.1177/1524839913507578

Hibel, L. C., Boyer, C. J., Buhler-Wassmann, A. C., & Shaw, B. J. (2021). The psychological and economic toll of the COVID-19 pandemic on Latina mothers in primarily low-income essential worker families. *Traumatology, 27*(1), 40–47. https://doi.org/10.1037/trm0000293

Hoover-Dempsey, K. V., & Sandler, H. M. (1995). Parental involvement in children's education: Why does it make a difference? *Teachers College Record, 95*(2), 310–342.

Hoover-Dempsey, K. V., & Sandler, H. M. (1997). Why do parents become involved in their children's education? *Review of Educational Research, 67*(1), 3–42. https://doi.org/10.3102/00346543067001003

Howland, A., Anderson, J. A., Smiley, A. D., & Abbott, D. J. (2006). School liaisons: Bridging the gap between home and school. *School Community Journal, 16*(2), 47–68.

Ijadi-Maghsoodi, R., Harrison, D., Kelman, A., Kataoka, S., Langley, A. K., Ramos, N., ... Bath, E. (2020). Leveraging a public–public partnership in Los Angeles county to address COVID-19 for children, youth, and families in underresourced communities. *Psychological Trauma: Theory, Research, Practice, and Policy, 12*(5), 457–460. https://doi.org/10.1037/tra0000880

Ingraham, C., Hokoda, A., Moehlenbruck, D., Karafin, M., Manzo, C., & Ramirez, D. (2016). Consultation and collaboration to develop and implement restorative practices in a culturally and linguistically diverse elementary school. *Journal of Educational and Psychological Consultation, 26*(4), 1–31. https://doi.org/10.1080/10474412.2015.1124782

Isobel, S., Goodyear, M., Furness, T., & Foster, K. (2019). Preventing intergenerational trauma transmission: A critical interpretive synthesis. *Journal of Clinical Nursing, 28*(7–8), 1100–1113. Retrieved from https://doi-org.libproxy.sdsu.edu/10.1111/jocn.14735

Janoff-Bulman, R. (1992). *Shattered assumptions: Towards a new psychology of trauma.* New York: The Free Press.

Jasis, P. M., & Ordoñez-Jasis, R. (2012). Latino parent involvement: Examining commitment and empowerment in schools. *Urban Education, 47*(1), 65–89. Retrieved from https://doi-org.libproxy.sdsu.edu/10.1177/0042085911416013

Jaycox, L. H., Kataoka, S. H., Stein, B. D., Langley, A. K., & Wong, M. (2012). Cognitive behavioral intervention for trauma in schools. *Journal of Applied School Psychology, 28*(3), 239–255. Retrieved from https://doi-org.libproxy.sdsu.edu/10.1080/15377903.2012.69576

Kataoka, S., Stein, B. D., Jaycox, L. H., Wong, M., Escuerdo, P., Tu, W., ... Fink, A. (2003). A school-based mental health program for traumatized Latino immigrant children. *Journal of the American Academy of Child and Adolescent Psychiatry, 42*(3), 311–318.

Knotek, S. E., & Sánchez, M. (2016). Madres para niños: Engaging Latina mothers as consultees to promote their children's early elementary school achievement. *Journal of Educational and Psychological Consultation.* https://doi.org/10.1080/10474412.2016.1185611

Krogstad, J. M., & Lopez, M. H. (2020). *Coronavirus economic downturn has hit Latinos especially hard.* Pew Research Center. Retrieved from https://www.pewresearch.org/hispanic/2020/08/04/coronavirus-economic-downturn-has-hit-latinos-especially-hard/

Landy, S. (2009). *Pathways to competence: Encouraging healthy social and emotional development in young children* (2nd ed.). Baltimore, MD: Paul H. Brookes Publishing.

Lehrner, A., & Yehuda, R. (2018). Trauma across generations and paths to adaptation and resilience. *Psychological Trauma: Theory, Research, Practice and Policy, 10*(1), 22–29. https://doi.org/10.1037/tra0000302

Lieberman, A. F., Van Horn, P., & Ippen, C. G. (2005). Toward evidence-based treatment: Child-parent psychotherapy with preschoolers exposed to marital violence. *Journal of the American Academy of Child and Adolescent Psychiatry, 44*(12), 1241–1248. https://doi.org/10.1097/01.chi.0000181047.59702.58

López, A., Anguiano, R. P. V., Galindo, R., Chibucos, T., & Atencio, A. (2018). Mennonite country: The role of school parent liaisons and school administrators connecting with immigrant Latino families in North Central Indiana. *School Community Journal, 28*(2), 139–158.

Loria, H., & Caughy, M. O. (2017). Prevalence of adverse childhood experiences in low income Latino immigrant and non-immigrant children. *Journal of Pediatrics, 192*, 209–215. Retrieved from https://doi.org10.1016/j.jpeds.2017.09.056

Lusk, M., Terrazas, S., Caro, J., Chaparro, P., & Puga Antúnez, D. (2021). Resilience, faith, and social supports among migrants and refugees from Central America and Mexico. *Journal of Spirituality in Mental Health, 23*(1), 1–22. Retrieved from https://doi-org.libproxy.sdsu.edu/10.1080/19349637.2019.1620668

Malchiodi, C. A. (2020). *Trauma and expressive arts therapy: Brain, body, and imagination in the healing process.* New York: The Guilford Press.

Mancini, M. A. (2020). A pilot study evaluating a school-based, trauma-focused intervention for immigrant and refugee youth. *Child and Adolescent Social Work Journal, 37*(3), 287–300. Retrieved from https://doi-org.libproxy.sdsu.edu/10.1007/s10560-019-00641-8

Mapp, K. L., & Bergman, E. (2019). *Dual capacity-building framework for family-school partnerships* (Version 2). Retrieved from: www.dualcapacity.org

Marquez, D., Pell, D., Forster-Cox, S., Garcia, E., Ornelas, S., Bandstra, B., & Mata, H. (2017). Promoting health through policy and systems change: Public health students and mentors on the value of policy advocacy experience in academic internships. *Health Promotion Practice, 18*(3), 323–326. Retrieved from https://doi-org.libproxy.sdsu.edu/10.1177/1524839917699817

McDermott, H. W., & Ainslie, R. C. (2021). Multifaceted profiling and violence: Experiences of Mexican and Central American migrants to the United States. In P. Tummala-Narra (Ed.), *Trauma and racial minority immigrants: Turmoil, uncertainty, and resistance (cultural, racial, and ethnic psychology)* (1st ed., pp. 31–49). Washington, D.C.: American Psychological Association.

McMillan, D. W., & Chavis, D. M. (1986). Sense of community: A definition and theory. *Journal of Community Psychology, 14*(1), 6–23. Retrieved from https://doi-org.libproxy.sdsu.edu/10.1002/1520-6629

Mendelson, T., Tandon, S. D., O'Brennan, L., Leaf, P. J., & Ialongo, N. S. (2015). Brief report: Moving prevention into schools: The impact of a trauma-informed school-based intervention. *Journal of Adolescence, 43*, 142–147. Retrieved from https://doi-org.libproxy.sdsu.edu/10.1016/j.adolescence.2015.05.017

Morales, D. X., Morales, S. A., & Beltran, T. F. (2020). Racial/ethnic disparities in house-hold food insecurity during the COVID-19 pandemic: A nationally representative study. *Journal of Racial and Ethnic Health Disparities.* Advance online publication. Retrieved from https://doi-org.libproxy.sdsu.edu/10.1007/s40615-020-00892-7

Nagata, D. K., & Patel, R. A. (2021). "Forever foreigners": Intergenerational impacts of historical trauma from the World War II Japanese American incarceration. In P. Tummala-Narra (Ed.), *Trauma and racial minority immigrants: Turmoil, uncertainty, and resistance* (pp. 105–126). American Psychological Association. https://doi-org.libproxy.sdsu.edu/10.1037/0000214-007

National Association for the Education of Young Children-NAEYC. (2009). *Developmentally appropriate practice in early childhood programs serving children from birth through Age 8.* Position Statement. National Association for the Education of Young Children.

National Child Traumatic Stress Network, Justice Consortium, Schools Committee, and Culture Consortium (NCTSN). (2017). *Addressing race and trauma in the classroom: A resource for educators.* Los Angeles, CA and Durham, NC: National Center for Child Traumatic Stress.

Norman, P. J., & Siller, M. (2018). Structuring field-based university methods courses in a PDS: A Win-Win for teacher candidates and elementary students. *School–University Partnerships, 11*(3), 76–85. Retrieved from https://search-ebscohost com .libproxy.sdsu.edu/login.aspx?direct=true&db=aph&AN=135377601&site=ehost -live&scope=site

Perfect, M. M., Turley, M. R., Carlson, J. S., Yohanna, J., & Saint Gilles, M. P. (2016). School-related outcomes of traumatic event exposure and traumatic stress symptoms in students: A systematic review of research from 1990 to 2015. *School Mental Health: A Multidisciplinary Research and Practice Journal, 8*(1), 7–43. Retrieved from https://doi-org.libproxy.sdsu.edu/10.1007/s12310-016-9175-2

Pickens, I. (2020). A trauma-informed and culturally responsive approach in the classroom. In E. Rossen (Ed.), *Supporting and educating traumatized students: A guide for school-based professionals* (2nd ed., pp. 45–58). Oxford: Oxford University Press. https://doi -org.libproxy.sdsu.edu/10.1093/med-psych/9780190052737.003.0003

Ramirez, A. G., Gallion, K. J., Aguilar, R., & Swanson, J. (2017). The state of Latino early childhood development: A research review. Salud America! Institute for health promotion research (IHPR) at UT Health San Antonio. Retrieved from https://salud -america.org/wp-content/uploads/2017/11/Early-Child-Dev-Res-Review.pdf

Ritblatt, S. N. (2013). *Circle of Education® program.* San Diego, CA: Delibrainy.

Rossen, E. (2020). *Supporting and educating traumatized students: A guide for school-based professionals, 2nd ed* (E. Rossen, Ed.). Oxford: Oxford University Press. https://doi -org.libproxy.sdsu.edu/10.1093/med-psych/9780190052737.001.0001

Ruiz, J. M., Campos, B., & Garcia, J. J. (2016). Special issue on Latino physical health: Disparities, paradoxes, and future directions. *Journal of Latina/o Psychology, 4*(2), 61–66. Retrieved from https://doi-org.libproxy.sdsu.edu/10.1037/lat0000065

Sacks, V., & Murphey, D. (2018). The prevalence of adverse childhood experiences, nationally, by state, and by race/ethnicity (Research Brief No. 2018-03). (2018, February). Retrieved from Child Trends website: https://www.childtrends.org/pub-lications/prevalence-adverse-childhood-experiences-nationally-state-race-ethnicity

Sangalang, C., & Vang, C. (2017). Intergenerational trauma in refugee families: A systematic review. *Journal of Immigrant and Minority Health, 19*(3), 745–754. Retrieved from https://doi-org.libproxy.sdsu.edu/10.1007/s10903-016-0499-7

Santiago, C. D., Pears, G., Baweja, S., Vona, P., Tang, J., & Kataoka, S. H. (2013). Engaging parents in evidence-based treatments in schools: Community perspectives from implementing CBITS. *School Mental Health, 5*(4), 209–220.

Schiele, S. (2015). *Promoting school readiness for at risk children: An evaluation of the circle of education program in preschool and kindergarten classrooms.* Thesis project to fulfil the requirement for the degree Master of Science in Child Development.

Schore, A. N. (2001). Effects of a secure attachment relationship on right brain development, affect regulation, and infant mental health. *Infant Mental Health Journal, 22*(1/2), 7–66. Retrieved from https://doi-org.libproxy.sdsu.edu/10.1002/1097-0355(200101/04)22:1<7::AID-IMHJ2>3.0.CO;2-N

Smrekar, C., & Cohen-Vogel, L. (2001). The voices of parents: Rethinking the intersection of family and school. *Peabody Journal of Education, 76*(2), 75–100. Retrieved from https://doi-org.libproxy.sdsu.edu/10.1207/S15327930pje7602_5

Stein, B. D., Jaycox, L. H., Kataoka, S. H., Wong, M., Tu, W., Elliott, M. N., & Fink, A. (2003). A mental health intervention for schoolchildren exposed to violence: A randomized controlled trial. *JAMA: Journal of the American Medical Association, 290*(5), 603–611. Retrieved from https://doi-org.libproxy.sdsu.edu/10.1001/jama.290.5.603

Stein, B. D., Kataoka, S., Jaycox, L. H., Steiger, E. M., Wong, M., Fink, A., … Zaragoza, C. (2003). The mental health for immigrants project: Program design and participatory research in the real world. In M. D. Weist, S. Evans, & N. Lever (Eds.), *Handbook of school mental health: Advancing practice and research* (pp. 179–190). New York: Kluwer Academic/Plenum Publishers.

Stein, B., Kataoka, S., Jaycox, L., Wong, M., Fink, A., Escudero, P., & Zaragoza, C. (2002). Theoretical basis and program design of a school-based mental health intervention for traumatized immigrant children: A collaborative research partnership. *Journal of Behavioral Health Services and Research, 29*(3), 318–326.

Suárez-Orozco, C., López Hernández, G., &. Cabral, P. (2021). The rippling effects of unauthorized status: Stress, family separations, and deportation and their implications for belonging and development. In P. Tummala-Narra (Ed.), *Trauma and racial minority immigrants: Turmoil, uncertainty, and resistance (cultural, racial, and ethnic psychology)* (1st ed., pp. 185–203). Washington, D.C.: American Psychological Association.

Tang, S. (2015). Social capital and determinants of immigrant family educational involvement. *Journal of Educational Research, 108*(1), 22–34. Retrieved from https://doi-org.libproxy.sdsu.edu/10.1080/00220671.2013.833076

Triplett, K. N., Tedeschi, R. G., Cann, A., Calhoun, L. G., & Reeve, C. L. (2011). Posttraumatic growth, meaning in life, and life satisfaction in response to trauma. *Psychological Trauma: Theory, Research, Practice, and Policy, 4*(4), 400–410. Retrieved from https://doi-org.libproxy.sdsu.edu/10.1037/a0024204

Turney, K., & Kao, G. (2009). Barriers to school involvement: Are immigrant parents disadvantaged? *Journal of Educational Research, 102*(4), 257–271. Retrieved from https://doi-org.libproxy.sdsu.edu/10.3200/JOER.102.4.257-271

van der Kolk, B. (2014). *The body keeps the score: Brain, mind, and body in the healing of trauma.* New York: Penguin.

Villatoro, A. P., Wagner, K. M., Salgado de Snyder, V. N., Garcia, D., Walsdorf, A. A., & Valdez, C. R. (2021). Economic and social consequences of COVID-19 and mental health burden among Latinx young adults during the 2020 pandemic. *Journal of Latinx Psychology.* https://doi.org/10.1037/lat0000195

Warren, M. R., Mapp, K. L., & Kuttner, P. J. (2016). From private citizens to public actors: The development of parent leaders through community organizing. In M. P. Evans & D. B. Hiatt-Michael (Eds.), *The power of community engagement for educational change* (pp. 21–39). Charlotte, NC: IAP Information Age Publishing.

Whyte, M. K. (2020). Walking on two-row: Reconciling first nations identity and colonial trauma through material interaction, acculturation, and art therapy. *Canadian Journal of Art Therapy: Research, Practice, and Issues, 33*(1), 36–45. https://doi.org/10.1080/08322473.2020.1724745

Wight, V. R., Chau, M., & Aratani, Y. (2011). *Who are America's poor children? The official story.* New York: National Center for Children in Poverty, Columbia University.

Wolpow, R., Johnson, M. M., Hertel, R., & Kincaid, S. O. (2016). *The heart of teaching & learning: Compassion, resiliency, and academic success.* Olympia, WA: Washington State Office of Superintendent of Public Instruction (OSPI) Compassionate Schools. Retrieved from http://www.k12.wa.us/CompassionateSchools/Resources.aspx

Chapter 7

Pride and Shame

Working with Sexual and Gender Variance

Nicole M. Kent

> *As a high school student in San Diego County in the 1980s, I did not know a single adult who openly identified as a sexual or gender minority (SGM) personally. There were a few side characters on TV and in the movies, but they were usually villains or the target of jokes. Years after I graduated, there was an anti-defamation film distributed to high schools in an effort to decrease bullying against non-dominant students. The principal of my high school decided to edit the film before presenting it to students. He eliminated segments that showed a doctor and a police officer who identified as SGM. When asked why, the principal stated that he did not want to present SGM people in "professional or authority positions" because it might encourage students to become SGM. This perspective is based on the false but pervasive belief that sexual identity is a choice. The principal was attempting to protect the heterosexual kids from SGM influence, but instead further shamed and alienated the students in actual need of protection and inclusion.*

Though things have undoubtedly changed over the past 30 years, SGM individuals and families continue to face implicit and explicit biases on all levels of social, educational, medical, and legal life, often beginning in early childhood. These biases result in *minority stress*, a term coined by Meyer (1995) to

DOI: 10.4324/9781003046295-9

describe the impact of systemic marginalization and oppression on the physical and mental health of people who are members of non-dominant communities. Further research has also identified some of the strengths developed by coping with minority stress. This chapter will grapple with the risks, and explore affirming, trauma-informed, and resilience-building approaches to care at all levels.

Terms

At the time of this writing, the complete, accepted acronym for the SGM community is LGBTQIAP2+, which stands for lesbian, gay, bisexual, transgender, queer, intersex, asexual, pansexual, two-spirit, and the plus, for identities not identified by a letter. In an effort to be inclusive, the acronym has expanded over the years. For this chapter, I will use SGM, an increasingly used umbrella term that includes all sexual and gender minorities. The only actual connection between these identities is their exclusion from heterosexual and cisgender mainstream society and privilege. The shared umbrella has given these marginalized identities greater visibility and political and social power. That said, using an umbrella term for such a diverse group can lead to reductive generalizations that fail to recognize the unique and distinctive histories and experiences of individuals. Please note the limited scope of this chapter, and continue your exploration of the many facets within the SGM community.

SGM individuals are at higher risk of abuse, family alienation, trafficking, mood disorders, drug and alcohol dependence, home insecurity, incarceration, suicide, and school drop outs. It is important that the increased risks to social equity, mental, and medical health faced by SGM individuals and families are acknowledged and addressed not as intrinsic characteristics, but rather as a result of marginalization. Anti-SGM prejudice at all levels creates obstacles to high-quality and affirming medical and mental health care. These health disparities and outcomes have been well documented among oppressed and marginalized people, including sexual minorities (Herek & Garnets, 2007; Lewis, 2009; Meyer, 2003). The minority stress model purports that people in marginalized or non-dominant groups experience unique stressors that influence interactions, expectations, and experiences. The model describes not only experiences of prejudice, exclusion, and lack of access, but also explores the secondary adaptive and ameliorative responses associated with the experience of minority stress. These include internalized bias, expectations of rejection, hiding, concealing, and avoiding (Meyer, 2003), all of which can have negative effects on outcomes.

Anti-SGM bias generally centers on the idea that SGM individuals are immoral, criminal, mentally ill, traumatized, unnatural, or are being manipulated by others. Because there are many different identities and presentations under the

SGM umbrella, not all of the stereotypes are shared. Cisgender and heterosexual people may experience their sexual and gender identity as a constant known—an implicit knowing that is only forced to be explicit when running up against experiences of incongruence. This can make it difficult for them to interpret the decidedly explicit process required for SGM people, whose gender and sexual identity consolidation involves several stages and shifts. This may be one source of the judgment of "it's not natural." That which is implicitly known, feels like nature itself.

Anti-SGM bias comes in the form of micro- or macro-aggressions. Macro-aggressions are the "big T" traumas, like assault or rape, and are easily identified as traumas. A micro-aggression is a more subtle type of prejudice in the form of comments, jokes, or questions (Pierce et al., 1977; Sue et al., 2007). Though a single micro-aggression is unlikely to cause significant harm, frequent and insidious exposure to micro-aggressions can cause chronic stress, and may have a harmful impact on mental well-being, identity formation, and quality of life (Nadal et al., 2012). Hatzenbuehler (2009) identified increases in emotional dysregulation, depressogenic cognitions, and risk factors for internalizing psychopathology. Hatzenbuehler et al. (2008) found that these risks are present in early childhood. The development of sense of self is intrinsically a relational process. *When dissonance is present, a child must either sacrifice self, or connection. This type of double bind is possibly the most significant consequence of minority stress.* A further challenge, particularly for those whose marginalized identity is not shared with the family system, is that bias is rarely acknowledged by the offender, which interferes with identity consolidation and coping. SGM people are often accused of being angry, overly sensitive, or expecting "special treatment" by people unwilling to explore their own intrinsic bias.

Diagnoses

The history of SGM-related diagnoses provides a context for the experience of SGM people with the medical and mental health system, as well as within society. The decriminalization of homosexuality in 1973 led to a mental illness frame, in which SGM identity was labeled as sociopathy. Prior to the 1980s, when laws were put in place to increase the criteria for involuntary hospitalization, many SGM people were institutionalized for months or years by family members, solely based on gender or sexual identity. In 2013, the DSM changed the diagnosis for transgender individuals from gender identity disorder to *gender dysphoria*, which points to the incongruence between assigned sex and gender identity. The DSM has played a role both in normalizing and pathologizing SGM identities. This history of pathologizing identity can and does result in a client's reluctance to participate in therapy, the withholding of important information from the therapist, and increasing the likelihood of premature discontinuation of mental health treatment (The American Psychological Association 2012, 2015, 2017).

Many gender-variant clients continue to be harmed by the *gatekeeper model*, which dictates that the therapist must affirm the client's identity in order to move forward with medical care. This puts the therapist in a role that is contradictory to the therapeutic space in which a client is invited to show themselves authentically and openly. The gatekeeper model encourages clients to minimize or conceal psychiatric symptoms, self-harming behaviors and thoughts, and ambivalence regarding transition or gender identity. Within this model, clients also feel pressure to maximize the symptoms of gender dysphoria (F74.0) in order to meet medical necessity and to obtain "permission" to move forward. Affirming care is an alternative to gatekeeping that recognizes the client's agency and expertise over their own gender experience, and minimizes obstacles to gender-affirming care.

Though discredited by every major licensing board (the American Psychological Association, the American Psychiatric Association, the American Counseling Association, and the American Academy of Pediatrics) it is still legal in 30 states to subject perceived SGM children to *sexual orientation change efforts (SOCE)*, which are aimed at changing a person's sexual orientation to heterosexual. There have been an estimated 700,000 American adults who have undergone SOCE, half before the age of 18 (Mallory et al., 2018). Ryan et al. (2020) evaluated the impact of parent-initiated SOCE on SGM adolescents and found that, compared with SGM adolescents with no SOCE, they were more than three times as likely to have suicidal ideation and almost three times as likely to attempt suicide. Adolescents who were exposed to SOCE were also found to have higher rates of STDs, lower educational achievement, lower social support, and less life satisfaction. Conversion therapy is sometimes presented in disguise with names like re-integration therapy, or sexual attraction exploration therapy.

Research suggests that mental health professionals who have limited training and experience in *affirmative care* with transgender and *gender nonbinary* clients may cause significant harm (Mikalson et al., 2012; Xavier et al., 2012). According to the 2015 U.S. Transgender survey, many transgender individuals have had negative experiences with medical and mental health providers, with 28% avoiding going to the doctor out of fear of discrimination and 19% having had the experience of being refused care due to their gender identity or expression, 18% of transgender people who sought mental health services experienced a mental health professional attempting to change or discourage their identity as transgender. One-third of transgender individuals experienced discrimination in a healthcare setting. The settings with the greatest reported incidence of discrimination were mental health clinics (James et al., 2016).

Evidence-Based Practices

There has been a significant effort to improve consistency and efficacy of therapy by promoting the use of evidence-based practices (EBP). These are therapeutic models that have been studied and tested using randomized controlled trials. According to the APA (2019), the rise in EBPs over several years has not resulted in improvements in mental health incidence or outcomes. In fact, national mental illness prevalence is on the rise, while treatment outcomes are stagnant, particularly among marginalized groups, youth under the age of 25, and individuals with co-occurring disorders.

EBPs evaluate specific models of therapy, but there are other common factors that play a significant role in therapeutic efficacy. Across these studies, the factor of model or technique accounts for 15–30% of the effectiveness of treatment, whereas the relationship, expectancy, and extra-therapeutic factors account for 70–85% of therapeutic effectiveness. EBPs evaluate models and techniques for effectiveness, but do not adequately address other factors. Because EBPs have not been found to improve outcomes for marginalized people, it is suggested that therapists utilize practice-based evidence (PBE), which involves assessing and measuring client progress through the course of therapy. PBE provides real-time feedback about how the client is responding to all of the factors of therapy. The use of PBEs with a focus on relationship may be of particular importance given the history of harm caused by the medical and mental health community against SGM people, as well as high rates of familial and societal rejection.

Affirming School Policies

Because youth are required to attend school, discriminatory and unsafe school climates for SGM students have significant impact on mental health. Anti-bullying laws and policies are positively associated with student safety and adjustment (Hatzenbuehler & Keyes 2013, Russell et al., 2010) and a reduction in suicide (Meyer et al., 2019). Despite this clear evidence, there are only 20 states that specifically include SGM youth in anti-bullying policies. There are currently four states with so-called "No Promo Homo" laws, which restrict positive and affirming representations of SGM identities in K–12 education.

Connecting to history provides marginalized people with a greater sense of belonging and hope. There are four states that require inclusion of SGM figures and events in the teaching of history, while six states have laws prohibiting the inclusion of SGM history in K-12 curricula. In South Carolina, health education "may not include a discussion of alternate sexual lifestyles from heterosexual relationships including, but not limited to, homosexual relationships except in the context of instruction concerning sexually transmitted diseases" (Kosciw et al., 2020).

These laws, which are put in place as a response to SGM-affirming laws, have serious implications for the lives of SGM people. A study done by GLSEN found that SGM people who live in states with anti-SGM inclusion laws experience higher levels of minority stress, have less access to affirming care, and have less protection and support from the community. In these states, as compared to states that do not have anti-SGM inclusion laws, there are fewer teachers who offer overt support for SGM students, fewer GSA (Gender and Sexuality Alliance) clubs, and less access to appropriate and accurate sexual health information (2019).

Strength and Resiliency

Most SGM people live happy and healthy lives, despite the prevalence of anti-SGM bias. It is extremely important to shift our approach away from a pathology and deficit model toward a more strength, pride, history, and community-based approach. When provided with strong protective factors, the impact of minority stress is decreased, and may lead to stress-related growth (SRG) (Park et al., 1996). Vaughan and Rodriguez (2014) reviewed qualitative and quantitative research on LGBT strengths, and found that SGM individuals exhibited "perceived gains in authenticity, creativity, positive affect/emotion, life satisfaction, identity, social intelligence, social support, as well as awareness of/commitment to social justice" (e.g., Cass, 1979; Coleman, 1982; Riggle et al., 2008; Savin-Williams, 2001; Troiden, 1979) (p. 357). Kwon (2013) noted higher rates of hope and optimism, and Brown (1989) discussed the creativity of SGM people, noting that SGM identity is "something we invent for ourselves by actively deconstructing and reconstructing our vision of human behavior" (p. 452).

Organizational and Practitioner Guidelines

Self-Reflection

Becoming competent to serve the SGM community does not simply entail the learning of terms and techniques, but also requires self-exploration and processing.

> Being a gender-affirming clinician requires a commitment to ongoing self-reflection and concrete actions. Being a gender therapist ... with trans people means understanding systems of power and privilege,

not just those related to gender but those related to race and class. This is a necessity; it is not optional.

(Chang et al., 2018, p.17)

Clinical expertise requires the ability to reflect on one's own experience, knowledge, hypotheses, inferences, emotional reactions, and behaviors, and to use that reflection to modify one's practices accordingly APA (2015). "It is essential that you view clients as existing within a social system, but also understand how you are part of this system and influenced by the social and political climate that dictates how care is conceptualized and provided" (Chang et al., 2018). Even those who identify as SGM are not automatically qualified to provide affirming care.

First Contact

When working with SGM clients, a therapist must also be aware of a client's potential expectation of bias. For example, gender expansive people face inappropriate questions about their genitalia, sexual encounters, and roles. It is especially important to communicate the client's agency in choosing not to answer questions when they are not comfortable. The therapist's language should communicate support for the client's self-determination, a nonbinary view of gender, and present SGM identity as a normal variation of human experience rather than as "other." To form a safe therapeutic alliance, it is important for the therapist to be able to address historical and contemporary SGM bias in society as well as within the fields of psychology and medicine.

> *Martin was a 52-year-old gay man who decided to seek therapy for support with grief after the death of his mother. During his initial phone call with a prospective therapist, he was mistaken for a woman. After correcting the therapist, he went on to describe that his husband had recommended he seek therapy. The therapist asked, "husband?" It was clear that this therapist was confused or taken aback by the Martin's identity. This awkward interaction was enough for Martin to drop his interest in seeking therapy for another two years.*

Legal and Ethical Practice

Ethical practice requires one to gain the knowledge, experience, and supervision required to provide beneficial counseling or therapy for a client, without causing harm. It is incumbent on all clinicians to know the legal and ethical guidelines for treating SGM individuals, couples, and families in their state of licensure. Refer to the licensing board under which you practice for specific considerations.

If these have not been adequately defined, seek information from organizations that promote ethical and affirming SGM care.

Client as Informant, Not Educator

Your client will teach you about their own unique experiences, reactions, dreams, hurts, etc. They should not be expected to educate you about SGM identity. In my experience, when a client is put into a teacher role, they are forced to move away from the processing of their own experience and emotions. Clients who have had this experience with mental health professionals have shared feeling frustrated and unsafe regarding the therapist's competence, which discourages openness and vulnerability. It is also important to remember that people who identify as SGM may have only a nascent understanding of their own identity, inaccurate information, and be influenced by internalized shame that results in cognitive dissonance. For this reason, the therapist's competence cannot be limited to being client-lead.

Avoid the Single Story Trap

Working with an SGM individual is not a singular experience by any means. Within the SGM community, there are an endless number of unique experiences, attachment styles, cultures, parenting styles, religions, and trauma histories, as well as the intersectionality of gender and sexual identity with race, religion, national origin, immigration history, and ability. A client is a whole person made up of a multitude of identities. These *intersectionalities* may involve increased risk, increased protection, or a variety of influences on social, emotional, psychological, and relational experiences. Intersectionalities may also influence one's experience of minority stress, access to care, and experiences with systems of care. Interventions must also be selected with consideration to contextual factors.

Believe Your Client

SGM individuals often face the challenge of being believed. SGM youth are often dismissed as incapable of knowing their own sexual or gender identity, or accused of being influenced by peer or media pressure. This skepticism interferes with a youth's ability to explore their own identity—feeling pressure to either suppress identity, or, in contrast, to claim a rigid identity. It is common for SGM individuals to achieve clarity regarding their identity after a process of exploration and experience. Because the terms and descriptions may change during this process, parents and other non-SGM people may interpret the child's identity as a phase.

Even in current society, a majority of children do not have regular exposure to real or representational SGM figures in their lives. It is often unacknowledged that straight-cis development is strongly influenced by representations of straightness in family, community, and media. Without access to a variety of representations, children are unlikely to have a full understanding of the non-heteronormative identities.

(Chang et al., 2018)

Address Sexual and Gender Identity Separately

Byron is 17 and identifies as a transgender male who is attracted to males. Byron's parents express confusion about their child's gender identity, stating that it will be easier to attract males if Byron "stays female." This is a common misconception—implying that gender identity is only significant in relation to romantic and sexual attraction. People who identify as transgender may be straight, gay, pansexual, bisexual, asexual, etc.

Treatment Guidelines

There is no single approach to therapy for SGM clients. Trauma-informed, strength-based, and relationship and empowerment can be utilized and modified in response to practice-based evidence. The following treatment guidelines are based on TF-CBT principles and APA guidelines (2012).

Safety and Psychoeducation

Address any current safety concerns and obstacles to accessing therapy. Provide or refer for crisis care, if necessary. Providing clients with accurate and affirming information and language serves many purposes, including challenging gender stereotypes and biases, helping kids and parents to communicate more effectively, improving a family's ability to recognize non-affirming care, providing clients with a sense of mastery so that they gain confidence in establishing boundaries and addressing cisgenderism and heteronormativity, and normalizing the experiences of the family. Assist your client in locating and accessing community-based resources and services.

Explore and Reduce Avoidance

Differentiate between adaptive and maladaptive avoidance.

Avoidance is a common symptom of minority stress. It can be an effective and adaptive method for steering clear of harmful situations. Like many coping strategies, it can be over-used, resulting in the avoidance of many aspects of life.

> **Benita** is a 17-year-old transgender female. Her parents were worried about her because she didn't seem interested in the normal milestones of late adolescence. Benita's parents accepted their daughter's identity, but insisted that she not pursue legal or medical transition until she turned 18. Benita shared that she wanted very badly to have a driver's license, to get a job, and apply for college, but that she couldn't face the humiliation in processes that involved showing legal identification, which "dead name" and misgender her. It was critically important for her treatment to include strategies for coping with anxiety as well as advocacy for limiting obstacles to accessing social, educational, and career opportunities without the threat of danger, rejection, or overwhelming dysphoria.

Address Mourning and Losses

Trauma and minority stress involves grieving. Helping clients to process the losses they have experienced is an important component of trauma-informed care. Mourning losses involves meaning making, which is central to a person's spirituality.

> **Aiden** was a 19-year-old transgender male who was raised in a family he described as "Evangelical Christians." When he was 14, and had not yet consolidated his gender identity, he told his parents that he was a lesbian. The following Sunday, the minister of their church called Aiden up to the pulpit, and announced to the congregation, "Satan has entered this young girl, and we must expel him!" The congregation proceeded to lay hands on Aiden, praying and chanting for his "release from the grips of Satan." As Aiden became more aware of his male identity, he felt forced into a false self, concealing himself from his family and church community. As he neared his 18th birthday, and planned to move away, he not only faced the challenge of taking care of himself, but had to grieve the loss of the only community he had ever known; the church had been the center of his social life, education, and family connection.

Restructure Minority Stress and Trauma Cognitions and Beliefs

Trauma and minority stress can result in shame in the form of internalized bias and self-blame (see Figure 7.1).

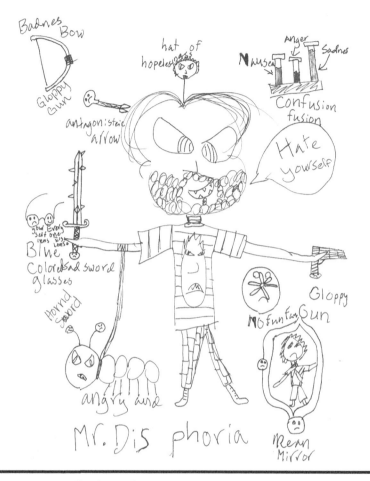

Figure 7.1 Externalized Dysphoria.

This is a picture drawn by a 10-year-old transgender child asked to draw dysphoria. This exercise allows the child to externalize dysphoria, as well as exploring the impact of dysphoria on physical, emotional, mental, perceptual, relational, and behavioral spheres. Expressive and creative techniques are often helpful ways to explore experiences, while also making the activity relaxing and even enjoyable. When an activity allows for positive affect, the "problem" being addressed feels more manageable, increasing confidence, competence, and integration.

Identify Strengths and Practice Coping Skills

Healthy coping strategies to manage stressors, not only helps with current stressors, but can also be used to avoid or prepare for future stressors. For SGM people, coping must be addressed within the specific context of the client's life. Provide clients with tools for stress management, relaxation, and mindfulness. Teaching clients about assertive communication and boundaries are also important and empowering elements of coping.

Connection

The strongest mitigating factor for the risks faced by SGM individuals is the quantity and quality of relationships with safe and caring others. This is particularly important for youth. Research demonstrates a strong link between family rejection of youth who identify as SGM and negative mental and medical health outcomes (Poirier et al., 2014; Ryan et al., 2009, 2010, SAMHSA, 2014). In contrast, family acceptance can serve as a protective factor against depression, substance use, and suicidal ideation and attempts; 25% of 10,000 SGM youth, ages 13–17, identified non-accepting families as the most salient challenge in their lives (youth.gov). It is important to note that parental rejection or acceptance is not a binary. Rejecting and accepting behaviors can coexist within a parent and within a family. Connections in the SGM community (Zimmerman et al., 2015) were found to compensate for parental rejection or provide an important adjunct to family support (Shilo et al., 2015), and virtual communities appeared particularly important for cultivating these SGM social ties where immediate family roles make it difficult to integrate sexuality and sexual identity with traditional social expectations (Chong et al., 2015). It is also worth considering that resilience may not be shown in all areas of SGM persons' lives. Gray et al.'s (2015) intersectional approach helps illustrate some of this complexity wherein different aspects of identity (being gay or being Latino) may be challenged depending on the environment. Acceptance in a "gay" environment may be conditioned on how behavior comports to a larger culture's notion of "gay."

Trauma and Identity Narrative

Discuss a client's identity as a journey or a process rather than a singular discovery or shift. "Tell me about your identity journey" rather than asking "when did you come out?" Coming out is an ongoing and complex process, not a singular event. A chronological and cohesive narrative, with the appropriate affect, serves as an important step for the integration of traumatic experiences.

SGM individuals and families are at greater risk due to the continued prevalence of anti-SGM bias in the United States. Providing people who are SGM with opportunities for psychoeducation, connection to the community, historical context, safe spaces, legal protection, and access to affirming care can mitigate the impact of minority stress, and amplify the many strengths that result from stress-related growth. This chapter is a brief introduction to some of the major considerations for working with the SGM community, but is by no means a comprehensive or complete picture of the complex and diverse needs of SGM individuals and families. I encourage you to continue your exploration and education about our LGBTQIA2+ siblings.

References

American Psychological Association. (2012). Guidelines for psychological practice with lesbian, gay, and bisexual clients. *American Psychologist, 67*(1), 10–42. http://doi.org/10.1037/a0024659

American Psychological Association. (2015). Guidelines for psychological practice with transgender and gender nonconforming people. *American Psychologist, 70*(9), 832–864. http://doi.org/10.1037/a0039906

American Psychological Association. (2017). *Guidelines and practice position statements.* Washington, DC: IPsyNet.

American Psychological Association. (2019). *Clinical practice guideline for the treatment of depression across three age cohorts.* Retrieved from https://www.apa.org/depression-guideline

Brown, L. S. (1989). New voices, new visions: Toward a lesbian/gay paradigm in psychology. *Psychology of Women Quarterly, 13*(4), 445–458. https://doi.org/10.1111/j.1471-6402.1989.tb01013.x

Cass, V. C. (1979). Homosexual identity formation: A theoretical model. *Journal of Homosexuality, 4,* 219–235. doi:10.1300/J082v04n03_01

Chang, S. C., Singh, A. A., & Dickey, L. M. (2018). *A clinician's guide to gender-affirming care: Working with transgender and gender non-conforming clients.* Oakland, CA: New Harbinger Publications, Inc.

Chong, E. S. K., Zhang, Y., Mak, W. W. S., & Pang, I. H. Y. (2015). Social media as social capital of LGB individuals in Hong Kong: Its relations with group membership, stigma, and mental well-being. *American Journal of Community Psychology, 55*(1–2), 228–238. https://doi.org/10.1007/s10464-014-9699-2

Coleman, E. (1982). Developmental stages of the coming out process. *Journal of Homosexuality, 7*(2–3), 31–43. doi:10.1300/J082v07n02_06

Gray, N. N., Mendelsohn, M. D., & Omoto, A. M. (2015). Community connectedness, challenges, and resilience among gay Latino immigrants. *American Journal of Community Psychology, 55,* 202–214. https://doi.org/10.1007/s10464-014-9697-4

Hatzenbuehler, M. L. (2009). How does sexual minority stigma "get under the skin"? A psychological mediation framework. *Psychological Bulletin, 135*(5), 707–730. http://doi.org/10.1037/a0016441

Hatzenbuehler, M. L., & Keyes, K. M. (2013). Inclusive anti-bullying policies and reduced risk of suicide attempts in lesbian and gay youth. *Journal of Adolescent Health, 53,* S21–S26.

Hatzenbuehler, M. L., McLaughlin, K. A., & Nolen-Hoeksema, S. (2008). Emotion regulation and internalizing symptoms in a longitudinal study of sexual minority and heterosexual adolescents. *Journal of Child Psychology and Psychiatry, 49*(12), 1270–1278. http://doi.org/10.1111/j.1469-7610.2008.01924.x

Herek, G. M., & Garnets, L. D. (2007). Sexual orientation and mental health. *Annual Review of Clinical Psychology, 3,* 353–375. https://doi.org/10.1037/0278-6133.27.4.455

James, S. E., Herman, J. L., Rankin, S., Keisling, M., Mottet, L., & Anafi, M. (2016). *The report of the 2015 U.S. transgender survey.* Washington, DC: National Center for Transgender Equality.

Kosciw, J. G., Clark, C. M., Truong, N. L., & Zongrone, A. D. (2020). *The 2019 national school climate survey: The experiences of lesbian, gay, bisexual, transgender, and queer youth in our nation's schools.* New York: GLSEN.

Kwon, P. (2013). Resilience in lesbian, gay, and bisexual individuals. *Personality and Social Psychology Review, 17*(4), 371–383. https://doi.org/10. 1177/10888683134 90248

Lewis, N. M. (2009). Mental health in sexual minorities: Recent indicators, trends, and their relationships to place in North America and Europe. *Health and Place, 15*(4), 1029–1045. https://doi.org/10.1016/j.healthplace.2009.05.003

Mallory, C., Brown, T. N. T., & Conron, K. J. (2018). Conversion therapy and LGBT youth. Los Angeles, CA: UCLA School of Law, The Williams Institute.

Meyer, I. H. (1995). Minority stress and mental health in gay men. *Journal of Health and Social Behavior, 36*(1), 38–56. http://doi.org/10.2307/2137286

Meyer, I. H. (2003). Prejudice, social stress, and mental health in lesbian, gay, and bisexual populations: Conceptual issues and research evidence. *Psychological Bulletin, 129*(5), 674–697. http://doi.org/10.1037/0033-2909.129.5.674

Meyer, I. H., Luo, F., Wilson, B. D. M., & Stone, D. (2019, January). Sexual orientation enumeration in state antibullying statutes in the United States: Associations with bullying, suicidal ideation, and suicide attempts among youth. *LGBT Health, 6*(1), 9109–9114. http://doi.org/10.1089/lgbt.2018.0194

Mikalson, P., Pardo, S., & Green, J. (2012). First, do no harm: Reducing disparities for lesbian, gay, bisexual, transgender, queer and questioning populations in California. California Reducing Disparities Project. Retrieved from https://www.nccdglobal.org/sites/default/files/publication_pdf/first_do_no_harm.pdf

Nadal, K. L., Skolnik, A., & Wong, Y. (2012). Interpersonal and systemic microaggressions towards transgender people: Implications for counseling. *Journal of LGBT Issues in Counseling, 6*(1), 55–82. https://doi.org/10.1080/15538605.2012.648583

Park, C. L., Cohen, L. H., & Murch, R. L. (1996). Assessment of prediction of stress-related growth. *Journal of Personality, 64*(1), 71–105. https://doi.org/10.1111/j.1467-6494.1996.tb00815.x

Pierce, C. M., Carew, J. V., Pierce-Gonzalez, D., & Wills, D. (1977). An experiment in racism: TV commercials. *Education and Urban Society, 10*(1), 61–87. https://doi.org/10.1177/001312457701000105

Poirier, J. M., Fisher, S. K., Hunt, R. A., & Bearse, M. (2014). *A guide for understanding, supporting, and affirming LGBTQI2–S children, youth, and families.* Washington, DC: American Institutes for Research. Retrieved from http://www.nasmhpd.org/content/LGBTQI2-S%20Guide,%2012-11-13.pdf

Riggle, E. D. B., Whitman, J. S., Olson, A., Rostosky, S., & Strong, S. (2008). The positive aspects of being a lesbian or gay man. *Professional Psychology: Research and Practice, 39,* 210–217. doi:10.1037/0735- 7028.39.2.210

Russell, S. T., Seif, H. M., & Truong, N. L. (2010). School outcomes of sexual minority youth in the United States: Evidence from a national study. *Journal of Adolescence, 24*(1), 111–127.

Ryan, C., Huebner, D., Diaz, R. M., & Sanchez, J. (2009). Family rejection as a predictor of negative health outcomes in white and Latino lesbian, gay and bisexual young adults. *Pediatrics, 123*(1), 346–352.

Ryan, C., Russell, S. T., Huebner, D., Diaz, R., & Sanchez, J. (2010). Family acceptance in adolescence and the health of LGBT young adults. *Journal of Child and Adolescent Psychiatric Nursing, 23*(4), 205–213. https://doi.org/10.1111/j.1744-6171.2010.00246.x

Ryan, C., Toomey, R. B., Diaz, R. M., & Russell, S. T. (2020). Parent-initiated sexual orientation change efforts with LGBT adolescents: Implications for young adult mental health and adjustment. *Journal of Homosexuality, 67*(2), 159–173. https://doi.org/10.1080/00918369.2018.1538407

Savin-Williams, R. C. (2001). A critique of research on sexual-minority youths. *Journal of Adolescence, 24,* 5–13. doi:10.1006/jado.2000.0369

Shilo, G., Antebi, N., & Mor, Z. (2015). Individual and community resilience factors among gay, bisexual, queer, and questioning youth and adults in Israel. *American Journal of Community Psychology, 54,* 3–4. https://doi.org/10.1007/s10464-014-9693-8

Substance Abuse and Mental Health Services Administration (SAMHSA). (2014). *SAMHSA's concept of trauma and guidance for a trauma-informed approach.* HHS Publication No. (SMA) 14-4884. Rockville, MD: Substance Abuse and Mental Health Services Administration.

Sue, D. W., Bucceri, J., Lin, A. I., Nadal, K. L., & Torino, G. C. (2007). Racial microaggressions and the Asian American experience. *Cultural Diversity and Ethnic Minority Psychology, 13*(1), 72–81. https://doi.org/10.1037/1099-9809.13.1.72

Troiden, R. (1979). Becoming homosexual: A model of gay identity acquisition. *Psychiatry: Journal for the Study of Interpersonal Processes, 42,* 362–373.

Vaughan, M. D., & Rodriguez, E. M. (2014). LGBT strengths: Incorporating positive psychology into theory, research, training, and practice. *Psychology of Sexual Orientation and Gender Diversity, 1*(4), 325–334. https://doi.org/10.1037/sgd0000053

Xavier, J., Bradford, J., Hendricks, M., Safford, L., McKee, R., Martin, E., & Honnold, J. A. (2012). Transgender health care access of Virginia: A qualitative study. *International Journal of Transgenderism, 14,* 3–17. http://doi.org/10.1080/15532739.2013.689513

Zimmerman, L., Darnell, D. A., Rhew, I. C., Lee, C. M., & Kaysen, D. (2015). Resilience in community: A social ecological development model for young adult sexual minority women. *American Journal of Community Psychology, 55*(1–2), 179–190.

Resources

Human Rights Campaign. (2017). Glossary of terms. Retrieved from www.hrc.org/resources/glossary-of-terms

Killermann, S. (2018). Comprehensive* list of LGBTQ+ vocabulary definitions. Retrieved from http://itspronouncedmetrosexual.com/2013/01/a-comprehensive-list-of-lgbt

https://store.samhsa.gov/sites/default/files/d7/priv/pep14-lgbtkids.pdf

National Center for Lesbian Rights #BornPerfect Toolkit.

Trevor Project Support Center.

National Suicide Prevention Lifeline.

GLAAD: Resources for Media Professionals.

SCHOOL AND COMMUNITY FOCUS

Chapter 8

Promoting Wellness with Native American Youth

Culturally Informed Resilience Practices to Reduce the Effects of Trauma

Carol Robinson-Zañartu, Ann Huynh, and Bryanna Kinlicheene

The well-being of our Native[1] youth draws on their rich traditions and values, the communities which nurture them, and the school personnel with whom they form meaningful relationships. All aspects of their wellness—the physical, social-emotional, cognitive, and spiritual—are complex and interrelated, as is the history that has influenced them. All too often that history involves complex trauma, which has deep roots in colonization and has been manifested in genocidal policies and practices, the outcomes of which have been passed down across generations. Thus, the nature of trauma-informed practices with Native populations is unique, complex, and must acknowledge historical and intergenerational trauma (Dunbar-Ortiz, 2019; Smith, 2012). Native traditions place high value on learning and creative inquiry, teachers and elders, the natural world and the spiritual, and health and vitality (Cajete, 2015). Often, these traditions are not accessible to our youth within a hegemonic, Eurocentric education system, especially when paired with the trauma they carry. Thus, trauma-informed practices which honor their cultural traditions support the strengthening of their

DOI: 10.4324/9781003046295-11

identities, voices, and senses of self as cultural and community-connected beings and learners.

In this chapter, we share and illustrate the reciprocal relationships between two frameworks. One guides culturally responsive work with Native youth who have been survivors of historical, intergenerational, and/or ongoing trauma. The second guides the preparation of professionals who will work with Native youth, in this case school psychology and school counseling graduate students, in which decolonizing their own identities for resilience is central. The two inform one another and are integrated in the model and in practice.

Beyond Individual Trauma: Critical Background

When trauma is related to major oppressive events perpetrated on a specific cultural, racial, or ethnic group of people it is called historical trauma (US Department of Health and Human Services [DHHS], n.d.). But the effects are not simply historical—they are far reaching. A long history of violent dismantling of Native communities, languages, and cultures has profoundly affected Native families and communities, including the lives of their children and youth. It has left a legacy of intergenerational trauma, which by Brave Heart (2003) describes as a cumulative emotional and psychological wounding emanating from massive group trauma experience. Duran (2006) refers to this profound historical trauma as a soul wound.

What Results from Historical Trauma/Soul Wound?

The wide-ranging results of historical trauma include "poor overall physical and behavioral health, including low self-esteem, depression, self-destructive behavior, marked propensity for violent or aggressive behavior, substance misuse and addiction, and high rates of suicide and cardiovascular disease" (DHHS). Traumatic stress indicators for youth, also called Adverse Child Experiences (ACEs), include witnessing violence against the mother, living with substance abusers, family members imprisoned, family members institutionalized, family members with mental health concerns, or experience of physical or psychological abuse. Children often have attention problems, emotional reactivity, withdrawal, or thought problems. They may seem disengaged, defiant, or aggressive (Wolpow et al., 2009). The prevalence rates in Native American populations are significantly higher than for the general population (Ehlers et al., 2013; Koss et al., 2003). These outcomes are often mistakenly attributed to individual effort, to parenting, or to students' cultures in general; thus, it is important to realize that very often they are in fact products of colonization and intergenerational trauma.

Many Native youth experience or act out from anger, much of which also has roots in historical trauma. Atkinson (2017) links anger and grief, saying that beneath all anger is grief. According to Brave Heart (2010), historical unresolved grief is the associated affect that accompanies Historical Trauma Response. When that anger and grief are turned inward, the epidemic levels of suicide found in this group result (American Psychiatric Association, 2017). Chandler and Lalonde (2008) found that the rate of youth suicide actually varied significantly from one First Nations community to the next. Their study led to the important finding that those bands that practiced more substantial ties to their cultural past and collective future also experienced youth suicide rates that were vanishing to absent. Thus, they named culture as a protective factor.

Historical Trauma Linked to Disruption of Identity

Compounding this intergenerational trauma, historical trauma often involves the additional challenge of a disrupted cultural identity (Sotero, 2006; Volkan, 2011). One of the things that makes a traumatic event so damaging is its violation of what Aydin (2017) refers to as primordial assumptions that people have about themselves and the world. Traumatized individuals and groups must try to reconcile the harsh and perhaps incomprehensible reality of extreme adversity with previously held, more benign assumptions about oneself, other people, and the world. After the traumatic event, the world never seems the same again. Integrating the atrocities into an intelligible narrative is profoundly difficult and can cause a discontinuity and rupture in identity formation. This in turn triggers a search for meaning and closure: "Why did this event happen to me/us/our people?" "How could somebody kill so many human beings?" … and hopefully, "What can we do to cope with it?" (Aydin, 2017, p. 129).

Critical Importance of Knowing Local Context

Over 570 tribes are federally recognized in the United States. Over 60 others are recognized by individual states. Each tribe has unique belief systems, ceremonies, languages, and customs. In addition, although federal government policies drove genocidal practices and tribes do have shared experiences such as the boarding schools, local and regional experiences have also been uniquely impactful. Thus, it is important not to over-generalize, but to know that each tribe and community has its own history and story based on what occurred within that region. For example, Brave Heart (2010) found that

> the Lakota suffer from impaired grief of an enduring and pervasive quality … [resulting] from massive cumulative trauma associated with such cataclysmic events as the assassination of Sitting Bull, the Wounded Knee Massacre, and the forced removal of Lakota children to boarding schools.
>
> (Brave Heart, 2010, p. 287)

In California, the state literally declared a war of extermination, with the purpose of making the Native peoples extinct. Militias murdered men, women, and children. City governments paid bounties on heads or scalps of Indians (Dunbar-Ortiz, 2019). In addition, the cruel history of enslavement, torture, and death of tens of thousands of California Natives at the hands of the California Mission priests and their soldiers became twisted into a tale of passive happy helpers. Propagated by tourist agencies and public schools, this lie became enshrined in California's fourth grade Mission unit. Stories of ugly truths and of powerful resistance remain untold and contribute to historical trauma (Miranda, 2013). Each community's stories must be heard.

Healing the Healer Framework

To work with youth whose communities have survived and even thrived despite these realities, those in the position of doing the intervention or healing work must come to understand and to work through their own histories, to understand the truth behind them with the aim to decolonize. Working with the effects of trauma can trigger traumatic memories and experiences in anyone. If the healers carry similar histories as those with whom they work, those triggers are more intense, which can seriously interfere with connection and effectiveness. Thus, a process which promotes a healing journey can lead to those experiences becoming reframed memories that are part of the tapestry of one's history rather than potentially obstructing effective youth and community work. Doing so in the context of a safe community, components of this process include truth seeking, truth telling, deep listening and reflecting, and emerging strengthened identity. This work then informs the resilience work with youth, characterized by belonging, mastery, independence, and generosity (Brokenleg, 2015), discussed in the next section of this chapter. Figure 8.1 illustrates the integration of the two frameworks.

San Diego State University's Native American and Indigenous Scholars Collaborative (NAISC) project uses this model to support graduate student scholars as they earn advanced degrees and credentials in school psychology and school counseling with a specialization in work with Indigenous youth and communities. Through reading, listening, reflecting, and telling our own truths, scholars and project faculty confront the effects of our own colonization, privilege, and resilience. We meet weekly, forming a community to understand more deeply and to contextualize our own stories while learning from one another, Indigenous literature, local leaders, and elders. This non-linear process is both integrative and iterative. The experiences contribute to the re-emergence of a stronger renewed identity and resilience from a strength-based and culturally grounded perspective. Before asking our youth to tell their deep stories and to

Figure 8.1 A Decolonizing Model of Reciprocal Identity and Resilience Building.

build resilience through healing, we do the same for ourselves (Duran, 2006). Four phases are described briefly below: Truth seeking, truth telling, deep listening, and identity and resilience.

> *Truth seeking.* Today's Indigenous peoples reflect both the strengths of their cultural traditions and resilience of survivors of genocidal policies and practices which left the wounds of intergenerational trauma. Not only has the truth been the source of profound wounds, but the whole truth has not been told—not told by communities whose fear of unearthing the pain or of passing it on keeps it hidden, nor in schools, where the guilt of its uncovering or the ignorance to it is so deep that they remain satisfied to live with and pass on blatant untruths or glossed-over versions of colonization. We must first seek truth to understand in depth who we are (Atkinson, 2017; Duran, 2006) and to confront rather than bury the trauma. We access multiple sources of information in this process: Our stories, knowledge from elders, film, trusted literature, ceremony, dreams, and immersion in our home community. Over time, we reframe our stories to reflect our truths and our resilience. We bring new understandings back into our community.
>
> *Truth telling.* Deep storytelling (Cajete, 2015; Duran, 2006; Smith, 2012) involves telling one's story in depth and reflecting learned truths, grieving

injustices, and emerging from trauma over time. Within that process, grieving facilitates a new understanding of anger, and empowerment emerges through truth acknowledged—often through embracing grounding aspects and inherent resilience within one's culture. We tell our stories seasonally and in community, as well as writing and revising them over time.

Deep listening. Within the context of our healing community (Duran, 2006; Sharing Culture, n.d.) the truth is acknowledged. Deep listening involves a reciprocal relationship with the teller and with the community of healers. The act of deep listening itself has healing properties. Being listened to with reflection on one's assets and strengths also contradicts the isolation of shame, uncertainty, or lack of belonging often associated with trauma.

Identity and resilience. Identity unburdened by negative stories about oneself, one's culture, and the deep wounding of historical trauma begets resilience. Identity reclaimed from an asset base and culturally grounded perspective breathes deeper, stands taller, and gives back. This strengthened or renewed identity also acts as a critical model for the youth with whom we will work.

Context of community. Cajete (2015) describes the affective component of community as a matter of heart and soul, and one of the most important. It arises from a "deep intuitive often subconscious understanding that self-interest is inseparably connected with community interest" (Hock, 2000, p. 35). The healing community creates safety and belonging. Within this community we find an environment in which risk taking and vulnerability are safe, learning and people's voices find expression, and questioning everything supports the shaping of each one's evolving identity.

Healing the Healer: Two Journeys

An Indigenous Scholar's Story

Yá'át'èèh. Bryanna Kinlicheene yinishyé. *Tábaahá* nishłį, *Tséńjíkiní* báshishchíín, *Ma'ii deeshgiizhinii* dashicheii, *Tó Dích'íi'nii* dashinálí. Hello. My name is Bryanna Kinlicheene. I am of the Water's Edge Clan, born for the Honey Combed Rock People Clan. My maternal grandfather is of the Coyote Pass Clan, and my paternal grandfather's clan is the Bitter Water People. I am a Diné (Navajo) woman whose family is from the Diné Nation, where I lived until the age of five.

To embrace identity from a decolonized perspective for me means first embracing my language, my traditional way of introduction, my maternal and paternal lineages, and relationship with the land. This is a form of *truth seeking*. *Truth telling* means acknowledging how at an early age I roamed the corn fields, rode horses, herded sheep, hauled water, and helped my grandmother cook, respecting the hard work of the adults around me. It has also meant acknowledging that when I later went to school off the reservation, others saw my home as a place of poverty. My truth as it emerges is to reject that interpretation. When I lived with my grandparents, we understood and respected the environment, sustaining our resources and only using and consuming what was essential. Our homes were built for shelter and safety, not for materialistic reasons. My truth telling is to share that the depth of their knowledge and resourcefulness and their relationship with all things was anything but a place of poverty.

Truth seeking has also meant acknowledging the hurt and confusion of depictions in my textbooks, in films, and sports mascots of Native people as violent. As a young student, I bore the burden of hearing negative stereotypes of Natives being alcoholics, drug abusers, or suffering from depression. Thus, I found myself trying to adapt to Western culture under the false assumption that White people did not feel the effects of mental illness or of these other stereotypes—the destructive assumption that by giving up my identity, my culture, my survival would be ensured. I was taught lies about my history from a colonialist perspective in school. There was no space for me to practice my language and I quickly lost the most important tie to my culture. Little did I know that the trauma my ancestors felt was being reinforced by the very people who were supposed to help me—my teachers.

A new level of truth seeking began in conjunction with this project and my graduate program. I began unlearning the colonialist beliefs that were instilled in me and immersing myself into my cultural traditions and beliefs again. I have read articles and books written from a Native perspective that addressed genocide, colonialism, effects of intergenerational trauma, systemic racism, and cultural inequities. I have heard creation stories from Native speakers and elders from my own as well as from other Native cultures. I have engaged in discussions on diverse cultural histories and challenged my colonized way of thinking.

I began learning deeply about my ancestral history. A powerful part of my learning came from family members who told me stories which reinforced the beliefs we had valued across decades. I advocated for my mental, physical, and spiritual well-being by participating in Diné ceremonial practices. The peace I felt being on the reservation motivated me to return home more often to engage in traditional events. At family gatherings, I listened to my aunts and uncles tell stories of their upbringing in Navajo. Their stories I hold close to my heart.

The NAISC project community became a safe haven for me—a place of *truth sharing*, where I was able to tell my own story and express what I was feeling. I was met with kindness and understanding. I recognized my anger at the lies that were taught to me and was able to release that tension. I felt discomfort and relief at the same time as I was sharing my experiences. Never before had someone asked me to share my perspective of my heritage, and provided this space, this healing community.

Each time I expressed my grief, anger, heartache, and confusion, I felt the resilience of my own story. Each time I felt lighter. I desperately grasped onto the values my family taught me and learned to express those values every day. Through the work of decolonizing my mindset, emotions, behaviors, and experiences, I have been able to see clearly the racial disparities of the society we live in. Through *truth seeking* and *truth telling*, I Walk in Beauty (a concept embedded in Diné/Navajo tradition) and feel confidence. As a Diné woman, mother, and educator, I realize how important it is to confront my historical trauma so I can continue my journey of decolonization.

Deep listening requires compassion, empathy, mindfulness, respect, and connection, which were concepts instilled in me from a young age. I feel these values inherently when I hear others tell their stories. It is the authenticity of the person's voice and hearing how they perceive themselves. It reminds me of the sacredness I feel when I am in ceremony. Hearing the songs of our Holy Deities, I hear the messages of healing they convey while focusing on the rhythm of the songs. When listening to other scholars within the project, it is a sacred time for the person sharing their story. It is important to hold space for them to feel their unique emotions at their own pace. Through listening to other stories, I set aside my beliefs and be there for them.

A strong sense of *Identity and Resilience* have emerged. Being Diné, I feel a sense of belonging through our Four Sacred Mountains which set the foundation to Diné life. Through this context, I recognize the power of traditional healing and knowledge that stems from my ancestors and from our four sacred mountains. This allows me to shape my mindset for the day, plan, reflect on my decisions, and finally to feel gratitude and protection for who I am (Carey, 2013). Through this traditional framework, I feel connected to my ancestral teachings. I practice strategies such as deep breathing, smudging, prayer, and connecting with Mother Earth to support myself.

How Does My Own Healing Journey Connect to My Work with Youth?

Being engaged in decolonization while learning about intergenerational trauma, I can be free of the troubling emotions that might have otherwise impeded my work with Native youth on a reservation. I do not hide or forget that I was once in their shoes. I lived on a reservation and felt happiness. This work also allows me to connect with Native youth on a level that some educators cannot. When I hear students talking about "going to town to go shopping," or "running the hills," I think of how I used to say those exact words when I was younger.

When I find myself in classrooms with teachers from the dominant culture, I can empathize with their Native students. I have heard some of their teachers say, "Those kids will never understand math or science, why bother?" It brings me back to when I was in grade school and I would hear the voices of teachers who doubted me. In reality, Native students like me do understand. I reflect deeply on concepts and sometimes have to translate ideas through my own cultural lens. Being able to understand that now helps me support Native youth. I recognize the looks that some teachers give students, and as much heartache as it has brought me in the past, it now motivates me to tap into and build resilience and strength within those students. I feel a deep imperative for Native students to engage in truth seeking, truth telling, and deep listening as well.

A Scholar Ally Story

As a Vietnamese American woman, I (co-author and project scholar Ann Huynh) come from a long line of ancestors who have embodied resilience, ingenuity, and compassion despite all odds. My parents and grandparents came to America as refugees of the Vietnam War. My family faced a plethora of challenges, from living in poverty to feeling isolation and discrimination in the American education system and workforce. Despite the adversity my family has faced, I have lived a relatively privileged life. Growing up in a middle-class family, my parents were able to provide me with what I needed, and more. My parents drilled the importance of education into me and I internalized this message. As a result, I thrived in school. My family's successes were due in part to our resilience and hard work, but also due to the systemic supports afforded to us (e.g., refugee resettlement programs, material support from community sponsors, the "model minority" myth). Recognizing these privileges and reflecting on their impact on my work has been critical. When I ignore them, I am liable to blame students and families for their challenges and act paternalistically; that is, in ways that reinforce systems of oppression. When I recognize my privileges, I recognize students' and families' structural barriers, center their experiences, and work to dismantle systemic obstacles.

The most critical aspect of my professional development has been coming to terms with how my identity impacts my work. Over the years, I have realized that in order to truly make a difference in the lives of those I serve, I must confront both privileges and traumas, heal, educate myself, and decolonize. Personally, this work has been difficult and sometimes painful, but also necessary and liberating. Reflecting on who I was and who I am now, I am proud of the work I have done thus far. The person I was a decade ago internalized colonized ways of being, engaged in problematic behaviors, and didn't recognize how identity impacted my work.

Truth Seeking, Truth Telling, and Deep Listening

Healing myself began with *truth seeking* and then *truth telling* about the ways in which colonialism has shaped me. Growing up, I had internalized the mainstream American values of individualism and competition. Like most others, I had been inundated with messages that conflate our productivity with our value—tricked into thinking that if we work longer hours and sacrifice our physical and mental well-being, we are somehow better people. Throughout my life, this message has manifested in my overworking, feeling like I have to do it all on my own, and lacking healthy boundaries. In order to heal, I have had to embrace rest, set boundaries, ask for help, and collaborate. Not only has this been personally restorative, but also it has allowed me to have the energy and compassion to truly show up for my community in meaningful ways.

Healing has also meant working through my own trauma. What has been fundamentally healing has been sharing my story, or *truth telling* in the *context of community*. Telling my story out loud has allowed me to process my traumas, recognize my strengths, and reflect on my growth. Additionally, relating to other people's stories despite our being from different cultures or life circumstances has been deeply therapeutic. Knowing that I am not alone, as well as hearing the ways in which others have dealt with pain has been empowering. This has made a difference in the way I approach my work with my community, and how I work with Native youth. I understand on a deeper level what it takes to tell one's story, to process trauma, and to heal.

A deep examination of my cultural *identity and resilience* has been critical. Growing up, despite my academic successes, I navigated school with feelings of self-hatred as an Asian person in a White-dominant community. The microaggressions I experienced, paired with how I saw others treat Asians who had not acculturated, pushed me to blend in and distance myself from my culture. One way I have been able to unlearn this self-hate and explore my identity was through an immersion to Vietnam, which I undertook with the intention to explore the meaning of "home" as someone who is the product of a diaspora, strengthen my Vietnamese language skills, reconnect with my cultural roots, and build relationships with Vietnamese people. My immersion allowed me to see that colonization and war were not enough to dismember my cultural roots. I realized that my home and my identity are deeply embedded in food, nature, language, and relationships. These truths have given me a greater sense of cultural pride and appreciation for everything my ancestors endured, and everything passed on to me. This has allowed me to empathize with others' journeys of exploring their own identity and resilience, including those of the youth with whom I worked.

Identity and Resilience Work with Indigenous Youth

Resilience has been described as an antidote to trauma (Jamieson, 2018). Resilience is found throughout the field of trauma-informed care as central. Although we use the term resilience for its accessibility, ultimately, we are seeking more a sense of survivance, both for our healers and our youth. As described by Vizenor (1999), survivance has "an active sense of presence, the continuance of native stories, not a more reaction ... Native survivance stories are renunciations of dominance, tragedy and victimry" (p. vii). Thus, the Decolonizing Model of Reciprocal Identity and Resilience Building (Figure 8.1) links that survivance to the resilience of both healer and client. Through modeling integrated with direct interventions, the school psychologists and counselors working with Indigenous youth can recognize and further foster their resilience. When youth build resilience, mental health and behavioral outcomes improve. With Native youth, strengthening identity, or enculturation, is strongly associated with enhanced resilience (Kahn et al., 2016; LaFromboise et al., 2006). Because the work of our project ultimately is for the youth, we work with our local Native youth, giving back to the community on whose land we reside and study. Our scholar graduates will return to their home communities with meaningful experiences and a framework for engaging with their own communities and youth. The following framework outlines the premises and processes that support that level of identity and resilience building with the youth.

Identity and Resilience Building Groups

Our work with youth builds on an Indigenous resilience framework called *Circle of Courage* (Brendtro et al., 2005; Brokenleg, 2015), which was designed to counteract the legacy of historical trauma. We incorporate locally informed and culturally grounded activities and identity work into this model, along with culturally mediated thinking skills (Robinson-Zañartu & Aganza, 2019) to counteract the cognitive interference that often accompanies trauma.

Brokenleg (2015) talks about four conditions within which Native youth will begin to learn beyond the unidimensional learning from the "head" to learn from the heart. In this way, they may attain the teachings of the four directions of the *Circle of Courage* model: Belonging, mastery, independence, and generosity. Our resilience group lessons and activities guide youth through the process of understanding and embodying those four concepts.

Belonging. Every human being naturally wants and needs to belong. Often our Native youth do not feel they belong in their schools. Especially when youth are in crisis, schools can create alienating experiences, from time-outs to suspensions (Brokenleg, 2015). Belonging creates a level of safety critical when working to counteract the effects of trauma. It lets youth know that they are significant (Brokenleg, 2015). Our youth begin their groups in a way consistent with local traditions, smudging with sage, then sit together in circles with scholar mentors to establishing ways they want to be together. This centers an Indigenous perspective rather than making it peripheral. They name their own groups, drawing on their assets. Facilitators draw on the wisdom of local elders and mentors and the experiences of the youth themselves. This work fosters excitement and empowerment in identity—the sense of belonging.

Mastery. Within this model, mastery refers to how the youth experience what they know (Brokenleg, 2015). Discovering what they can do or believe rather than being told what to do or what to think is key. The scholars or healers are mediators. One of the cognitive outcomes of trauma is difficulty with key executive functions like cognitive and emotional self-regulation, attention, flexible thinking, planning, organizing, planning, and goal setting. Thus, we integrate the mediation of culturally grounded thinking skill development (Robinson-Zañartu & Aganza, 2019) into our group experiences, which supports youth to discover their capabilities of critical thinking within cultural contexts. We then help them bridge those capabilities into new contexts, such as school or future plans.

Independence. In this context, independence means being able to take responsibility for oneself (Brokenleg, 2015). Scholar facilitators use a coaching and facilitation model to foster independence. Rather than use a passive learning model in which a teacher "tells" some truth, and the student is expected to absorb it, the facilitator asks the learner to form ideas, questions, opinions, and connections. They coach youth to make decisions on their own. This level of independence is empowering and leads youth toward giving back to their communities.

Generosity. Giving in a sacred way is embedded in the traditions of most Native peoples. It may bring people together, honor people, share with those who are in need, be a restorative act, or may be an exercise of spiritual humility. Brokenleg (2015) says that generosity is "how I will know my goodness." These acts of generosity are believed to be able to turn one's life in a positive direction. Being generous is integral to Native resilience. Each of our groups plans an activity of generosity to community, school, or elders.

Case[2] Examples

Rowan (sixth grade) and Easton (third grade) are siblings, Native youth who live in a rural reservation community in southern California. Each elected to participate in one of our project's school-based resilience groups, with their mother's consent. Their histories are intertwined with that of their family, their tribal community, and larger context of Native communities in general. Thus, their stories are situated in a history of colonial genocide, violence, and subjugation, with clear effects of intergenerational trauma. Like many Native families, their stories also reflect a remarkable history of Indigenous resistance and resilience.

Within their greater family constellation, trauma indicators were high; family members had experienced drug use, incarceration, and mental health challenges. The children had witnessed relational violence at home, volatile fights which paralleled those which their mother and her siblings witnessed from their adult figures. Their mother had graduated from high school hoping to attend college, but was too occupied as caretaker for her siblings, and then became pregnant with Rowan and other siblings to follow. Her partner was in the home inconsistently. Thus, she raised her children and siblings largely on her own with little support and few resources.

Nonetheless, she was a fierce advocate for her children. Along the way, she had distanced herself from her Native culture. Because of this, Rowan and Easton had not participated in tribal community events, although both expressed a desire to be more involved. Nonetheless, she was open to her children being part of our identity and resilience groups at school.

Rowan and Easton: Initial Interviews

Initial interviews produced a picture of Rowan, a sixth grader, as a young man proud about his cultural heritage, but thirsty for more knowledge about his roots. He held a vision of passing this knowledge on to others. Yet in the classroom, he was often off-task and engaged in or making jokes about serious topics. In response to a recent crisis, he had retreated inward and refused to do work at school. His younger brother Easton, now in third grade, presented himself as a wanderer, silly and active in school, while at home his family valued his help with household duties. In response to that recent crisis, he had become hyperactive and struggled to focus or to contain his energy in the classroom. In the interview, he shared that he felt calmed by tending his garden or running the hills. Easton knew little about his identity but was eager to learn more.

Developing Culturally Responsive Curriculum for Resilience Building

Each of the boys was in a resilience/identity group with same-aged peers. The overall conceptual foundation of both resilience groups built on Brendtro, Brokenleg, and Van Brockern's (2005) *Circle of Courage*, an Indigenous framework for youth resilience. Facilitators for the younger group used this model directly, helping students discover their own meanings and assets in its four directions of belonging, mastery, independence, and generosity. The sixth-grade facilitators selected *The Sacred Tree: Reflections on Native American Spirituality* (Lane et al., 1984) to guide their work for its indigenous representations of life and its use of the medicine wheel. The four directions of the medicine wheel became guides to help the youth seek balance across the physical, mental, emotional, and spiritual aspects of their lives. They incorporated teachings of local tribal elders. Using such culturally grounded and strength-based models with Native youth becomes critical to achieve that balance.

Resilience Building through Belonging, Mastery, Independence, and Generosity

> *Easton's journey in group.* For the younger group, *belonging* was initiated through opening the space in a circle and smudging with sage. Initially, Easton's behavior mirrored his classroom antics and jokes. Rather than responding with a punitive approach, the facilitators asked him to explain his choices, fostering *independence*. Easton reflected as he explained that his "silliness" brought him attention from his classmates, avoiding what he anticipated as being called bad or stupid because of being unprepared. He was unfamiliar with smudging. Given the opportunity to learn and to help in the process, to work toward *mastery*, he volunteered immediately.

As the group established norms early on, Easton expressed his need to keep things shared in the group inside the room. Given his family history, his reasons were evident, yet it took strength to voice this concern to his peers and to two adults new to him. His trust and feeling of safety in the group were building. The feeling of safety was facilitated by the co-facilitators sharing their own identities openly and creating a space for reciprocal learning and discussion.

Initially, Easton spoke about his inability to express himself in class the way he wanted to. He believed that his teachers had no interest in what he thought was interesting. He said, "they (teachers) don't understand me … they just think we can learn what they're telling us, but it's hard." This illustrates his perception that in his classroom, teaching was a form of "teaching at" instead of a shared or reciprocal learning between adult and student. This set the stage for further work with Easton on *mastery*. Easton showed a connection to his Indigenous views and intuitively knew how to advocate for himself when given the space to do so. He took leadership in a sage-planting project, demonstrating goal setting and planning skills. It was important to allow Easton to see that he was a capable thinker, to begin to contradict his feelings of incompetence as a learner in the classroom. He began to view himself as competent. The facilitators listened to his stories and validated his voice. As Indigenous scholars themselves, they recognized the power in that validation and in allowing Easton to be fully himself.

One of Easton's life goals was to teach Native students, which fit well with the group goal of engaging our students in the fourth dimension of Indigenous resilience, *generosity*. The group decided to create and pass on a book to the next generation of Native students. This gave Easton the motivation to contribute during every discussion.

In our effort to help him transfer those skills to the classroom, his own ideas became central in his plan—contributing to small groups and speaking up more often to share his thoughts. As the year went on, he demonstrated this sense of *independence* by sharing his ideas, asking questions, and forming and sharing his own opinions. Initially, Easton's teacher had described him using solely negative behavioral characteristics; however, as the year progressed, those descriptions gradually disappeared as his behavior changed. He showed more interest in academic work and willingness to participate in class. At the end of the year, Easton talked about how much he had learned and that he felt more connected to his culture.

> *Rowan's journey in group.* Facilitators for the older group consciously built genuine relationships and fostered reciprocity to help build the trust that comes with a sense of *belonging*. For Rowan, trust did not come easily, and in his first two weeks, his behavior paralleled a lack of focus and seemingly random comments seen in the classroom. In fact, he commented "this group is overrated." Drawing on the notion of giving youth the *independence* to think for themselves, the facilitator asked him to stay back and talk. She assured him that she valued his voice and honesty. She wanted to understand his perspective and be sure the space could be meaningful for him. Rowan insisted that he didn't mean anything by his statement about the group being "overrated," and that he couldn't think of ways to improve the group. When reassured that his voice would always be welcomed, this conversation became an important building block in his sense of belonging, and the relationship began to grow.

To foster self-efficacy, facilitators asked the students to develop personal goals. Rowan wanted to work on his spirit of mastery. In his words, "I want to believe in myself more. I want to feel confident in myself." As a child who had a history of academic struggles, who had learned to avoid challenges and give up or disengage (a typical trauma response), it was obvious why Rowan wanted to feel a sense of mastery. He wanted to feel valuable and to be someone who could contribute something to his classroom, his community. One of the ways the facilitators established *mastery* and *independence* was to provide students with the space to share their knowledge, ask questions, challenge ideas, and ponder new ones. It gave them thoughtful voice.

Rowan and the facilitator discussed ways he could work toward his goal in the classroom and in our group; they brainstormed how he could step outside of his comfort zone and take more risks (e.g., raise his hand, offer ideas, ask questions), ask for help, and learn more about his Native culture so that he could offer ideas. Throughout the year, Rowan made genuine efforts to take risks in the group. He consistently and actively participated, asked questions, shared ideas even when he was unsure of his responses, bringing in his knowledge, telling stories, and demonstrating critical thinking. He persevered through difficult activities that required academic skills including reading and writing. Rowan was able to demonstrate this mastery because he was given opportunities to do so in meaningful ways. He was already a smart, curious child. He had needed to feel a *sense of belonging* as a valued individual to feel safe enough to participate.

As a final project, Rowan's group engaged in a storytelling project grounded in the four directions. Students were to identify a gift they embodied in each direction and to illustrate or write a story about how they exemplified that gift. This was meant to foster their sense of *mastery and independence*. Before starting their medicine wheels, the group discussed the tradition and purpose of storytelling as Native people. Facilitators shared their own medicine wheel illustrations and personal stories of resilience to model vulnerability, self-reflection, and growth to the students, and to foster reciprocity.

Ann Huynh's observation of one example of Rowan's growth portrays a young man coming into his own: As the students scattered around the room and drafted their medicine wheels to the faint sound of Native American flute music in the background, I found Rowan laying on his belly under a desk deep in thought. He was looking at a model with the gifts of the four directions listed, carefully brainstorming which ones he would choose for his medicine wheel. This was certainly a different sight than the Rowan we had seen early in the year, who was easily distracted and didn't take things seriously. I sat down on the floor and brainstormed with him. As we talked, he came up with amazing examples of times he exemplified the gifts. For the West, he chose "respect for spirituality." He told me the story of how he refused to let his father chop down a tree in their garden. He stood in front of the tree and said, "This tree is me." His dad let the tree stand. This powerful story exemplified Rowan as a Native person—one who intuitively and spiritually knew that he was connected to that tree, and who protected its life.

Implications for Policy and Practice

Social justice is at the heart of our work; thus, in addition to our critical local action and work, to influence systemic change, we also engage with broader implications for policy and practice. Five themes emerge.

Centering Indigenous Culture and Frameworks

Supporting Native students' resilience, and ultimately their survivance, through trauma-informed and culturally responsive care becomes critical when considering the effects of historical, intergenerational, and ongoing trauma. Across settings— from counseling groups to classrooms—Indigenous frameworks such as the *Circle of Courage* allow Native youth to connect their learning to their everyday lives and goals. Interventions become culturally responsive when grounded in trauma-informed practices which consider or include cultural adaptations.

Historical Education

Education about the history of Indigenous peoples is critical to decolonizing and to challenging White supremacist underpinnings. This entails actively educating oneself through reading texts by Indigenous authors, following the work of Indigenous scholars and activists, and connecting with Indigenous communities. While it is critical to learn from Indigenous people, it is also important not to place the burden of education on them.

Relationship Building

Trusting and respectful relationships sit at the heart of Native learning. Thus, relationship building with Native youth should support their development, learning, well-being, and resilience. Indigenous students thrive when they are seen, and their voices are heard. Critical one-on-one relationships, whether built by teachers, counselors, or psychologists must complement critical attention to systemic practices, as in well-designed, school-wide positive behavior interventions and supports. Relationships must be reciprocal and collaborative so that we ponder different ideas, challenge different perspectives, and make connections together.

Advocacy at Every Level

Advocate for Indigenous students and families in the classroom, in your community, federally, and globally. Stand in solidarity with Indigenous peoples in their fight for sovereignty. This may range from advocating for Indigenous history being taught in schools, to standing with water protectors in their fight against the Dakota Access Pipeline.

Mutual Aid

Mutual aid provides collective care within communities (e.g., distributing material resources, care networks for disabled individuals). It is critical to survival—a political act that recognizes that often the government does not provide the care needed for survival. For example, the COVID-19 pandemic disproportionately affected the Navajo Nation, with some of the highest rates of infection in the United States and slowest government response (Doshi et al., 2020). People mobilized mutual aid efforts across the nation to provide resources. These efforts are consistent with the Indigenous value that we are all interconnected beings and rely on one another.

Conclusion

Altogether, putting these practices into action within an oppressive, hegemonic education system has its limitations. If we are to truly decolonize our practice, we must completely transform the education system to honor Indigenous knowledge and ways of being. We propose this model as a component of that transformation. The ultimate act of decolonization is Indigenous sovereignty and the dismantling of oppressive systems at large.

Notes

1. Native American, Indigenous, American Indian, and Native are all terms used to describe the original peoples of what is now the United States. In this chapter, we chose to use the term "Native" to the US Indigenous population; however, we use "Indigenous" to indicate the broader group of Indigenous peoples across the globe.
2. The case examples presented used pseudonyms to protect the identities of the youth and their families.

References

American Psychiatric Association. (2017). *Mental health disparities: American Indians and Alaska Natives*. Washington, DC: Author. Retrieved from https://www.psychiatry .org/File%20Library/Psychiatrists/Cultural-Competency/Mental-Health -Disparities/Mental-Health-Facts-for-American-Indian-Alaska-Natives.pdf

Atkinson, J. (2017). *The value of deep listening – The aboriginal gift to the nation.* TEDxSydney. Retrieved from https://www.youtube.com/watch?v=L6wiBKClHqY

Aydin, C. (2017). How to forget the unforgettable? On collective trauma, cultural identity, and mnemotechologies. *Identity, 17*(3), 125–137. https://doi.org/10.1080 /15283488.2017.1340160

Brave Heart, M. Y. H. (2003). The historical trauma response among natives and its relationship to substance abuse: A Lakota illustration. *Journal of Psychoactive Drugs, 35*(1), 7–13.

Brave Heart, M. Y. H. (2010). The return to the sacred path: Healing the historical trauma and historical unresolved grief response among the Lakota through a psychoeducational intervention. *Smith College Studies in Social Work, 68*, 287–305. Retrieved from https://www.tandfonline.com/doi/abs/10.1080/00377319809517532

Brendtro, L., Brokenleg, M., & Van Bockern, S. (2005). The circle of courage and positive psychology. *Reclaiming Children and Youth, 14*(3), 130.

Brokenleg, M. (2015). First people's principles of learning. Retrieved from https://www.youtube.com/watch?v=0PgrfCVCt_A

Cajete, G. A. (2015). *Indigenous community: Rekindling the teachings of the seventh fire*. St. Paul, MN: Living Justice Press.

Carey Jr., H. (2013, January 7). Mount Blanca (sisnaajini) Navajo sacred mountain. Retrieved from http://navajopeople.org/blog/mount-blanca-sisnaajini-navajo-sacred-mountain/

Chandler, M. J., & Lalonde, C. E. (2008). Cultural continuity as a protective factor against suicide in first nations youth. *Horizons, 10*(1), 68–72.

Doshi, S., Jordan, A., Kelly, K., & Solomon, D. (2020). The COVID-19 response in Indian country: A federal failure. Center for American Progress. Retrieved from https://www.americanprogress.org/issues/green/reports/2020/06/18/486480/covid-19-response-indian-country/

Dunbar-Ortiz, R. (2019). *An Indigenous peoples' history of the United States for young people*. Boston, MA: Beacon Press.

Duran, E. (2006). *Healing the soul wound: Counseling with American Indians and other native people*. New York: Teachers College Press.

Ehlers, C. L., Gizer, I. R., Gilder, D. A., Ellingson, J. M., & Yehuda, R. (2013). Measuring historical trauma in an American Indian community sample: Contributions of substance dependence, affective disorder, conduct disorder and PTSD. *Drug and Alcohol Dependence, 133*(1), 180–187.

Hock, D. (2000). *Birth of the chaordic age*. San Francisco, CA: Berrett-Koehler Publishers.

Jamieson, K. (2018). Resilience: A powerful weapon in the fight against ACEs. Center for Child Counseling. Retrieved from https://www.centerforchildcounseling.org/resilience-a-powerful-weapon-in-the-fight-against-aces/

Kahn, C. B., Reinschmidt, K., Teufel-Shone, N. I., Oré, C. E., Henson, M., & Attakai, A. (2016). American Indian elders' resilience: Sources of strength for building a healthy future for youth. *American Indian and Alaska Native Mental Health Research, 23*(3), 11–133.

Koss, M. P., Yuan, N. P., Dightman, D., Prince, R. J., Polacca, M., Sanderson, B., & Goldman, D. (2003). Adverse childhood exposures and alcohol dependence among seven native American tribes. *American Journal of Preventive Medicine, 25*(3), 238–244.

LaFromboise, T. D., Hoyt, D. R., Oliver, L., & Whitbeck, L. B. (2006). Family, community, and school influences on resilience among American Indian adolescents in the upper Midwest. *Journal of Community Psychology, 3*(2), 193–209. https://doi.org/10.1002/jcop.20090

Lane, P., Bopp, J., Bopp, M., Brown, K., & elders (1984, fourth edition 2012). *The sacred tree*. Twin Lakes, WI: Lotus Press.

Miranda, D. A. (2013). *Bad Indians: A tribal memoir*. Berkeley, CA: Heyday.

Robinson-Zañartu, C., & Aganza, J. S. (2019). Culturally responsive mediated learning in 21st century schools. In B. L. Chua & I. W. Yuen Fun (Eds.), *Advances in mediated learning experience for the 21st century: Competencies, contexts and culture* (pp. 1–22). Singapore: Cengage Learning Asia Pte Ltd.

Sharing Culture: Healing Historical Trauma. (n.d.). *Aboriginal healing, historical trauma.* Retrieved from http://www.sharingculture.info/index.html

Smith, L. T. (2012). *Decolonizing methodologies: Research and Indigenous peoples* (2nd ed.). New York: Zed Books.

Sotero, M. M. (2006). A conceptual model of historical trauma: Implications for public health, practice and Research. *Journal of Health Disparities Research and Practice, 1,* 93–108.

U. S. department of health and human services website/Administration for Children and Families. *Trauma.* Retrieved from https://www.acf.hhs.gov/trauma-toolkit/trauma -concept

Vizenor, G. (1999). *Manifest manners: Narratives on postindian survivance.* Lincoln, NE: University of Nebraska Press.

Volkan, V. D. (2011). Transgenerational transmissions and chosen traumas: An aspect of large-group identity. *Group Analysis, 34,* 79–97. https://doi.org/10.1177 /05333160122077730

Wolpow, R., Johnson, M. M., Hertel, R., & Kincaid, S. O. (2009). The heart of learning and teaching: Compassion, resiliency, and academic success. Retrieved from http://www.k12.wa.us/compassionateschools/pubdocs/TheHeartofLearningandTe aching.pdf

Chapter 9

Centering the Community's Voice and Needs in Gang Prevention and Intervention through a Trauma-Informed Lens

Joey Nuñez Estrada Jr., Edwin Hernandez, and Jesus Sandoval Hernandez

> *The pain of the community's voice leads us to the wound. Let us listen with compassion so we can be guided to the sacred place of healing and strength. We hear you! We see you! We are with you!*
>
> —*Steven Kim, Executive Director of Project Kinship*

Introduction

In this opening vignette, Steven Kim, Executive Director of Project Kinship, an organization that provides support services to individuals impacted by gangs

DOI: 10.4324/9781003046295-12

and incarceration, offers a critical message that drives our work in this chapter by incorporating a community-centered approach in trauma and healing. Rather than us informing the communities about their trauma, the community is aware of their trauma and we are learning from them as they teach us what is needed (Trauma-Informed LA, 2020). Hence, we open up with Steven's quote as it lends educators and clinical professionals an opportunity to understand that healing and transformation from the multiple layers of trauma occurs in collaboration, in a community of kinship. This chapter brings attention to compassionate listening to support the emotional well-being of young people impacted by the trauma integrated within the gang culture. The working definition of trauma used in this chapter is defined as

> Individual trauma results from an *event*, series of events, or set of circumstances that is *experienced* by an individual as physically or emotionally harmful or life threatening and that has lasting adverse *effects* on the individual's functioning and mental, physical, social, emotional, or spiritual well-being.
>
> Substance Abuse and Mental Health Services
> Administration (SAMHSA, 2014)

The focus on young people navigating the gang culture is important, as they represent our family and friends, and oftentimes their life experiences make them more likely to be exposed to higher levels of trauma than non-gang-involved peers (Estrada et al., 2017). For this reason, it is important to understand the multiple layers of trauma and how we can respond through a healing-centered lens so we can support our community members as they move from surviving to thriving.

Jesus's Narrative: The Events, Experiences, and Effects of Trauma

Guided by Steven's reflection of centering the experiences and knowledge of the community, we share the story of our friend, colleague, and honorary co-author Jesus, a formerly gang-involved Latino male, who vividly narrates his early memories of trauma. As Jesus described,

> By the age of sixteen, I had been shot by a double barrel shotgun on my chest, and six months later I got stabbed. I still question why I survived. During that time, I lost most of my friends to the grave or to prisons.

In a very short span of time, Jesus had experienced multiple series of events with trauma as he had experienced various life-threatening encounters and losing close friends, which had a tremendous effect on his mental, physical, and spiritual well-being. Recollecting on these events and experiences of his childhood trauma, Jesus noted, "You can say, by today's Adverse Childhood Experience (ACE) score standard, I answered yes to 9 out of the 10 questions." The ACE study has been widely used to demonstrate the effect of trauma on children over their lifespan, in which the higher the score, the worse the health outcomes over their life trajectory (Felitti et al., 1998).

In the case of Jesus, research from the National Child Traumatic Stress Network (2009) has shown how young people navigating the gang lifestyle are exposed to physical and sexual abuse, neglect, and maltreatment, and have observed extensive levels of community violence, resulting from another being murdered or dramatically injured. Therefore, this shows how young people involved with gangs are more likely to have experienced multiple types of trauma in the various ecological spaces they navigate. Kira (2001) has shown a comprehensive development-based taxonomy of trauma that includes individual (e.g., attachment trauma), single (e.g., car accidents) and complex traumas (e.g., repetitive ongoing), and cross-generational traumas that transmit through family or collectively (historical and social structural) (Kira, 2001). In listening and learning from Jesus, his story demonstrates the various types of trauma that can impact young people within the gang culture at an early age. These multiple occurrences with trauma can tremendously impact the mental health and wellness of young people involved in gangs, as in the case of Jesus who encountered emotional and physical violence. Thus, for Jesus and many gang-involved youth, to encounter these experiences with trauma at an early age can have a significant effect on their mental health, wellness, and success.

System-Induced Traumatization and Re-traumatization Leading to Gang Involvement

We draw on a system-induced traumatization and re-traumatization theoretical framework that lends itself to understand gang involvement as a larger macro-level consequence, rather than a micro-level decision (Estrada et al., 2017). Racial and cultural motivated forces that have occurred throughout violent historical events, discrimination, and oppression of various generations has impacted the lives of past, present, and future generations, in which various forms of unresolved grief and system-induced trauma have yet to be addressed (Oversreet, 2000). As a result of the lack of institutions to address the system-induced trauma, the cycle of perpetuated re-traumatization persists and further hinders an individual's

Figure 9.1   Traumatization and Re-traumatization.

psychological wounding (Estrada et al., 2017). In Figure 9.1, we present the progression toward system-induced traumatization and re-traumatization, which builds off the work of Vigil's Multiple Marginality Framework (1983, 1988, 2002, 2010). First, historical context has shown how legislative policies such as racial segregation have contributed to racial and economic disparities, which led to communities of color being placed in impoverished, clustered enclaves. As a result of these clustered enclaves, many communities of color have little to no resources, including social institutions that have failed to appropriately respond to the needs of groups within these communities. Consequently, resources toward social services and programs that have been significant toward vulnerable youth have been trimmed, thus this has further contributed to widening the economic and social gap among disenfranchised groups. Given the challenges as a result of lack of opportunities and financial insecurity, it directly creates psychological and emotional strain on systems, which causes traumatic experiences for children and families living under these conditions. As a result, the multidimensional psychological and emotional strain experienced further contributes to traumatic experiences and often further reproduces re-traumatization for the most vulnerable youth living in under-resourced communities (Estrada et al., 2017).

Risk and Protective Factors for Youth Gang Involvement

Research has documented the various risk and protective factors for youth gang involvement (see Huerta et al., 2019). The process that leads individuals to join a gang is not homogenous, as there are various internal and external factors connected to one's socioeconomic status, family composition, social networks, and their experiences with marginalization (Curry & Spergel, 1992; Estrada et al., 2018). Many gang-involved youth might be experiencing marginalization in various contexts, including their homes, schools, and communities which pushes them to find alternative forms of support. Therefore, the decision for a youth to pursue and join a gang oftentimes is a reaction due their traumatic experiences they have been exposed to in their environments (Calabrese & Noboa, 1995; Estrada et al., 2017). Individuals that are at greater risk of being associated with gang-involvement are those who come from single-parent households, homes with a high substance abuse, physical and/or sexual abuse, and those with family members involved in gangs (Estrada et al., 2018; Shelden et al., 2013; Vigil, 2016). One of the prevailing concerns is the impact of poverty on youth and families, as the socioeconomic status of families' might hinder their ability to experience resources or opportunities that are essential to the needs of youth. The issue with poverty has direct implications on housing, attention to medical and nutrition, and other resources that children need (Halpern, 1990; Lareau, 2011). Specifically, for low-income, youth of color, and working-class communities who do not have equitable access to health care, employment opportunities, or free and high-quality afterschool programs (Huerta & Rios-Aquilar, 2018). Yet, instead gang-involved youth might have more direct experiences with a heavy presence of police in their schools and communities that often mistreat, label, and punish them (Alexander, 2010; Huerta & Rios-Aquilar, 2018; Rios, 2017). As a result, Conchas and Vigil (2012) have noted that individuals might pursue gangs to find a place of inclusion, love and support, and affirmation of their self-identity given the constant marginalization they have faced in other contexts.

Many of the protective factors that gang-involved youth experience also come from their homes, schools, and communities (Huerta & Rios-Aquilar, 2018). For instance, in the home context the role of family plays an important part in the socio-emotional and academic development of children and adolescents, through their direct involvement that provides youth with the direction, attention, love, and support (Estrada et al., 2018; Vigil, 2016). Considering how family plays an important role in the protective factors, any individual support for gang-involved youths should expand to also include the family. In the school context, rather than excluding gang-involved youth through the use of disciplinary practices, schools need to invest in more opportunities and resources for gang-involved youth to be connected to the school (Huerta & Rios-Aquilar, 2018). Lastly, protective factors in the community, such as those provided by community-based organizations, churches, and other agencies should consider including effective gang prevention and intervention services (Howell & Griffiths, 2016). In the next section, we expand on the work that has focused on prevention and intervention services for gang-involved youth.

The Community-Based Gang Intervention Two-Prong Approach

There have been various prevention and intervention strategies that have attempted to curtail youth gang-involvement. Some of our previous work highlights the need for a holistic comprehensive multidimensional model that addresses the complex systemic and institutional impediments that young people involved in gangs and their families confront daily (Estrada et al., 2018). We have also uplifted the need to consider a culturally based, trauma-informed approach focused on the trauma of poverty and the multiple marginality factors that exacerbate the psychological strain, economic status frustration, dominant culture value conflict, and identity confusion of young involved in gangs from a biological, psychological, and social perspective (Estrada et al., 2017). What we want to amplify in this chapter is that gangs are not going away; gangs are woven into the fabric of the community and we need to embrace the funds of knowledge those with lived experience bring to this work (Huerta & Rios-Aguilar, 2018). As our mentor Father Greg Boyle, the founder of Homeboy Industries—the largest and most successful gang intervention program in the world—proclaims, transformational healing requires

> moving ourselves closer to the margins so that the margins themselves will be erased. We stand there with those whose dignity has been denied. We locate ourselves with the poor and the powerless and the voiceless. At the edges, we join the easily despised and the readily left out. We stand with the demonized so that the demonizing will stop.
> (Boyle, 2011, p. 190)

This work requires meeting people where they are with compassion and taking time to listen to those on the margins. Elevating the indomitable spirits that have survived the historic intergenerational cultural trauma marginalities and the school and community violence of neighborhood rivalries of survival, will only enhance intervention strategies by allowing those like Jesus to contribute to both his own and his community's transformational healing.

Figure 9.2 depicts a Community-Based Gang Intervention Two-Prong Approach created by the community, for the community (for a detailed description, see Cárdenas 2008). Between the years of 2006 through 2008, Los Angeles City Council member Tony Cárdenas (now U.S. Representative for California's 29th Congressional District), provided space for community members to have a voice at the policy-making table by convening a series of meetings where community intervention workers shared their wealth of knowledge and expertise on the subject of gang intervention. Consequently, in a unanimous vote in 2008, the Los Angeles City Council passed the Community-Based Gang Intervention

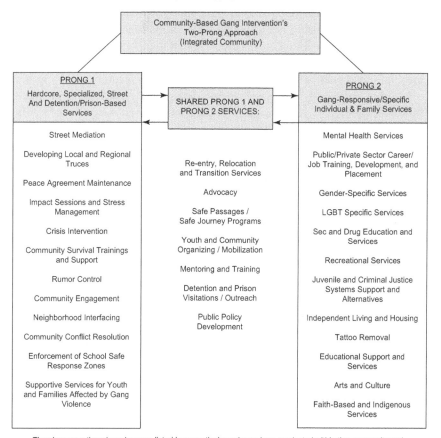

Community-Based Gang Intervention Definition and Diagram

Gang Intervention is a two-prong approach that providers hardcore, specialized, street-based mediation and mitigation to stop or prevent violence between gangs and the concurrent redirection of individual gang members and their families in ways that bring progress to themselves and their communities.

Community-Based Gang Intervention's
Two-Prong Approach
(Integrated Community)

PRONG 1
Hardcore, Specialized, Street And Detention/Prison-Based Services

SHARED PRONG 1 AND PRONG 2 SERVICES:

PRONG 2
Gang-Responsive/Specific Individual & Family Services

PRONG 1	SHARED PRONG 1 AND PRONG 2 SERVICES	PRONG 2
Street Mediation		Mental Health Services
Developing Local and Regional Truces	Re-entry, Relocation and Transition Services	Public/Private Sector Career/ Job Training, Development, and Placement
Peace Agreement Maintenance	Advocacy	Gender-Specific Services
Impact Sessions and Stress Management	Safe Passages / Safe Journey Programs	LGBT Specific Services
Crisis Intervention	Youth and Community Organizing / Mobilization	Sec and Drug Education and Services
Community Survival Trainings and Support	Mentoring and Training	Recreational Services
Rumor Control	Detention and Prison Visitations / Outreach	Juvenile and Criminal Justice Systems Support and Alternatives
Community Engagement	Public Policy Development	Independent Living and Housing
Neighborhood Interfacing		Tattoo Removal
Community Conflict Resolution		Educational Support and Services
Enforcement of School Safe Response Zones		Arts and Culture
Supportive Services for Youth and Families Affected by Gang Violence		Faith-Based and Indigenous Services

The above-mentioned services are listed in no particular order and are conducted within the community and in the juvenile halls, camps, division of juvenile justice (DJJ) facilities, county jails, and state prisons.

Figure 9.2 Community-Based Gang Intervention's Two-Prong Approach (Integrated Community).

Two-Prong Approach, which provided the city known as the gang capital of the world and the rest of the country a blueprint for understanding community-based gang intervention. Prong I provides hard-core, specialized, street- and detention/prison-based crisis intervention services, and Prong II provides concurrent ongoing gang-responsive specific individual and family services (Cárdenas, 2008). This two-prong approach promotes the co-elevation of the community members that directly interface with community violence as first responders, practitioners that provide ongoing support services, as well as system stakeholders that support sustainable community healing and restoration.

One may ask, why highlight an approach that is over a decade old? We feature this Community-Based Gang Intervention Two-Prong Approach because it can be viewed as a seminal piece that has been the springboard for many effective gang intervention models being implemented on a national and international scale. What is most noteworthy about this model is that it utilizes "skilled intervention specialists who have personal knowledge, understanding, and experience of gang life and thereby offer the greatest likelihood for gaining, building, and maintaining trust and confidence among active and former gang members" (Cárdenas, 2008, p. 5). This two-prong approach has served as a guide in building the current Credible Messenger movement across cities like Los Angeles, Santa Ana, San Diego, Oakland, New York, New Jersey, Chicago, South Carolina, and the District of Columbia (Austria & Peterson, 2017). As Austria and Peterson (2017) suggest, "Young people receive guidance from believable sources, opportunities to form healthy relationships in safe, supportive environments, and tools to replace negative attitudes and behaviors with productive practices and relationships" (p. 1). This movement is beginning to transform systems as large governmental agencies like the New York City Department of Probation, the District of Columbia Department of Youth Rehabilitation Services, the County of San Diego Probation Department, and others have invested financially in this cost-effective approach. Preliminary research on the Credible Messenger model supports gains in key attitudinal and behavioral indicators, including improvements in self-perception and relationships with others, emotion regulation, positive future orientation, and a reduction in recidivism (Lynch et al., 2018). "Credible messengers—people who are recognized and validated by a community—can spread a message of hope and change to young people who trust them" (Austria & Peterson, 2017, p. 2).

Furthermore, the Community-Based Gang Intervention Two-Prong Approach serves as the foundational core of the Professional Community Intervention Training Institute (PCITI). Our dear friend and mentor, Dr. Aquil Basheer, played a pivotal role in the creation of the two-prong approach and developed the PCITI in 2006 as a "practitioner driven" community-based gang outreach intervention, first-responder violence deterrence, and crisis abatement training institute. PCITI has trained over 15,000 gang intervention specialists, university students, mental health professionals, social service experts, emergency first responders (including law enforcement officers, firefighters) and public safety professionals in 60 U.S. and 14 international cities. Therefore, we uplift the Community-Based Gang Intervention Two-Prong Approach because over the last decade we have witnessed firsthand how the collaborative efforts of the community in the implementation of the hardcore gang intervention services of Prong I first responders, along with the continuous support services of Prong

II service providers, as well as support from system partners, has significantly promoted healing that is transforming lives and communities through trauma resiliency. In the next section, we revisit the narrative of Jesus to demonstrate how the Community-Based Gang Intervention Two-Prong Approach aligns well with the Substance Abuse and Mental Health Services Administration (SAMHSA, 2014) key components of a trauma-informed approach to provide a seamless response to addressing the events, experiences, and effects trauma that impact young people in gangs.

Key Components of a Trauma-Informed Gang Intervention Approach

As one begins the journey of healing from traumatic experiences of a gang lifestyle, it is important to consider the four key assumptions (the 4 Rs) in a trauma-informed approach (SAMHSA, 2014). Additionally, since the overall intervention goal is to support transformational change, infusing the five Stages of Change in this work is also critical (Zimmerman et al., 2000).

The first key assumption in a trauma-informed approach includes having a basic *realization* about trauma and how it affects individuals, families, and communities. When supporting young people involved in gangs, one must realize that the negative behaviors often displayed (i.e., violence, crime, drug use, etc.) are usually a survival response to adverse systemic conditions, emotional psychological distress, and other traumatic pressures and threats. It is important to point out that these responses are regular and acceptable within the gang culture and often encouraged and praised by others. As Jesus shared,

> When I was gang banging, hustling drugs, and putting in work, I was building up my street credibility and making a name for myself and my gang. I was living the dream, earning recognition, respect, influence, trust, and loyalty. You did what you needed to survive.

Unfortunately, many young people in this situation do not realize the impact their actions are having and far too often put their lives and that of others at risk. The hyper-focus on survival places young people in the *precontemplation* stage of change where they are not even thinking about making a change since thoughts and behaviors are occupied with building street credibility and staying alive (Zimmerman et al., 2000). It is during this critical time that the Prong I hardcore street gang interventionists, credible messengers, and community mentors "who come from the same communities and have shared similar experiences have an especially powerful role to play" (Austria & Peterson, 2017, p. 2). These community leaders realize the traumatic experiences young people are navigating because they too have survived the difficulties these young people are up against. As first responders to gang violence, these individuals provide life-saving crisis intervention efforts as they interrupt potential retaliations, dispel rumors, and work to establish safety, which is the first key principle of a trauma-informed approach (SAMHSA, 2014).

The second assumption in a trauma-informed approach includes *recognizing* the signs of trauma. Again, Prong I hardcore street gang interventionists, credible messengers, and community mentors have their own lived experiences with trauma so recognizing it is second nature. As pillars of the community, they engage and interface with key players of the streets to screen, assess, and recognize pivotal signs of trauma. This requires a structured methodological protocol, because without this lives could be lost (Basheer & Hoag, 2014). Sadly, recognizing the signs of trauma within the gang culture often occurs in emergency rooms when victims are trying to survive a gunshot wound, or as trained community interventionists respond to a drug overdose because the family is too afraid to call 911, or when they have to secure the perimeter of a funeral service so a family can bury their loved one in peace. During these crucial times, interventionists use transformation mentoring and motivational interviewing skills to share strategies they have used to overcome similar situations in hopes that it encourages young people to move toward the contemplation stage of change where one begins to consider an alternative path (Austria & Peterson, 2017; Zimmerman et al., 2000). In Jesus' case, he shared how, "by the age of eighteen, I became a teen father and decided to leave the gang life and integrate into my new faith-life." Fatherhood was a significant event in his life that prompted change, yet he also recalled the importance of mentorship during that time. Jesus described, "being in the living room with my mentor and seeing the family pictures on his wall. I felt peace, love and security every time I was in that setting."

Being present, running toward rather than away from young people as they confront the signs of trauma, helps strengthen relationships and builds *trustworthiness* and *peer support*, which are the second and third key principles of a trauma-informed approach (SAMHSA, 2014). Again, these Prong I hardcore street gang interventionists, credible messengers, and community mentors are part of the fabric of the community.

> They are trained and paid to develop authentic long-term relationships with young people. They stay connected, serving as real and present guides as youth navigate the difficult path of life change. They offer firsthand wisdom about down-to-earth challenges youth face.
>
> (Austria & Peterson, 2017, p. 2)

Trust and peer support are the salient instruments needed to increase safety and hope, and the lived experiences and narratives of interventionists move the pendulum toward healing (SAMHSA, 2014). The mentorship Jesus received had an immense effect on what he had envisioned for himself and his family, as he shared, "I saw a vision of what I wanted, a family that I could call my own. A healthy family away from the drugs, the streets, and the gangs, so I decided to give my life to the lord." Fatherhood, receiving mentorship, and becoming involved in faith-based organizations were the important *events, experiences,* and *effects* in his transition, transformation, and healing process from the trauma he was exposed to from a young age.

The third assumption in a trauma-informed approach is to *respond* by fully integrating "an understanding that the experience of traumatic events impacts all people involved, whether directly or indirectly" (SAMHSA, 2014, p. 10). It is at this point, that holistic and comprehensive gang-responsive specific individual and family services of Prong II are infused in the intervention approach. Once a sense of safety, peace, and trust are established by Prong I hardcore street gang interventionists, they can then fully assess the responsivity needs and socio-ecological factors that are contributing to traumatic events and experiences. Through *collaboration and mutuality,* which is the fourth key principle of a trauma-informed approach, interventionists leverage their Prong II partnerships and alliances to connect young people through a "warm-handoff" to community services that will best support their healing and transformational change (SAMHSA, 2014). Young people are often more willing to engage in services when hardcore street gang interventionists, credible messengers, and community mentors they now trust are encouraging them to try it out and can vouch that the service provider is a supportive ally in the healing process. For instance, Jesus now utilizes his lived experiences to transform systems. His healing journey has been a long process. In 2003, his change began when his pastor took him under his wing and mentored him to be a youth leader for his church. Shortly thereafter, the church fellowship bent the rules and ordained Jesus as a pastor based on his lived experiences, rather than the traditional formal education of a seminary or university training. This is considered the preparation stage of change where one is preparing for action to alter their thinking process toward sustainable change (Basheer & Hoag, 2014; Zimmerman et al., 2000). Trained counselors, social workers, and other Prong II service providers are able to assess a young person's commitment to change and work with and support them on the most culturally sustaining treatment plan. A menu of healing practices are explored, which may include strategies guided by the neurological effects of trauma and attachment, such as self- and community-reflection activities, interactive journaling, narrative storytelling, or creative expression, right-brain artistic activities (e.g., yoga, music, dance, drama, painting, script writing, acting/role-play) (Clark et al., 2019; Jordan, 2010; Lapum et al., 2019; Macy et al., 2018; Rolbiecki et al., 2016; Stenman et al., 2019; Williams et al., 2009).

At this point, young people are often ready to move into the *action* stage of change where one actively implements a treatment plan for change as they strengthen positive coping strategies and identify new sources of support (Zimmerman et al., 2000). Jesus transferred the skills he used as a gang leader in the streets, to the servant leadership he now provides to his church and community. As he recalls,

> Getting high and loaded was replaced with prayer, meditation and worship services. Dealing dope was replaced with dealing hope to the homies. Earning my stripes in the hood was replaced with growing within the ranks and leadership of the church and community.

He shares his funds of knowledge and elevates that of others in his co-authored book *Hidden Treasures: Find Yours!* that uncovers how people formerly in "the life" now work alongside the Probation Department, law enforcement, churches, schools, local universities, and a multitude of non-profit organizations to intervene and educate others (Sandoval et al., 2017). For roughly nine years he provided comprehensive wraparound services to youth and families, using the same model that transformed his life. Community wraparound services take into consideration the biological, psychological, and social components of all socio-ecological systems to strengthen change at the individual, family, peer, school, community, and organizational level (Estrada et al., 2018). Relationship-based, cognitive behavioral intervention strategies that sensitively mend the wounds of trauma may include individual and family counseling, social competence training, academic support, parent/child conflict management training, multisystemic therapy, restorative justice practices, hip-hop therapy, Trauma-Focused Cognitive Behavioral Therapy, or other cultural traditions and rituals that support healing (Foa et al., 2009; Lieberman et al., 2006; Lieberman et al., 2005). Within the fifth key principle of a trauma-informed approach, young people are *empowered, and their voice and choice* are uplifted as they are supported "in shared decision-making, choice, and goal setting to determine the plan of action they need to heal and move forward" (SAMHSA, 2014, p. 11). Elevation of the cognitive and behavioral discourses that inspire young people to liberate themselves from the intrinsic and extrinsic pressures through acceptance of resilience, strengths, and supportive resources should be applied (Estrada et al., 2017).

The fourth and last assumption in a trauma-informed approach includes *resisting re-traumatization* (SAMHSA, 2014). The healing and recovery process is a lifelong journey surrounded by constant trigger points. Organizations need to be aware of the various practices that intend to be helpful, but are sometimes more hurtful, as they inadvertently precipitate distressful memories that penetrate deep into the wounds of young people with traumatic histories (SAMHSA, 2014). The organizational support systems operating from the Community-Based Gang

Intervention Two-Prong Approach need to recognize that not only are the young people out of the gang lifestyle vulnerable to re-traumatization, but their staff with lived experience are navigating the environments and experiences which may re-trigger pain points as well. Therefore, identification of people, places, and things that could pose as triggers to relapse is critical. This is the work required in the *maintenance* stage of change where continuous support of the healthy lifestyle changes made is imperative because the temptations of the streets and forceful pull of a criminogenic mindset are ever-present (Zimmerman et al., 2000). However, when organizations understand that setbacks are embodied in the process of healing and recovery and continue to embrace and support young people through the struggle, it provides a safe space of unconditional love and belonging, which was previously provided by the streets. As Jesus describes, "this is the difference between transactional and transformational healing touch points."

While Jesus has encountered adversity in his journey, he recollects the support available to him from multiple individuals and organizations that have contributed to his transformation, as he recounts, "My Pastor always told me, my adversity was my university." His lived experiences have contributed to him dedicating his life to inspiring others to step out of the quicksand of self-destruction onto the solid ground of productivity. In December of 2018, Jesus was appointed by the Mayor of San Diego as the Executive Director of the Commission for Gang Prevention & Intervention, whose vision is

> to develop a more strategic, coordinated, and collaborative effort between the City, law enforcement agencies, social service providers, and the general public with the objective of significantly curtailing gang involvement, and its negative impact, in the City of San Diego.
> (www.sandiego.gov/gangcommission/about)

His lived experiences, trauma recovery, and transformational change not only provided him a seat at a table, but has led him to directing the efforts for the entire City of San Diego. Jesus proclaims, "My goal now is to bring forth a wraparound model into a policy level to bring healing and hope to all our communities that have been impacted and devastated from trauma so they can experience triumph."

For sustainable maintenance, organizations need to leverage the healing benefits of *cultural-*, *historical-*, and *gender*-responsive services, which is the sixth key principle of a trauma-informed approach (SAMHSA, 2014). At a micro-level, this entails addressing the intersections of trauma with culture, history, race, gender, location, and language (National Child Traumatic Stress Network, n.d.), which are all factors in the Community-Based Gang Intervention Two-Prong Approach. At a systemic macro-level, trauma care advocates need to be conscious of and work to rectify the compounding impact of structural inequity and the system-induced trauma of multiple marginalities often perpetuated by systems of power and oppression, which contributes to young people seeking asylum within the street socialization of gangs (Estrada et al., 2018; Huerta et al., 2019; National Child Traumatic Stress Network, n.d.; Vigil 1988, 2002, 2010).

Implications

While we center the narrative of Jesus and the hidden treasures of his transformational healing, it is imperative to reiterate that safe and supportive systems and environments of authentic compassion and kinship are critical for healing and transformation to occur (Estrada et al., 2017; 2018). The success of any gang intervention model is highly dependent on whether care advocates, educators, counselors, and other clinical professionals are able to cultivate an unconditional positive regard through a healing-centered lens for young people involved in gangs (Estrada et al., 2017). Additionally, a holistic model of prevention and intervention services like the Community-Based Gang Intervention Two-Prong Approach must work to abolish the countless systemic impediments that young people involved in gangs and their families encounter repeatedly. Such a comprehensive model needs to consider the complex interplay between individuals, peers, families, the community, school, and other historical, cultural, and societal elements that have an impression on young people involved in gangs (Cárdenas 2008).

We uplift some of the organizations functioning from the Community-Based Gang Intervention Two-Prong Approach that are beacons of hope and healing for their communities. Places like Project Kinship (https://projectkinship.org/) and Underground Grit (https://undergroundgrit.org/) in Orange County, CA, which provides both the critical life-saving efforts of Prong I services and specialized community responsive services of Prong II. For instance, with the majority of staff having lived experiences with gangs and the carceral system, Project Kinship provides Prong I outreach in schools, neighborhoods, and partnering agencies with the purpose of connecting, engaging, and linking individuals to appropriate Prong II services, such as counseling, intensive case management, health and well-being programming, family support service, recovery groups, tattoo removal, legal clinics, workforce development, etc. Underground Grit provides a voice to men, women, and youth who have been system-impacted and who are breaking cycles perpetuated by trauma. Through the personal and professional experiences of their staff, they are able to recognize the gaps in the system to offer innovative services that include groundbreaking, trauma-specific therapies that integrate holistic care with trauma-informed yoga, reiki, mindfulness, and the art mediums of fashion, music, and poetry to support transformational change and healing.

In San Diego, CA, Project Aware (www.projectawareenterprises.org/), Paving Great Futures (www.pavinggreatfutures.org/), and the San Diego Compassion Project are all staffed by care advocates who reside in the same communities and come from the same backgrounds and whose lived experiences allow them to connect with and motivate the young people who are navigating system-induced traumas. Project Aware utilizes restorative practices to build social capital with a primary focus on emotional literacy skills, social development, and problem-solving techniques. Paving Great Future's comprehensive work experience programs, which operate from six core competencies (Entrepreneurship, Job Readiness, Financial Literacy, Responsible Life Skills, Community Service, and Civil Engagement) transform misguided young people into productive and empowered community leaders. Whereas the San Diego Compassion Project is a volunteer-driven program that started in 2008 as a crisis-response group working with victims' assistance and the San Diego Police Department to provide support for families dealing with sudden loss and overwhelming grief. The San Diego Compassion Project works with organizations to support families in crisis by providing both faith-based assistance with the goal of helping to calm tensions and reduce or remove the potential for gang retaliation, as well as help families access services and facilitate community unification to restore peace and regain a sense of security in their own and surrounding neighborhoods. Again, the uniqueness of these programs lies with the staff of the program. They bring their own lived experiences with trauma, gangs, and incarceration to the heart of the program. These hardcore street gang interventionists, credible messengers, and community mentors have transformed their lives and continue their healing journeys by helping to restore the communities they once destructed.

Future directions in this work requires the importance of understanding the various layers of trauma that directly impact gang-involved individuals to effectively respond through a healing-centered lens. Policy recommendations must take into account the System-Induced Traumatization and Re-traumatization theoretical framework, which was offered earlier in this chapter, as it provides an account of the various forces that contributed to gang involvement given the unaddressed grief and system-induced trauma that has been dismissed. Given the lack of institutions to respond to the system-induced trauma, policy makers should consider providing more resources and opportunities to social institutions and organizations to effectively respond to the needs of groups within these communities. Therefore, any broader recommendations must be offered at multiple levels from the macro to the micro level in healing the psychological wounding and providing structures of support for transformation to take place by also centering those directly impacted. For instance, as the Executive Director of the Commission for Gang Prevention & Intervention, Jesus has engaged in policy work by directly collaborating with the Clinton Foundation, the San Diego Foundation Strong Families, Thriving Communities

Coalition, and with dozens of youth who have lived experience in child welfare and juvenile justice systems to develop a Trauma-Informed Code of Conduct, which provides government agencies, non-profit organizations, and communities with a framework on how to support youth in building resilience, and in being balanced, healthy, and empowered (The San Diego Foundation, 2019). This approach and involvement of Jesus in policy work demonstrates the critical work of trauma-informed approaches, in which collaboration takes place among trauma survivors, community members, and other social institutions to foster empowerment, healing, and recovery.

Future research is needed to understand how a trauma-informed gang intervention approach is implemented by educators and clinical professionals. This will contribute to the understanding of their pedagogical approaches and the ways in which they collaborate with credible messengers and those directly impacted by trauma. In addition, future research is needed to document the ways in which organizations employ the Community-Based Gang Intervention Two-Prong Approach to support young people involved in gangs through hope and healing as they find ways to further their education and engage civically with their communities. Yet, as we have discussed in this chapter, it is critical to involve those directly impacted in the decision-making process, thus, we elevate the narrative of Jesus to demonstrate that change is possible when structures of opportunities are presented. As a servant leader with lived experiences, Jesus compassionately listens to the pain of the community's voice, he bears the scars of traumatic wounds from the gang lifestyle, he was previously guided and now guides others to the sacred place of healing and strength. In closing, we acknowledge all the young people navigating the gang culture as they represent our family and friends. "We hear you! We see you! We are with you!"

References

Alexander, M. (2010). *The new Jim Crow: Mass incarceration in the age of colorblindness.* New York: New Press.

Austria, R., & Peterson, J. (2017). Credible messenger mentoring for justice-involved youth. Retrieved from https://www.thepinkertonfoundation.org/wp-content/uploads/2017/02/Pinkerton-Papers-credible-messenger-monitoring.pdf

Basheer, A., & Hoag, C. (2014). *Peace in the hood: Working with gang members to end the violence.* New York: Turner.

Boyle, G. (2011). *Tattoos on the heart: The power of boundless compassion.* New York: Free Press.

Calabrese, R. L., & Noboa, J. (1995). The choice for gang membership by Mexican-American adolescents. *High School Journal, 78*(4), 226–235.

Cárdenas, T. (2008). *A guide for understanding effective community-based gang intervention.* Los Angeles, CA: Office of Los Angeles City Councilmember Tony Cárdenas.

Clark, R., Gehl, M., Heffron, M. C., Kerr, M., Soliman, S., Shahmoon-Shanok, R., & Thomas, K. (2019). Mindful practices to enhance diversity-informed reflective supervision and leadership. *Zero to Three, 40*(2), 18–27.

Conchas, G. Q., & Vigil, J. D. (2012). *Streetsmart schoolsmart: Urban poverty and the education of adolescent boys.* New York: Teachers College Press.

Curry, G. D., & Spergel, I. A. (1992). Gang involvement and delinquency among hispanic and African-American adolescent males. *Journal of Research and Delinquency, 29*(3), 273–291.

Estrada, J. N., Hernandez, R., & Kim, S. (2017). Considering definitional issues, cultural com-ponents, and the impact of trauma when counseling vulnerable youth susceptible to gang-involvement. In J. G. Ponterotto, J. M. Casas, & L. A. Suzuki (Eds.), *Handbook of multicultural counseling* (4th ed., pp. 332–340). Thousand Oaks, CA: Sage.

Estrada, J. N., Huerta, A. H., Hernandez, E., Hernandez, R., & Kim, S. (2018). Socioecological risk and protective factors for youth gang involvement. In H. Shapiro (Ed.), *The Wiley handbook on violence in education: Forms, factors, and preventions* (pp. 185–202). Hoboken, NJ: Wiley-Blackwell.

Felitti, V. J., Anda, R. F., Nordenberg, D., Williamson, D. F., Spitz, A. M., Edwards, V., & Marks, J. S. (1998). Relationship of childhood abuse and household dysfunction to many of the leading causes of death in adults. *American Journal of Preventive Medicine, 14*(4), 245–258.

Foa, E. B., Keane, T. M., Friedman, M. J., & Cohen, J. A. (2009). *Effective treatments for PTSD: Practice guidelines from the international society for traumatic stress studies* (2nd ed.). New York: The Guilford Press.

Halpern, R. (1990). Poverty and early childhood parenting: Toward a framework for intervention. *American Journal of Orthopsychiatry, 60*(1), 6–18.

Howell, J. C., & Griffiths, E. (2016). *Gangs in America's communities* (2nd ed.). Thousand Oaks, CA: Sage.

Huerta, A. H., Hernandez, E., & Estrada, J. N. (2019). "I am somebody": Gang membership. In D. Capuzzi & D. R. Gross (Eds.), *Youth at risk: A prevention resource for counselors, teachers, and parents* (pp. 281–302). Alexandria, VA: American Counseling Association.

Huerta, A. H., & Rios-Aguilar, C. (2018). "Treat a cop like they are God": Exploring the relevance and utility of funds of gang knowledge among Latino male students. *Urban Education.* https://doi.org/10.1177/0042085918794766

Jordan, K. (2010). Vicarious trauma: Proposed factors that impact clinicians. *Journal of Family Psychotherapy, 21*(4), 225–237. https://doi.org/10.1080/08975353.2010.529003

Kira, I. A. (2001). Taxonomy of trauma and trauma assessment. *Traumatology, 7*(2), 73–86. https://doi.org/10.1177/153476560100700202

Lapum, J. L., Martin, J., Kennedy, K., Turcotte, C., & Gregory, H. (2019). Soul expression: A trauma informed dance intervention. *Journal of Aggression, Maltreatment, and Trauma, 28*(5), 566–580.

Lareau, A. (2011). *Unequal childhoods: Class, race, and family life* (2nd ed.). Berkeley, CA: University of California Press.

Lieberman, A. F., Ippen, C. G., & Van Horn, P. (2006). Child-parent psychotherapy: 6-month follow-up of a randomized controlled trial. *Journal of the American Academy of Child and Adolescent Psychiatry, 45*(8), 913–918.

Lieberman, A. F., Van Horn, P., & Ippen, C. G. (2005). Toward evidence-based treatment: Child-parent psychotherapy with preschoolers exposed to marital violence. *Journal of the American Academy of Child and Adolescent Psychiatry, 44*(12), 1241–1248.

Lynch, M., Astone, N. M., Collazos, J., Lipman, M., & Esthappan, S. (2018). *Arches transformative mentoring program: An implementation and impact evaluation in New York City.* Washington, DC: Urban Institute.

Macy, R. J., Jones, E., Graham, L. M., & Roach, L. (2018). Yoga for trauma and related mental health problems: A meta-review with clinical and service recommendations. *Trauma, Violence, and Abuse, 19*(1), 35–57.

National Child Traumatic Stress Network. (2009). Trauma in the lives of gang-involved youth: Tips for volunteers and community organizations. Retrieved from http:// www.nctsn.org/sites/default/files/assets/pdfs/trauma_and_gang_involved_youth .pdf

National Child Traumatic Stress Network. (n.d.). Culture and trauma. Retrieved from https://www.nctsn.org/trauma-informed-care/culture-and-trauma

Overstreet, S. (2000). Exposure to community violence: Defining the problem and understanding the consequences. *Journal of Child and Family Studies, 9*(1), 7–25.

Rios, V. M. (2017). *Human targets: Schools, police, and the criminalization of Latino youth.* Chicago, IL: The University of Chicago Press.

Rolbiecki, A., Anderson, K., Teti, M., & Albright, D. L. (2016). "Waiting for the cold to end": Using photovoice as a narrative intervention for survivors of sexual assault. *Traumatology, 22*(4), 242.

Sandoval, J., Soriano, A., Brown, D., Freedman, A., Gomez, S., Sandoval, L., ... Torres, C. (2017). *Hidden treasures: Find yours!* Bowman Publishing.

Shelden, R. G., Tracy, S. K., & Brown, W. B. (2013). *Youth gangs in American society* (4th ed.). Wadsworth, CA: Belmont.

Stenman, K., Christofferson, J., Alderfer, M. A., Pierce, J., Kelly, C., Schifano, E., ... Kazak, A. E. (2019). Integrating play in trauma-informed care: Multidisciplinary pediatric healthcare provider perspectives. *Psychological Services, 16*(1), 7–15.

Trauma Informed LA. (2020). Steve Kim and Mary Vu: Healing through re-entry activism (No. 8) [Audio podcast episode]. *In Our Stories matter.* Trauma Informed LA. Retrieved from https://traumainformedla.org/our-work/our-stories-matter-podcast/our-episodes/episode-seven/episode-eight/

Substance Abuse and Mental Health Services Administration. (2014). *SAMHSA's concept of trauma and guidance for a trauma-informed approach.* HHS Publication No. (SMA) 14-4884. Rockville, MD: Substance Abuse and Mental Health Services Administration.

The San Diego Foundation. (2019). Creating San Diego's first trauma-informed care code of conduct. Retrieved from https://www.sdfoundation.org/news-events/sdf -news/creating-san-diegos-first-trauma-informed-care-code-of-conduct/

Vigil, J. D. (1983). Chicano gangs: One response to Mexican urban adaptation in the Los Angeles area. *Urban Anthropology, 12*(1), 45–75.

Vigil, J. D. (1988). *Barrio gangs: Street life and identity in Southern California.* Austin, TX: University of Texas Press.

Vigil, J. D. (2002). *A rainbow of gangs: Street cultures in the mega-city.* Austin, TX: University of Texas Press.

Vigil, J. D. (2010). *Gang redux: A balanced anti-gang strategy.* Long Grove, IL: Waveland Press.

Vigil, J. D. (2016). Multiple marginality: A comparative framework for understanding gangs. In M. Cameron Hay (Ed.), *Methods that matter: Integrating mixed methods for more effective social science research* (pp. 284–305). Chicago, IL: University of Chicago Press.

Williams, G. B., Gerardi, M. B., Gill, S. L., Soucy, M. D., & Taliaferro, D. H. (2009). Reflective journaling: Innovative strategy for self-awareness for graduate nursing students. *International Journal for Human Caring, 13*(3), 36–43.

Zimmerman, G. L., Olsen, C. G., & Bosworth, M. F. (2000). A 'stage of change' approach to helping patients change behavior. *American Family Physician, 61*(5), 1409–1416.

Chapter 10

Children Experiencing Loss and Deprivation of Parental Care

Shulamit N. Ritblatt, Audrey Hokoda, Nory Behana, Barbara Wojtach, Christopher Walsh, and Christina Gonzalez

> *What a different picture of the world an infant receives when quiet, patient, careful, yet secure and resolute hands take care of her—and how different the world seems when these hands are impatient, rough, or hasty, unquiet, and nervous.*
>
> *—Dr. Emmi Pikler (The Pikler Collection, Hands)*

Abandonment and/or loss of a parent(s) is a major traumatic event that affects the physical and mental health of an estimated 153 million children worldwide; every day, about 10,000 children become orphans (United Nations Children's Emergency Fund—UNICEF). According to the Orphan Report 2021 (Nar, 2021), physical orphans are under 18 years old and have lost both parents due to reasons that include war, natural disasters, chronic illnesses, disease outbreaks, poverty, and lack of resources. A social orphan is a child under the age of 18 who has at least one parent alive who fails to meet their parental duties due to reasons that include extreme poverty, domestic violence, substance abuse, mental illness, and other family problems. According to the 2021 Orphan Report, the long-term impact of the traumatic neglect and deprivation experiences includes major mental health problems such as regression, depression, isolation and loneliness, low self-esteem and a sense of worthlessness, as well as exposure to other major risks such as prostitution, substance abuse, gangs, and criminal behaviors (Nar, 2021).

Throughout history, people have taken in and raised children whose parents either died or were unavailable for some other reason. This "informal" arrangement of foster/kinship/adoption caregiving did not have government involvement and still occurs throughout the world. For example, according to Generation United (May 2020), in the US over 2.7 million children are raised by their grandparent(s) or other relative. In the foster care system in the US, for every child in the welfare system cared for by a relative, there are 19 children outside the system being raised by a relative. However, "formal" placement such as orphanages, institutional care, foster care, kinship care, and adoption, involves a governmental system put in place to protect the well-being of the children involved.

The purpose of this chapter is to describe the effects of trauma and loss on children who have experienced the loss of their parent(s), and to review formal and informal arrangements of care that best meet their needs. We highlight the importance of high-quality relationships and sensitive, responsive care that can promote resilience and describe trauma-informed interventions that may help these vulnerable children heal and thrive.

Impact of Trauma and Loss on Children

The absence of the family impacts the development of the child and causes major traumatic experiences and long-term mental health problems (Nar, 2021). Orphans experience more traumas than the loss of their parents, with most children experiencing at least one additional traumatic event and more than half experiencing four or more (e.g., child abuse, exposure to family violence, other family deaths) (Whetten et al., 2011). Adverse childhood experiences (ACEs) have long-lasting physical and mental outcomes that are associated with the number, severity level, and duration of the traumas (Felitti et al., 1998).

Neurobiological Effects of Trauma

There are negative lasting effects in brain development among children who have experienced adverse trauma in their early years (Corbin, 2007; Schore, 2001). The brain is much more malleable as the neural circuits or pathways are forming during early childhood than later in life after the circuits have become established (Schore, 1994; Siegel, 1999). If a child experiences early parental loss and deprivation, abuse, and other forms of relational trauma in this sensitive period of development, this can alter both the structure and the function of the brain. Specifically, the connections between the prefrontal cortex (i.e., orbitofrontal region) and the limbic structures such as the amygdala can become compromised. This results in the more primitive subcortical-driven states (e.g., fear, hyperarousal) to be expressed without the benefit of the higher cortical functioning that can help the child cognitively process their experiences, regulate their bodily states, and self-soothe when stressed (Perry, 2009; Schore, 2001).

Research also shows that the chronic increase in cortisol levels in response to trauma causes one's hippocampus and visual gray matter in the prefrontal cortex to decrease in volume, thus, impacting the structure of the brain as well. These neurobiological disruptions primarily affect the hypothalamic–pituitary–adrenal axis, impacting how well children can regulate their emotions and behaviors (Burri et al., 2013; Humphreys & Zeanah, 2015; McLaughlin et al., 2014; Owen, 2020; Sheridan et al., 2012; Shimada et al., 2015). Trauma disrupts a child's developing brain that can lead to their stress-management systems responding at lower thresholds; that is, they are prone to react as if there is a threat even when there is minimal threat. Left alone to try to manage relational traumas, a child's immature regulatory system can be easily overwhelmed without the benefit of co-regulatory support of responsive, consistent caregiving. Thus, supportive strong attachment relationships offer protection from the effects of stress and the absence of such relationships can imperil the child's neurobiological capacities for managing it.

Another neurological theory, the Polyvagal Theory (Porges, 2004), described the role of the vagus nerve in influencing a traumatized person's ability to form attachments. The theory focuses on the autonomic nervous system, particularly the role of the vagus nerve, part of the parasympathetic nervous system, in determining one's ability to regulate one's emotions and socially engage with others. The nervous system is composed of the sympathetic nervous system, involved in preparing for "fight or flight" responses in stressful situations, and the parasympathetic nervous system, that is associated with recovery or "rest and digest" functions. Porges' theory (Porges, 2004) distinguishes two roles of the parasympathetic nervous system that include immobilization and primitive freeze reactions that depend on the unmyelinated brain stem area called the dorsal motor nucleus of the vagus nerve, and the myelinated vagus that is called the nucleus ambiguous or "smart vagus" that helps regulate the sympathetic system of "fight or flight" behaviors and opens the way for social affiliative behavior to take place. When the neuroception system senses danger and threat, the primitive parts of the brain respond to the threat and do not allow the formation of attachment relations. Influential in therapy for trauma, the theory emphasizes the importance of creating a safe caregiving environment so that one does not need to utilize the primitive immobilization or mobilization systems to respond to threats but rather can remain regulated, calm, and open to engaging in forming relationships.

Systems of Care for Children Experiencing Parental Loss

The debate about what is the best way to care for children who have lost their parents or their primary caregivers has been going on for centuries. In 2021 orphanages are very common in Eastern Europe, Asia, Central and South America, despite many studies pointing to challenges institutions face in providing the consistency in caregiving conducive to building healthy social-emotional growth and attachments in children. Children in orphanages could possibly have over 100 caretakers by the time they are 19 months (McCall, 2013). Their early trauma and loss combined with multiple placements and high turnover of caregivers affect their ability to form secure attachments and a sense of safety (Dozier et al., 2012; van IJzendoorn et al., 2011). As many as 65% of orphaned, abandoned, and maltreated children living in residential institutions have disorganized attachments, and nearly half of them show high levels of indiscriminately sociable behavior (Dozier et al., 2012).

Secure Attachments Support Resilience

Several studies provide evidence that consistency with primary caregivers is important in predicting outcomes for orphans. In a study conducted in a Romanian orphanage (Smyke et al., 2002), three groups of toddlers were compared; two were institutionalized children and the third group had never been institutionalized. In the institutionalized groups, the standard-unit group was run with rotating shifts of multiple care providers (20 providers) for a large group of toddlers (ratio of 30 children to 3 care providers), while the pilot group included 10 institutionalized children with 4 consistent care providers. The results showed that the children who had experienced multiple inconsistent care providers had higher rates of reactive attachment disorders than the pilot group or non-institutionalized children. Another study, examining children in residential care in Europe, concludes that it is the lack of a one-to-one relationship with a primary caregiver that is the major cause of delays in physical growth and abnormal brain development (Johnson et al., 2006). Similarly, the St. Petersburg–USA Orphanage Research Team (2008) raised concerns of a lack of social and emotional adult–child interactions, high turnaround of caregivers, high child–adult ratio and large groups contributing to negative outcomes in orphans.

Studies comparing orphanages to foster care have proposed eliminating orphanages and increasing placements in foster care as it tries to emulate family life and provide a child with consistent high-quality caregiving. Barth (2002), comparing institutionalized care (e.g., residential group homes) to foster care in the US on service outcomes (e.g., safety, permanence of care, long-term child outcomes, costs), concluded there is no place for residential care in the welfare system.

> What I learned about institutionalized orphans in Mexico, is they greeted us and clung to us as if they knew us for years (indiscriminate attachment behaviors). While engaging with them on a consistent basis, their emotional needs became clearer. Most children needed a lot of regulation from adults, whether it was a hug, physical contact, eye contact, or even comforting words. There were a lot of moments where they would want to cling on us. Then, other times, they didn't want us to hug them and that was usually when we were leaving. Transitions were hard for them as they needed a lot of warning signs when things were ending. I learned that some children cannot be held while others need constant physical touch.
>
> (Gonzalez, 2018)

Other studies similarly provide evidence to the benefits of foster care and placements in family-like settings versus orphanages in promoting better outcomes for children. In Chile, children raised in large impersonal institutions have more difficulties forming secure attachments, regulating their behaviors and are more aggressive or withdrawn than children who are placed in foster care (Garcia Quiroga & Hamilton-Giachritsis, 2016; 2017; Garcia Quiroga et al., 2017). Results of a meta-analysis looking at a total of 23 studies and a sample size of 13,630 children in the US (7,469 in foster care; 6,161 in residential care) indicated that children in foster care have less internalizing and externalizing behaviors and have better experiences and positive perceptions of care (Li et al., 2019). Although children in foster care can also experience multiple placements and inconsistency of care (Jones-Harden, 2004; Pew, 2004) and there are multiple ways to improve the system (see Font & Gershoff, 2020), it does provide a better environment than orphanages for children who have lost their parents.

Positive, sensitive parenting in foster parents is critically important to developing secure parent–child attachments (West et al., 2020). An inspiring motivational speaker, Josh Shipp, highlights the positive impact foster care parents can have when they build caring relationships and a home that ensures stability and safety. Josh's quote "Every kid is one caring adult away from being a success story" reflects on his own experiences growing up in the foster care system, moving from one placement to the other due to his challenging behaviors. At his last placement at age 14, he kept on trying to push their buttons so they would send him away. At age 17, when he was held at juvenile hall for driving without a license, he was certain that he is going to be sent away. However, his foster father's life-changing response was "there is nothing you can do that will make us send you away! We are here for you." Josh credits that demonstration of commitment to his turnaround into a more productive and secure life (Shipp, n.d.).

In the US, the Family First Prevention Services Act 2018 emphasizes the importance of preserving families first and providing parents with the needed support to keep children safe and at home. When this is not possible, due to abuse, neglect, incarceration, or other reasons, they need to be placed in the least restrictive, most family-like environment that can meet their needs and that is near to their parents' home and their school, with the aim of returning the child to his or her birth parent home with supportive family services. The act emphasizes prevention in order to keep children safely within their birth families, as well as placement in kinship care with siblings when there is a need to intervene as this helps children maintain connections to their family, school, and community (Children's Defense Fund, 2018). When reunification with family is not possible, children are then best served in family settings, such as with foster or adoptive parents. In December 2019, the United Nations General Assembly (all 193 member states) adopted a Resolution on the Rights of the Child that officially stated that orphanages should be progressively eliminated globally, and children should be supported to remain with families over being raised in institutional care (United Nation General Assembly, 2020). In the US orphanages have been mostly replaced by foster care, group homes, residential treatment centers (RTCs) facilities and institutional care such as "Child Abuse Shelters." In every type of placement for children experiencing parental loss, policies must prioritize the "best fit" to meet the specific needs of the child (Font & Gershoff, 2020), with the knowledge that high-quality, relationship-based adult–child interactions and sensitivity of care are the most critical factors needed to promote their secure attachment and positive developmental outcomes.

Trauma-Informed Care and Relationship-Based Practices

> The relationship between adults, particularly caregivers, and children must never have the character of a struggle for authority and rights: caregivers have an obligation to skillfully arrange conditions under which children may freely develop in the fullness of their rights.
>
> (from "A Child as an Individual" by Janusz Korczak)

When working with traumatized children who have experienced the loss of their parents, it is important to utilize trauma-informed care (TIC) which is defined as a strengths-based framework that is grounded in an understanding of and responsiveness to the impact of trauma, that emphasizes physical, psychological, and emotional safety for both providers and survivors, and that creates opportunities for survivors to rebuild a sense of control and empowerment.

(Hopper et al., 2010, p. 82)

A trauma-informed approach to care perceives trauma not simply as a past event but as a formative one that may be contributing to the child's current state or circumstances. The first step is promoting the sense of safety and building trusting relationships. Adult–child consistent, positive, and predictable interactions can set the foundation for relationship building.

Around the world, there are examples of institutionalized care that have utilized these relationship-based interactions and trauma-informed principles. The Pikler Institute in Hungary, for example, was designed to be a family structured environment that would help foster social-emotional development and attachment. The environment Dr. Pikler created was designed to help nurture the child, allow children to grow at their own pace, and to provide a safe place to explore (Horm et al., 2012). Another example can be found in the SOS Villages. In India, for example, the village uses the caretakers as "Mothers" of their cottage. They place children in small groups with "Mothers" in order to develop a sense of family and culture within groups (Lassi et al., 2011). There are SOS Villages around the world including the US and all are guided by its founder Hermann Gmeiner's four principles: (1) Each child needs to have a loving parent, a trained SOS Mother; (2) siblings are important to socializing as a family and building relationships, each home in the village has several children assigned to the SOS Mother. It is also a way to keep biological siblings together; (3) each family has their own home and they can work together to form routines and share responsibilities; and (4) the home is an integral part of a community of Mothers, children, youth leaders, SOS Aunts, family assistants, a management team including a director, administrative and maintenance staff, child-development educators, psychologists, and social workers who support one another and prepare the children to become positive, active members (Lukaš, 2014). A study evaluating children living at a SOS Village showed positive effects on their mental and social development compared to children living at other orphanages in Karachi (Lassi et al., 2011). In a meta-analysis comparing physical growth and mental health of SOS Children versus children raised in families (biological, foster, adoptive, kinship), although SOS Children have major delays in both physical and mental health, compared to children in typical large-group institutions, SOS Children were found to do better on mental health but worse on physical growth (Van IJzendoorn & Bakermans-Kranenburg, 2021).

To build trauma-informed, relationship-based systems for children who have lost their parent(s) or their parental care, it is paramount to provide care providers with education, mentoring, and training for them to be attuned and responsive to the child's needs, provide appropriate adult–child interactions, and support the child's behavior and emotion regulation (McCall & Groark, 2015). Care providers, either in institutions, in foster or kinship care, or adoptive parents, can trigger the child's symptoms and intensify the reliving of the traumas when their behaviors and expression of emotions are inappropriate (Owen, 2020). Every transition of a child to a new care provider requires educating the new adult about the past traumatic experiences of the child as well as providing guidance on how to support and address the child's challenging behaviors while providing the child with the sense of safety and security. This therapeutic process involves the understanding of the attachment style and working models of the child as well as comprehension of the challenging behaviors as the manifestation of the traumas they have experienced (Owen, 2020; Vasquez & Stensland, 2016). In recent years, a new term has been introduced. "Resource" family care refers to the need to place a child who has experienced the trauma of abuse and/or neglect with a trained family that can meet the child's needs—whether that be foster care, kinship care, or adoption. It requires foster care parents to be well-trained and equipped with the needed skills to decrease challenging behaviors and enhance relationship formation (Fisher et al., 2009; Goemans et al., 2015).

A training program uniquely designed to help resource parents provide a trauma-informed response to their foster or adopted child's behaviors is called "Caring for Children Who Have Experienced Trauma: A Workshop for Resource Parents" (often referred to as the Resource Parent Curriculum—RPC). Developed by over 30 experts at the National Child Traumatic Stress Network (NCTSN, 2016), essential elements of the training include educating resource parents to recognize the effects of trauma on children as well as triggers or reminders that children may associate with their previous traumas. Learning about the impact of trauma on the brain, resource parents are taught the importance of creating safety before the child can socially engage and regulate their emotions and behaviors. An example of a sensitive foster parent who recognized trauma symptoms and prioritized safety is the foster mother who recalled how a four-year-old, new to the foster family's home, changed from a quiet and compliant child to a flailing, screaming, and biting one when the foster parent attempted to help her into the bathtub. Rather than resort to power struggles and respond in a judgmental, punitive way, the resource parent started with sponge bathing, and then set up a shower stall to be child-friendly with special soap and toys. It was later discovered that the four-year-old had been molested in a bathtub, thus the foster mother shielded the little girl by being sensitive to trauma effects and creating safety, even though she did not understand that the bathtub was a trauma trigger.

Resource parents are taught to be attuned to their child's emotions and create safety for them by remaining calm and regulated themselves when dealing with challenging situations. They learn about the negative messages traumatized children have developed about themselves and others through a series of interactive lessons called the Invisible Suitcase. The lessons give resource parents tools to help their children analyze the negative beliefs they have about themselves and others. One four-year-old boy said, "I'm such a bad boy. I should just throw myself in front of that truck." He was in care because he lit a fire in the apartment closet that sparked a bigger fire that killed his mother who was passed out in the next room. He felt responsible and unworthy after years of neglect by his mother. The goal of his future resource parents was to help him "unpack" those negative beliefs and "repack" the suitcase with more realistic and positive beliefs, such as "I am a good person who had some bad things happen to me." The Invisible Suitcase lessons also incorporate self-reflection exercises that encourage resource parents to explore their own invisible suitcases and to think about how their own beliefs and past experiences influence how they respond to their children. Recognizing that secondary trauma and compassion fatigue are experienced by caregivers who work with traumatized children (Hannah & Woolgar, 2018; Whitt-Woosley et al., 2020), self-care (e.g., rest, socialization, exercise) is emphasized in the RPC program. Support groups of resource parents are often formed to provide a place where they can build friendships, learn from others, and share practical trauma-informed strategies that help with their children.

Creating safety and supporting positive and stable relationships in the life of the foster child can take the form of staying in touch with birth parents, siblings, past foster homes, neighbors, teachers, and other important people in the foster child's life. An example of resource parents going to extraordinary lengths to provide this stability is seen in the case of a family of five children, who ranged in age from preschoolers to teens. No resource family was available to take in all five children; however, the five resource families who each had one of the children, became a network and facilitated frequent visits and activities with all of the children. Together, they worked to create an extended family for the children, respecting the importance of the siblings' relationships and the shared understanding of the traumas the children had experienced.

Another essential element of the RPC curriculum provides tools for resource parents to be advocates for their children. The importance of preparing resource parents to be active advocates for their children is shown in a foster mother who began to care for a 12-year-old boy who had most recently been in a group home after multiple foster homes. Physically, he appeared to be 12; however, cognitively, he was closer to 6 as he could barely read. Socially, he was inappropriate when trying to get attention, such as popping out from a door to say "boo" to strangers, and emotionally, he continually craved the resource mother's attention and wanted to constantly sit on her lap. The foster mother addressed his needs one at a time. Physically, she worked with doctors to have him evaluated by a brain trauma specialist who discovered latent brain injury—probably from shaking or beating in early childhood. She worked tirelessly with the school system to improve his disjointed special education services which were in disarray due to the many moves, and she also communicated with the boy's therapist to learn how to help him develop more socially appropriate peer interactions. At home, she began reading preschool-level books to him, gradually moving to books for older children. The activity provided an opportunity to have close one-on-one time together while also helping the boy with his reading. Her training in the RPC program helped her become a successful advocate and work collaboratively with a whole team of professionals (i.e., social workers, teachers, doctors, therapists) to help the boy. Most importantly, she offered security and commitment, providing him with a safe home where he could thrive.

Several studies provide evidence that the RPC program is successful in increasing resource parents' knowledge of trauma-informed parenting and their self-efficacy in handling challenges associated with trauma (Murray et al., 2019; Sullivan et al., 2016). Knowledge of trauma-informed parenting includes recognizing the impact of trauma on children, understanding the importance of building positive, stable relationships and safety, and having a toolkit of strategies to help children manage overwhelming emotions and decrease problem behaviors (Murray et al., 2019). Gigengack et al. (2019) also provide evidence that the RPC program is successful in increasing resource parents' ability to recognize trauma symptoms and in decreasing their stress levels dealing with problem behaviors. In addition, although children continued to display high levels of trauma symptoms, the RPC program appeared to decrease child trauma symptoms over time as well (Gigengack et al., 2019). *Fostering Connections*, a similar program implemented in Ireland, has also produced positive effects for both the foster care providers and the children; foster parents showed an increase in knowledge on trauma-informed parenting and in their tolerance to children's misbehavior, and the children showed improvement in emotional and behavioral functioning (Lotty et al., 2020).

Relational therapeutic interventions have also incorporated these trauma-informed principles. For example, the *Trust-Based Relational Intervention (TBRI)* is a model that uses a two-pronged approach to training and supporting both caregivers and the children. The intervention focuses on three principles: 1) Empowerment, that is, providing the child with a new home to feel safe and physically well-cared for; 2) connection, that is, a focus on building a trusting relationship within the new family; and 3) correction, that is, providing caregivers with cognitive behavioral strategies to help the child regulate their emotions and behaviors (Howard et al., 2014; Purvis et al., 2013). The intervention provides intensive family preservation support with 15–20 in-home sessions by licensed clinical counselors, as well as group sessions. An evaluation of this trauma-informed parent training intervention with at-risk adopted children and their families supports that it is successful in reducing children's behavioral problems and trauma symptoms (Purvis et al., 2015).

Expressive arts like music, drawing/painting dance, play, and drama have been frequently used with trauma survivors (Malchiodi, 2020). Despite a lack of well-designed studies providing empirical evidence that the arts are effective (Baker et al., 2018; McFerran et al., 2020), they are widely used by clinicians and several neurological theories (e.g., Perry, 2009; Porges, 2004; van der Kolk, 2014) support the use of music-based activities when working with individuals who have experienced trauma. For example, music that provides consistent rhythms may be effective in treating traumatized individuals as music bypasses higher cognitive functioning and makes connections in the primitive, undamaged parts of the brain. Music with slower tempos (80–100 bpm) lowers heartrate and blood pressure and can help trauma survivors who are anxious and hypervigilant (Perry, 2006) and loud music with fast tempos can create arousal and more intense emotions. Use of music combined with cognitive behavioral strategies can be used in therapies to expose and desensitize survivors to trauma cues in a non-threatening way, and to help them feel in control as they learn to regulate their emotions. Trauma interferes with survivors' abilities to access areas of the brain that govern language skills (van der Kolk, 2014) and so music, rhythmic drumming, and movement can be helpful for survivors who cannot participate or do not benefit from talk-based interventions (Faulkner, 2017).

A ten-week therapeutic intervention (Creative Arts in Psychotherapy—CAP) that uses a variety of expressive art strategies has been developed for traumatized children in South Africa (van Westrhenen et al., 2017). The program integrates group participatory music and movement activities that help create an environment where the children have fun, feel safe, and develop relationships. The program infuses art, music, and role-playing lessons that focus on helping children identify and express emotions, and in reflective writing and creative music activities, the children build a narrative that focuses on the "hero's journey" and their strengths as survivors (van Westrhenen et al., 2017). An evaluation study supports that the program is successful in reducing hyperarousal and avoidant trauma symptoms in children (van Westrhenen et al., 2019). In Denmark, an intervention was developed for emotionally neglected children using music therapy, and an evaluation supports that the program was successful in building positive attunement and communication between parents and children (Jacobsen et al., 2014).

An example of a relationship-based intervention using expressive arts, the Circle of Education (COE) peaPods (Ritblatt, 2015), was implemented with young children (birth–three years old) in an orphanage in Mexico. The program uses music, movement, puppets, books, and play to build socio-emotional skills and enhance adult–child interactions. Over a two-year period of consistent visits by two volunteers (Spanish-speaking child-development and counseling professionals), trust and relationships were formed. As orphanage staff spent time with the volunteers, they began sharing their needs for providing better care for the children. The volunteers tried to bring some needed supplies (e.g., clothes that fit the sizes of the children living at the orphanage, fresh fruit) as they made regular visits, built relationships with the children and staff, and learned the routines of the orphanage. They led activities that included yoga ball exercises, singing and dancing, painting, bubbles, and games of chasing, modeling for staff how to integrate these kinds of activities into the orphanage's structured schedule.

Over many months, staff identified challenges they faced with the children, that included transitioning from one activity to another, completing routine activities, and becoming more independent with self-help skills. COE lessons that address these issues were then introduced. For example, *El Circulo de las Routinas* (The Circle of Routines) includes a song, *Mi Carril de la Memoria* (My Memory Lane), that introduces toddlers to the notion of routines and a schedule. The children are shown pictures from magazines of materials (e.g., toothbrushes, a bed, play food) and the children talked about routines they did as they prepared for bedtime and in the mornings. They were encouraged to help create a routines pictorial board in which they could use safety scissors to cut the magazine pictures and paste them on a cardboard. The lessons helped meet the needs of staff who could use the song and pictorial board to help the children more cooperatively transition through daily activities, and the lessons were fun and engaging for the children. For traumatized children, a structured schedule with predictability provides safety and a sense of control. Another set of lessons, *Mi Pequena Oruga*, included a song, *Aprendo a Comer Alimentos Saludables* (I Learn to Eat Healthy Food), as well as the book, *La Oruga Muy Hambrienta* (The Very Hungry Caterpillar) by Eric Carle. An activity involves making a caterpillar out of cut fruits and veggies with children given food that required different levels of skills (e.g., unpeeled bananas) as they were supported in being independent. The book *Cuando Yo Era Pequena* (When I Was Little) by Jamie Lee Curtis was also read to them to further promote self-help skills and pride in becoming more independent. COE is an example of an early childhood program that uses a variety of methods (e.g., music, art, books) to build socio-emotional skills and enhance adult–child interactions when working with orphans. As the toddlers prepared fruit, they were provided an opportunity to explore and problem-solve how different shapes come together to create a caterpillar. They were learning about healthy eating and math concepts, developing self-help, language, and fine motor skills, while positively interacting with adults.

Conclusion and Recommendations

The US Family First Prevention Services Act (2018) emphasizes the importance of preserving and supporting families to provide safety and stability for children. The current recommendation is to minimize institutionalized residential care and invest in parental support and kinship care (e.g., Osborne et al., 2021), with the United Nations (2019) calling for the eventual elimination of institutional care across the world. Wherever they are placed, children who have experienced parental loss can benefit from trauma-informed programs that incorporate research on early brain development and attachment, and provide caregivers with an understanding of how trauma and loss affect the children they care for (Owen, 2020). The programs emphasize the importance of caregivers providing safety with consistent, calm responses, understanding that traumatized children may respond to stress with more primitive mobilization and immobilization brain responses (e.g., hyperarousal, fear, dissociation), making them less able to regulate their emotions, problem-solve, or self-soothe. Trauma-informed programs emphasize safety and relationship building, teaching caregivers ways to help children reduce arousal and fear, remain regulated, and help them with social-emotional skills affected by trauma (McCall & Groark, 2015; Owen, 2020).

Using an eco-system approach, we need to create coordinated systems of care with all families and professionals who serve children who have experienced parental loss, providing education and support to deliver trauma-informed services. Strong parent–school partnerships are key to promoting educational success in foster children (Stapleton & Chen, 2020) as teachers and staff who have daily contact with the children and are trained in ways to address challenging behaviors, can make the school a safe place where foster children can continue to develop trusting relationships while learning academic skills. Attorneys representing children in dependency court (Miller et al., 2020), public health nurses (Carabez & Kim, 2019), and others all play important roles in providing the best care for children who have experienced the loss of parental care.

Science-based policies and programs across disciplines should be implemented to facilitate healthy brain development and provide protection for children who have experienced adversities (National Scientific Council on the Developing Child, 2020). In addition to focusing on educating caregivers on the importance of safety and supportive relationships for the children, an emphasis must also be to provide this type of support for the caregivers as well. Foster care providers experience high levels of secondary traumatic stress and compassion fatigue (Hannah & Woolgar, 2018; Whitt-Woosley et al., 2020), and Goemans et al. (2020) highlight the importance of attending to parental stress as it is the strongest predictor of foster children's positive developmental outcomes. It is also well-documented that social workers and professionals working in child welfare have high levels of work-related stress, secondary trauma, and burnout (Letson et al., 2020; Tullberg & Boothe, 2019).

To create science-based systems of care that best serve children who have faced adversities, many program and policy changes are recommended that include changes in professional training and support, and macro-level changes in funding allocation and accountability (National Scientific Council on the Developing Child, 2020). For example, to increase stability for children in foster care, better data collection and tracking with technologically advanced predictive modeling methods can be used to improve placement decisions on where the "best fit" is to meet the specific needs of a child (Font & Gershoff, 2020). Increasing data tracking, developing statewide databases on foster homes, and creating more rigorous standards for potential caregivers' past history of violent and criminal behaviors are other examples of recommended changes that can better ensure that children are safe in their placements (Font & Gershoff, 2020).

Within organizations, improvement in practices can help professionals better serve children who have lost their parents. For example, relationship-based practice in the welfare system and the inclusion of reflective practice has been found to facilitate awareness, insights, and the ability of the workers to process their emotions and be more effective in their difficult work (Ferguson, 2018; Russ et al., 2020). Agencies implementing new trauma-informed assessment and intervention practices need to provide extra support for the staff expected to provide these new services (Dunkerley et al., 2021). For example, the frontline child welfare service providers report the need for agencies to provide specialized positions (such as an intake and assessment team), post-training coaching and supervision to help with challenging cases, as well as policies that provide structure and accountability for the new practices (Dunkerley et al., 2021). With improved programmatic and organizational policies, we can better protect children who have lost their parents, as well as the caregivers and professionals who care for them.

> *Children without families are the most vulnerable people in the world.*
> —*Brooke Randolph*

> *The most terrible poverty is loneliness and the feeling of being unloved.*
> —*Mother Teresa*

This chapter described the effects of trauma and loss on children without families, who are among the most vulnerable people in our world and who risk growing up lonely and feeling unloved. We highlight the importance of stability and responsive caregiving and present trauma-informed strategies and principles that we hope families and professionals can use to work together to provide the best care for their well-being.

References

Baker, F. A., Metcalf, O., Varker, T., & O'Donnell, M. (2018). A systematic review of the efficacy of creative arts therapies in the treatment of adults with PTSD. *Psychological Trauma: Theory, Research, Practice, and Policy, 10*(6), 643–651. https://doi.org/10.1037/tra0000353

Barth, R. P. (2002). *Institutions vs. Foster homes: The empirical base for the second century of debate*. Chapel Hill, NC: UNC, School of Social Work, Jordan Institute for Families.

Burri, A., Maercker, A., Krammer, S., & Simmen-Janevska, K. (2013). Childhood trauma and PTSD symptoms increase the risk of cognitive impairment in a sample of former indentured child laborers in old age. *PLOS ONE, 8*(2), 1–8. https://doi.org/10.1371/journal.pone.0057826

Carabez, R., & Kim, J. E. (2019). Part I: The role of public health nursing in addressing health care needs of children in foster care. *Public Health Nursing, 36*(5), 702–708. Retrieved from https://doi-org.libproxy.sdsu.edu/10.1111/phn.12647

Children's Defense Fund. (2018). The family first prevention services act. Retrieved from https://www.childrensdefense.org/wp-content/uploads/2018/08/family-first -detailed-summary.pdf

Corbin, J. R. (2007). Reactive attachment disorder: A biopsychosocial disturbance of attachment. *Child and Adolescent Social Work Journal, 24*(6), 539–552. https://doi.org/10.1007/s10560-007-0105-x

Dozier, M., Zeanah, C. H., Wallin, A. R., & Shauffer, C. (2012). Institutional care for young children: Review of literature and policy implications. *Social Issues and Policy Review, 6*(1), 1–25.

Dunkerley, S., Akin, B. A., Brook, J., & Bruns, K. (2021). Child welfare caseworker and trainer perspectives on initial implementation of a trauma-informed practice approach. *Journal of Child and Family Studies*. https://doi.org/10.1007/s10826-021-01935-1

Faulkner, S. (2017). Rhythm2recovery: A model of practice combining rhythmic music with cognitive reflection for social and emotional health within trauma recovery. *Australian and New Zealand Journal of Family Therapy, 38*(4), 627–636. https://doi.org/10.1002/anzf.1268

Felitti, V. J., Anda, R. F., Nordenberg, D., Williamson, D. F., Spitz, A. M., Edwards, V., & Marks, J. S. (1998). Relationship of childhood abuse and household dysfunction to many of the leading causes of death in adults: The adverse childhood experiences (ACE) Study. *American Journal of Preventive Medicine, 14*(4), 245–258. https://doi.org/10.1016/s0749-3797(98)00017-8

Ferguson, H. (2018). How social workers reflect in action and when and why they don't: The possibilities and limits to reflective practice in social work. *Social Work Education, 37*(4), 415–427. Retrieved from https://doi-org.libproxy.sdsu.edu/10.1080/02615479.2017.1413083

Fisher, P. A., Chamberlain, P., & Leve, L. D. (2009). Improving the lives of foster children through evidence-based interventions. *Vulnerable Children and Youth Studies, 4*(2), 122–127.

Font, S. A., & Gershoff, T. E. (2020). Foster care: How we can, and should, do more for maltreated children. *Social Policy Report Society for Research in Child Development, 33*(3), 1–39.

Garcia Quiroga, M., & Hamilton-Giachritsis, C. (2016). Attachment in alternative care: A systematic literature review. *Child and Youth Care Forum, 45*(4), 625–653. http://doi.org/10.1007/s10566-015-9342-x

Garcia Quiroga, M., & Hamilton-Giachritsis, C. (2017). Getting involved: A thematic analysis of caregiver's perspectives in Chilean residential children's homes. *Journal of Social and Personal Relationships, 34*(3), 356–375. http://doi.org/10.1177/0265407516637838

Garcia Quiroga, G. M., Hamilton-Giachritsis, C., & Fanes, I. M. (2017). Attachment representations and socio-emotional difficulties in alternative care: A comparison between residential, foster and family based children in Chile. *Child Abuse and Neglect, 70*, 180–189.

Generation United. (2020, May). *Checklist: Family first prevention services act: Implementing the provisions that support kinship families.* Retrieved from https://www.grandfamilies.org/Portals/0/Documents/Grandfamilies-GeneralFactSheet%287%29.pdf

Gigengack, M. R., Hein, I. M., Lindeboom, R., & Lindauer, R. J. L. (2019). Increasing resource parents' sensitivity towards child posttraumatic stress symptoms: A descriptive study on a trauma-informed resource parent training. *Journal of Child and Adolescent Trauma, 12*(1), 23–29. https://doi.org/10.1007/s40653-017-0162-z

Goemans, A., Buisman, R. S. M., van Geel, M., & Vedder, P. (2020). Foster parent stress as key factor relating to foster children's mental health: A 1-year prospective longitudinal study. *Child and Youth Care Forum, 49*(5), 661–686. Retrieved from https://doi-org.libproxy.sdsu.edu/10.1007/s10566-020-09547-4

Goemans, A., van Geel, M., & Vedder, P. (2015). Over three decades of longitudinal research on the development of foster children: A meta-analysis. *Child Abuse and Neglect, 42*, 121–134.

Gonzalez, C. (2018). *An ethnographic reflective journey in understanding children and staff in an orphanage and exploring trauma-informed practices to promote attachment and social emotional development.* Thesis San Diego State University. ProQuest Dissertations Publishing, 2018. 10972979.

Hannah, B., & Woolgar, M. (2018). Secondary trauma and compassion fatigue in foster carers. *Clinical Child Psychology and Psychiatry, 23*(4), 629–643. https://doi.org/10.1177/1359104518778327

Hopper, E. K., Bassuk, E., & Olivet, J. (2010). Shelter from the storm: Trauma-informed care in homelessness services settings. *Open Health Services and Policy Journal, 3*(1), 80–100.

Horm, D. M., Goble, C. B., & Branscomb, K. R. (2012). Infant toddler curriculum: Review, reflection and revolution. In N. File, J. J. Mueller, & D. B. Wisneski (Eds.), *Curriculum in early childhood education: Re-examined, rediscovered, renewed* (pp. 105–119). New York and London: Routledge, Taylor and Francis Group.

Howard, A. R., Parris, S. R., Nielsen, L. E., Lusk, R., Bush, K., Purvis, K. B., & Cross, D. R. (2014). Trust-based relational intervention® (TBRI®) for adopted children receiving therapy in an outpatient setting. *Child Welfare, 93*(5), 47–64.

Humphreys, K. L., & Zeanah, C. H. (2015). Deviations from the expectable environment in early childhood and emerging psychopathology. *Neuropsychopharmacology, 40*(1), 154–170. https://doi.org/10.1038/npp.2014.165

Jacobsen, S. L., McKinney, C. H., & Holck, U. (2014). Effects of a dyadic music therapy intervention on parent-child interaction, parent stress, and parent-child relationship in families with emotionally neglected children: A randomized controlled trial. *Journal of Music Therapy, 51*(4), 310–332. https://doi.org/10.1093/jmt/thu028

Johnson, R., Browne, K., & Hamilton-Giachritsis, C. (2006). Young children in institutional care at risk of harm. *Trauma, Violence, and Abuse, 7*(1), 34–60. https://doi.org/10.1177/1524838005283696

Jones-Harden, B. (2004). Safety and stability for foster children: A developmental perspective. *Future of Our Children, 14*(1), 30–47.

Korczak, J. (1920). *How to love a child* (2nd ed.), Warsaw, Poland.

Lassi, Z. S., Mahmud, S., Syed, E. U., & Janjua, N. Z. (2011). Behavioral problems among children living in orphanage facilities of Karachi, Pakistan: Comparison of children in an SOS village with those in conventional orphanages. *Social Psychiatry and Psychiatric Epidemiology, 46*(8), 787–796.

Letson, M. M., Davis, C., Sherfield, J., Beer, O. W. J., Phillips, R., & Wolf, K. G. (2020). Identifying compassion satisfaction, burnout, & traumatic stress in Children's Advocacy Centers. *Child Abuse and Neglect, 110*(Part 3). Retrieved from https://doi-org.libproxy.sdsu.edu/10.1016/j.chiabu.2019.104240

Li, D., Chng, S. G., & Chu, M. C. (2019). Comparing long-term placement outcomes of residential and family foster care: A meta-analysis. *Trauma, Violence, and Abuse, 20*(5), 653–664.

Lotty, M., Dunn-Galvin, A., & Bantry-White, E. (2020). Effectiveness of a trauma-informed care psychoeducational program for foster carers – Evaluation of the fostering connections program. *Child Abuse and Neglect, 102.* https://doi.org/10.1016/j.chiabu.2020.104390

Lukaš, M. (2014). SOS children's friendly community historical overview. In E. Berbić Kolar, B. Bognar, M. Sablić, & B. Sedlić (Eds.), *Challenges in building child friendly communities: Proceedings of the international conference Zadar 2014, Croatia* (pp. 44–55). Slavonski Brod: Europe House Slavonski Brod.

Malchiodi, C. A. (2020). *Trauma and expressive arts therapy: Brain, body, and imagination in the healing process.* New York: The Guilford Press.

McCall, R. B. (2013). Review: The consequences of early institutionalization: Can institutions be improved?—Should they? *Child and Adolescent Mental Health, 18*(4), 193–201.

McCall, R. B., & Groark, C. J. (2015). Research on institutionalized children: Implications for international child welfare practitioners and policymakers. *International Perspectives in Psychology: Research, Practice, Consultation, 4*(2), 142–159.

McFerran, K. S., Lai, C. H. I., Wei-Han Chang, W. H., Acquaro, D., Chin, T. C., Stokes, H., & Crooke, D. H. A. (2020). Music, rhythm and trauma: A critical interpretive synthesis of research literature. *Frontiers in Psychology, 11.* https://doi.org/10.3389/fpsyg.2020.00324

McLaughlin, K. A., Sheridan, M. A., Winter, W., Fox, N. A., Zeanah, C. H., & Nelson, C. A. (2014). Widespread reductions in cortical thickness following severe early-life deprivation: A neurodevelopmental pathway to attention-deficit/hyperactivity disorder. *Biological Psychology, 76*(8), 629–638. https://doi.org/10.1016/j.biopsycho.2013.08.016

Miller, J. J., Donahue-Dioh, J., & Owens, L. (2020). Examining the legal representation of youth in foster care: Perspectives of attorneys and attorney guardians ad litem. *Children and Youth Services Review, 115.* https://doi.org/10.1016/j.childyouth.2020.105059

Murray, K. J., Sullivan, K. M., Lent, M. C., Chaplo, S. D., & Tunno, A. M. (2019). Promoting trauma-informed parenting of children in out-of-home care: An effectiveness study of the resource parent curriculum. *Psychological Services, 16*(1), 162–169. https://doi.org/10.1037/ser0000324

Nar, C. (2021). *Orphan report, INSAMER report,* April 2021. Retrieved from https://www.ihh.org.tr/public/publish/0/152/insamer-2021-yetim-raporu-eng-200425-n.pdf

National Child Traumatic Stress Network (NCTSN). (2016). Resource parent curriculum - RPC caring for children who have experienced trauma: A workshop for resource parents. Retrieved from https://www.nctsn.org/resources/resource-parent-curriculum-rpc-training-modules

National Scientific Council on the Developing Child. (2020). *Connecting the brain to the rest of the body: Early childhood development and lifelong health are deeply intertwined working paper no. 15.* Retrieved from www.developingchild.harvard.edu

Osborne, J., Hindt, L. A., Lutz, N., Hodgkinson, N., & Leon, S. C. (2021). Placement stability among children in kinship and non-kinship foster placements across multiple placements. *Children and Youth Services Review, 126.* https://doi.org/10.1016/j.childyouth.2021.106000

Owen, C. (2020). Obscure dichotomy of early childhood trauma in PTSD versus attachment disorders. *Trauma, Violence, and Abuse, 21*(1), 83–96.

Perry, B. D. (2006). Applying principles of neurodevelopment to clinical work with maltreated and traumatized children. In N. B. Webb (Ed.), *Working with traumatized youth in child welfare* (pp. 27–52). New York: Guilford Press.

Perry, B. D. (2009). Examining child maltreatment through a neurodevelopmental lens: Clinical applications of the neurosequential model of therapeutics. *Journal of Loss and Trauma, 14*(4), 240–255. https://doi.org/10.1080/15325020903004350

Pew Commission on Children in Foster Care (written by Hochman, G., Anndee Hochman, A., Miller, J.). (2004). *Foster care: Voices from the inside.* Retrieved from https://www.pewtrusts.org//media/legacy/uploadedfiles/wwwpewtrustsorg/reports/foster_care_reform/fostercarevoices021804pdf.pdf

Porges, S. (2004). Neuroception: A subconscious system for detecting threats and safety. *Zero to Three, 24,* 19–24.

Purvis, K., Cross, D. R., Dansereau, F. D., & Parris, S. R. (2013). Trust-based relational intervention (TBRI): A systemic approach to complex developmental trauma. *Child and Youth Services, 34*(4), 360–386.

Purvis, K., Razuri, E., Howard, A., Call, C., DeLuna, J., Hall, J., & Cross, D. (2015). Decrease in behavioral problems and trauma symptoms among at-risk adopted children following trauma-informed parent training intervention. *Journal of Child and Adolescent Trauma, 8*(3), 201–210. https://doi.org/10.1007/s40653-015-0055-y

Ritblatt, S. N. (2015). *Circle of education: PeaPod 4: Circle of exploration* (18–24 months) (English and Spanish).

Russ, E., Lonne, B., & Lynch, D. (2020). Increasing child protection workforce retention through promoting a relational-reflective framework for resilience. *Child Abuse and Neglect, 110*(Part 3). https://doi.org/10.1016/j.chiabu.2019.104245

Schore, A. N. (1994). *Affect regulation and the origin of the self: He neurobiology of emotional development.* Mahwah, NJ: Lawrence Erlbaum Associates, Inc.

Schore, A. N. (2001). The effects of early relational trauma on right brain development, affect regulation, and infant mental health. *Infant Mental Health Journal, 22*(1/2), 201–269.

Sheridan, M. A., Fox, N. A., Zeanah, C. H., McLaughlin, K. A., & Nelson, C. A. (2012). Variation in neural development as a result of exposure to institutionalization early in childhood. *Psychological and Cognitive Sciences, 109*(32), 12927–12932. https://doi.org/10.1073/pnas.1200041109

Shimada, K., Takiguchi, S., Mizushima, S., Fujisawa, T. X., Saito, D. N., Kosaka, H., ... Tomoda, A. (2015). Reduced visual cortex grey matter volume in children and adolescents with reactive attachment disorder. *NeuroImage: Clinical, 9*, 13–19. https:// doi.org/10.1016/j.nicl.2015.07.001

Shipp, J. (n.d.). Every kid is one caring adult away from being a success story. Retrieved December 4, 2021, from https://joshshipp.com/

Siegel, D. (1999). *The developing mind.* New York: Guilford.

Smyke, A. T., Dumitrescu, A., & Zeanah, C. H. (2002). Attachment disturbances in young children. I: The continuum of caretaking casualty. *Journal of the American Academy of Child and Adolescent Psychiatry, 41*(8), 972–982.

Stapleton, D. H., & Chen, R. K. (2020). Better outcomes for children in treatment foster care through improved stakeholder training and increased parent-school collaboration. *Children and Youth Services Review, 114.* Retrieved from https://doi -org.libproxy.sdsu.edu/10.1016/j.childyouth.2020.105010

St. Petersburg-USA Orphanage Research Team. (2008). The effects of early social-emotional and relationship experience on the development of young orphanage children. *Monographs of the Society for Research in Child Development, 73*(Serial Number 291), 1–260. http://doi.org/10.1002/9781444309683.fmatter

Sullivan, K. M., Murray, K. J., & Ake, G. S. (2016). Trauma-informed care for children in the child welfare system: An initial evaluation of a trauma-informed parenting workshop. *Child Maltreatment, 21*(2), 147–155. https://doi.org/10.1177 /1077559515615961

Tullberg, E., & Boothe, G. (2019). Taking an organizational approach to addressing secondary trauma in child welfare settings. *Journal of Public Child Welfare, 13*(3), 345–367. https://doi.org/10.1080/15548732.2019.1612498

United Nations General Assembly. (2020). Resolution adopted by the general assembly on 18 December 2019: Rights of the child. Retrieved from https://bettercarenet-work.org/sites/default/files/2020-01/A_RES_74_133_E.pdf

van der Kolk, B. (2014). *The body keeps the score: Mind, brain and body in the transformation of trauma.* London: Allen Lane.

Van IJzendoorn, M. H., & Bakermans-Kranenburg, M. J. (2021). Tear down your institutions. Empirical and Evolutionary Perspectives on Institutional Care in SOS Children's Villages. Psyarxiv [Preprint].

Van IJzendoorn, M. H., Palacios, J., Sonuga-Barke, E. J. S., Gunner, M. R., Vorria, P., McCall, B. R., ... Juffer, F. (2011). Children in institutional care: Delayed development and resilience. *Monographs of the Society of Research in Child Development, 76*(4), 8–30.

Van Westrhenen, N., Fritz, E., Vermeer, A., Boelen, P., & Kleber, R. (2019). Creative arts in psychotherapy for traumatized children in South Africa: An evaluation study. *PLOS ONE, 14*(2), e0210857. https://doi.org/10.1371/journal.pone.0210857

Van Westrhenen, N., Fritz, E., Oosthuizen, H., Lemont, S., Vermeer, A. & Kleber, R. J. (2017). Creative arts in psychotherapy treatment protocol for children after trauma. *The Arts in Psychotherapy, 54*, 128–135. https://doi-org.libproxy.sdsu.edu /10.1016/j.aip.2017.04.013

Vasquez, M., & Stensland, M. (2016). Adopted children with reactive attachment disorder: A qualitative study on family processes. *Clinical Social Work Journal, 44*(3), 319–332. https://doi.org/10.1007/s10615-015-0560-3

West, D., Vanderfaeillie, J., Van Hove, L., Gypen, L., & Van Holen, F. (2020). Attachment in family foster care: Literature review of associated characteristics. *Developmental Child Welfare, 2*(2), 132–150. https://doi.org/10.1177/2516103220915624

Whetten, K., Ostermann, J., Whetten, R., O'Donnell, K., Thielman, N., & Positive Outcomes for Orphans Research Team. (2011). More than the loss of a parent: Potentially traumatic events among orphaned and abandoned children. *Journal of Traumatic Stress, 24*(2), 174–182.

Whitt-Woosley, A., Sprang, G., & Eslinger, J. (2020). Exploration of factors associated with secondary traumatic stress in foster parents. *Children and Youth Services Review, 118.* https://doi.org/10.1016/j.childyouth.2020.105361

Chapter 11

Healing around the Table

A Trauma-Informed Approach to Community Nutrition Education

Monica Bhagwan and Adrienne Markworth

> *Putting it plainly in regard to obesity, we have seen that obesity is not the core problem. Obesity is the marker for the problem and sometimes is a solution. This is a profoundly important realization because none of us expects to cure a problem by treating its symptom.*
>
> —Dr. Vincent Felitti, "Obesity: Problem, Solution, or Both?" (2010)

> *"Every time, hot chips. Whenever she walks into my room, she acts panicked: "Do you have my hot chips?" But what I hear is, 'Did you remember me? Do I matter? Do you <u>care?</u>"'*
>
> —Dafna Lender, "Hot Chips" in Psychotherapy Networker (2020)

Led by Dr. Vincent Felitti and his team, the 1995/1997 Kaiser-CDC Adverse Childhood Experiences (ACEs) study was groundbreaking in its finding that trauma is a public health issue. This observation engendered transformations in healthcare, behavioral health, education, and social services. From this context emerged trauma-informed care, which seeks to account for the effect of trauma on individuals and the community, thereby providing more compassionate, effective, and integrated services.

This fundamentally person-centered approach has intriguing beginnings: Dr. Felitti had undertaken a wholly separate investigation that ultimately led to

DOI: 10.4324/9781003046295-14

the more extensive ACEs study. The former was a close examination of his own medically supervised obesity treatment protocol. Although the calorie-restrictive intervention was a medically sound weight loss intervention, Felitti noticed that patients were unconsciously sabotaging their initial success by discontinuing the program or regaining the weight. Through patient interviews, he discovered surprisingly high rates of trauma from early childhood experiences among those patients. This finding had significant implications for organizations working to curb the obesity epidemic, yet public health and community nutrition programs did not initially consider the implications of this original inquiry in the full ACEs study. However, the original study was bolstered by subsequent research which clarified the scientific relationship between ACEs, trauma, and toxic stress – ultimately changing how we define the issue of poor nutritional health. Moreover, these findings have altered our conceptualizations of related lifestyle habits, such as sleep and physical activity. For professionals engaged in nutrition education and dietary behavior change, these realizations necessitate a new approach.

Accordingly, this chapter introduces a framework we call Trauma-Informed Nutrition Security (TINS). The TINS approach integrates lessons from trauma research and trauma-informed best practices into nutrition and food security efforts (Coleman-Jensen et al., 2020). Moreover, it changes how we understand and promote healthy eating and food security by recognizing the relationship between adversity, illness, diet, and our relationship to food. In this framework, nutritional health and food security are inextricably linked.

Beyond detailing the TINS framework, this chapter introduces *Around the Table*: A trauma-informed nutrition and cooking curriculum for teens and young adults. In discussing this resource, the utility of the framework is illustrated: participant outcomes demonstrate the potential to inspire a shift in community nutrition and food security programs throughout the country.

Trauma-Informed Nutrition Security: A New Approach to Community Nutrition

A trauma-informed approach recognizes that disordered eating, unhealthy[1] dietary habits, chronic disease, and poor health outcomes result from a complex combination of factors (The Mayo Clinic, 2018). These contextual factors may include adverse experiences such as socioeconomic adversity (Robert Wood Johnson Foundation, 2017). Thus, the recent public health movement to emphasize socioeconomic adversity via the social determinants of health (SDOH) has been an essential step toward a trauma-informed perspective. The SDOH implicate community-level traumas, like social inequality and racism, in public health outcomes.

Emphasizing root causes of a systemic nature (environmental adversity), this approach deviates from traditional perspectives marked by excessive focus on individual eating habits (Baum & Fisher, 2014). Appropriately, public health programs now include both individual-level interventions (such as nutrition classes) and macro-level approaches, like policy, systems, and environmental interventions (PSEs). Examples of the latter include availing grocery stores to low-income neighborhoods and leveraging behavioral economics in school cafeterias, corner stores, and food pantries.

Notably, socioeconomic adversity is not the only form of trauma made salient when we apply the trauma-informed lens to nutritional health. As demonstrated by ACEs' research, the stress hormones released during trauma and toxic stress inspire neurobiological changes that affect the nervous, cardiovascular, immune, and endocrine systems. Trauma disrupts feelings of safety and attachment, resulting in a variety of traumatic adaptations that affect our diet. This includes changes in metabolism, inflammation, gut–brain circuitry, decision-making and planning, emotional regulation, and cravings. To fully appreciate this concept, one may consider how their diet shifts in even the briefest instances of heightened stress. Many people begin to crave foods with more sugar, salt, or fat, which they consume to feel better or calm themselves. This is perhaps exacerbated by the practical difficulties of planning, shopping, and meal preparation during stressful circumstances. Clearly, trauma and toxic stress may easily undercut one's ability to maintain a nourishing diet in the long term. Evidently, the trauma-conscious perspective presents an opportunity to address the full range of underlying barriers to good nutritional health.

Individuals are not at fault for their trauma nor its neurobiological implications. Accordingly, a trauma-informed approach implores nutrition and food security professionals to avoid shaming, stigma, and blame. For their part, nutritional health interventions must go beyond promoting healthy eating or increasing access to healthy food. Indeed, they must encourage a new perspective that considers food in relation to other aspects of well-being. This avails an opportunity to harness the broader power of nourishing food, which may be used to combat the physiological and socio-emotional impacts of trauma. Furthermore, incorporating mindfulness and stress-reduction strategies into nutrition education acknowledges that food choices are influenced by the mental state. Using these principles, prevention programs can address obesity, diabetes, cardiovascular disease, and other traditional targets of nutrition interventions more holistically and more effectively.

The table below presents some key questions related to community nutrition and demonstrates how a trauma-informed perspective adds depth to traditional assumptions (Table 11.1).

Table 11.1   Key Questions for Nutrition Education

	Traditional Assumptions	Trauma-Informed Perspective
What is a healthy diet?	Consuming a diet of various nutrient-rich foods and balancing calorie intake with calorie expenditure.	■ Nourishment is holistic and is dependent on the interconnectedness of multiple dimensions of health— physical, intellectual, social, spiritual, and emotional dimensions (Stoewen, 2017).
What are the causes of poor health outcomes?	1980s–1990s: Dietary fat and Cholesterol; Genetic predisposition; "Type-A" (high strung) personality 2000s: Poor lifestyle and dietary habits; Family history of disease as a strong predictor of health.	■ The relationship between dietary behavior, adversity, and health outcomes is multidirectional but not always causal. ■ Individual and community adversity are strong risk factors for diet-related disease, as they: ■ Impact relationship to food and dietary practices. ■ Influence multiple biological mechanisms (including metabolic health). ■ Have epigenetic and transgenerational impacts on health. ■ Community adversity correlates with proximity to unhealthy and obesogenic food environments.
Which public health nutrition and physical activity strategies are needed to improve health and well-being?	Disease prevention focused solely on messaging that promotes exercise and consumption of nutritious/low-calorie foods as the keys to reduced rates of illness and disease.	■ Nutrition messages broaden to include socio-emotional well-being and protective factors. ■ Providers' interpersonal skills, engagement strategies, and organizational processes are integral to effective programs and service delivery.

(Continued)

Table 11.1 (Continued)

	Traditional Assumptions	Trauma-Informed Perspective
What are the objectives of community nutrition programs?	Use programs to change personal behaviors across the population, or to improve environments and provide easier access to healthy foods.	■ Use trauma-informed approaches to enhance individual and community resilience and nurture opportunities for a positive relationship with food. ■ Work in alignment with other sectors to elevate community resilience factors.

The current mix of community nutrition education and structural interventions remains appropriate in a trauma-informed approach. However, program planners can redefine and expand education efforts to lend support to systems change. Moreover, program implementers can use trauma-informed nutrition education to empower community leaders to drive long-term engagement with systems change. Nutrition education then becomes a vehicle for a more impactful, multilayered approach in which trauma-informed nutrition program delivery can be integrated into PSE interventions more broadly—across health and human services.

Around the Table: A Trauma-Informed Nutrition and Cooking Curriculum

From this perspective, Leah's Pantry developed *Around the Table* in 2018, in partnership with the California Department of Social Services' (CDSS) CalFresh Healthy Living program. CalFresh Healthy Living, often referred to as SNAP-Ed in other states, is a federal program that serves as a companion to the SNAP program (currently referred to as CalFresh in California; formerly known as Food Stamps). The program funds various activities in all 58 California counties; these include nutrition classes, social marketing, and the aforementioned PSE interventions. The principal goal is to increase the nutritional health of Californians who meet the requirements for federal nutrition-assistance programs such as SNAP, the Special Supplemental Nutrition Program for Women, Infants, and Children, or the National School Lunch program. Trauma stemming from food insecurity can have a lasting impact on biological, cognitive, and psychological processes required for a healthy diet. Thus, federal nutrition-assistance programs provide protection from trauma but must consider these traumatic adaptations when implementing nutrition programs for populations with high food security rates. Furthermore, as much as people have come to rely on these programs for assistance and subsistence, they also have mistrust and suspicion of them. The historical and systemic oppression that many populations have experienced at the hands of government and other institutions must be acknowledged and repaired in order for community health programs to have meaningful impact.

Over the past decade, SNAP-Ed nutrition curricula have become increasingly learner-centered and interactive: Including cooking skills and group discussions in place of formal presentations. Moreover, PSE interventions have taken up a larger proportion of state SNAP-Ed budgets, and state-level conferences frequently include conversations about racial equity, health disparities, and SDOH. In this way, the system was primed for a trauma-informed pivot. These ideas gained further credibility when Governor Gavin Newsom appointed ACEs' pioneer Dr. Nadine Burke-Harris as California's first surgeon general.

A statewide training and technical assistance contract with CDSS put Leah's Pantry in a unique position to introduce ACEs' science- and trauma-informed approaches into the CalFresh Healthy Living program. We used this work to show community nutrition educators, program planners, evaluators, and administrators that trauma, toxic stress, and nutrition are connected. Based on conference attendance and training demand, there was tremendous interest in this framework. Additionally, our federal and state funders enthusiastically supported the creation of an explicitly trauma-informed nutrition curriculum for older youth and young adults—an age-group underserved by existing SNAP-Ed interventions.

Traditionally, nutrition education curricula prioritized standard messages that linked balanced diets, avoidance of sugary beverages, and budgeting to a healthy lifestyle (marked by lower risk of obesity and chronic disease). Existing curriculum options did not incorporate socio-emotional wellness, although we suspected this issue was important to young people. Furthermore, we understood that dietary habits were more likely to be impacted if participants' lived experiences fostered skills like reading nutrition labels or shopping with grocery lists. Accordingly, we theorized that this curriculum could better meet the needs of youth aged 14–25 if we used a trauma-informed lens to inform instructional strategy, messaging content, and evaluation. Thus, Leah's Pantry aimed to align *Around the Table* with the principles of trauma-informed care. Moreover, we sought to reframe the topic of dietary health to include stress awareness. The following section articulates how these ideas are essential to nutrition education, using *Around the Table* as a case study in implementation.

Centering Participant Perspectives

To maintain emphasis on program participants, we incorporated a strengths-based and participant-centered approach from the beginning. Before designing lessons or activities, we held paid focus groups with young "curriculum consultants" in San Diego and San Francisco. This initiative provided insight into themes that could potentially emerge regarding future participants' perspectives on: (1) nutritional health, (2) its relationship to stress, and (3) past experiences with nutrition programs. We then tested the focus group themes in curriculum testing workshops. The results indicated that youth participants most enjoyed group cooking. Accordingly, we chose to center the curriculum around a group meal, and *Around the Table* was born.

We enhanced this curriculum by limiting our topics and activities to allow for robust discussion and ensure that joyful experiences were not encumbered by time constraints. In a memorable example of the latter, a group of young men in San Diego (recruited for their efforts to reduce mental health stigma in refugee communities) exuberantly turned a yogurt parfait activity into an over-the-top competition. This occasion demonstrated that, given space and opportunity to do so, participants can use the raw material of nourishing food, conversation, and mindful interaction to create positive emotional experiences. Thus, our experience in developing *Around the Table* revealed that trauma-informed nutrition programs and education efforts must center participant and community experiences.

Notably, these experiences vary widely, even among members of vulnerable groups. Young people are especially susceptible to experiences of adversity, yet individual circumstances and contexts are rarely the same. Many have limited control over their food. Those living with guardians likely have less responsibility for shopping or cooking. Even young adults with more domestic independence may still be adjusting to the responsibility of making their own nutritional decisions. Furthermore, some youth routinely use food for emotional regulation, or show evidence of a disordered relationship with food, while others do not. Clearly, myriad contextual factors come together to shape individual relationships with food. For instance, many of our refugee and immigrant youth testers had rich and well-developed relationships with food tied to culture and family.

The decision to center the class around a group meal was indicative of this intersectional perspective. Indeed, this activity can easily accommodate differing culinary literacy levels, cultural backgrounds, and personality types. To this end, we also chose to incorporate opportunities for open-ended discussion. These exchanges honor different experiences and allow for individualized decision-making. For example, participants discuss their own shopping experiences and then select tips that would work for themselves or their families. A young person who participated in this curriculum disclosed that she was always beholden to the food choices made by her foster parents. Once out of their care, she felt transformed by the freedom and autonomy of purchasing food herself.

It is, of course, never easy to center multiple perspectives in a single resource. This is a challenge we certainly faced during curriculum development. Ultimately, we settled on a few core ideas that would drive this process, and determined that our curriculum must provide a positive and empowering experience that:

1. Explicitly incorporates an understanding of the psychological and physiological effects of stress and adversity on nourishment and health.
2. Utilizes trauma-informed strategies to facilitate the class.
3. Promotes a positive and healing relationship to food that enhances the vibrancy and vitality of people and communities.
4. Increases the food and cooking literacy of participants in tangible ways.
5. Provides specific pathways for youth leadership, voice, and choice throughout.

Guiding Framework

To maintain a consistent, disciplined approach to program development, Leah's Pantry used the Substance Abuse and Mental Health Services Administration's (SAMHSA) guidance on trauma-informed approaches as a starting template for the TSNS framework (2014). This report was written primarily for mental health services but is well-suited for non-clinical work. One major change embraced by many, ourselves included, is the inclusion of "resilience" as a fifth assumption. This reflects the national conversation about the role of resilience in trauma-informed care while honoring the public health mandate to help people find pathways to healing and well-being. As implementers, facilitators, and organizations committed to that cause, and to the fundamentals of trauma-informed care, we believe community nutrition work can promote positive and healing relationships with food and strengthen resilience at the individual and community levels (Figure 11.1).

Adapted from: SAMHSA's Concept Trauma and Guidance for a Trauma-Informed Approach.

Moreover, we contend that trauma-informed alignment with this guidance can create space for more authentic interactions that promote sustainable self-care practices and holistic nutritional well-being. Fundamental to this alignment is the aforementioned participant-centered approach. It has been a challenge for SNAP-Ed to remain participant-centered, as its curricula are message-driven and fail to consider lived experience. Overemphasis on messaging can forge a disconnect between a nutrition skill and dietary habits. Using *Around the Table* as an example, the following sections discuss how nutrition education can align with the SAMHSA process and the accompanying trauma-informed principles.

Realize...
that trauma impacts
our communities

Recognize...
the signs of trauma

Resilience...
and healing can happen
with prevention, support
and care

Respond...
using trauma-informed
practices, policies and
procedures

Resist...
re-traumatizing
clients and staff

Figure 11.1   The Five Rs of Trauma-Informed Care Diagram.

Realize That Trauma Impacts Individual and Community Nourishment

Since the ACEs study of the 1990s, the original ten adverse childhood experiences have expanded to include incidents in community and environmental settings. Although many forms of adversity cut across class and income levels, certain groups—especially those that serve as the primary audience for nutrition and food security initiatives—face higher degrees of adversity. This includes community adversity, which is particularly relevant for comprehensive nutrition programs that aim to influence individual behaviors and broader aspects of a community's food environment.

Limited food access and lack of food security are obvious forms of nutrition-related adversity, but there are other considerations to be made. For instance, in abusive environments, food can be used to control, punish, or shame. Furthermore, people often experience social stigma or judgment in relation to their familial or cultural food habits, or their need for food assistance. Finally, resource constraints typically inhibit choice and make shopping an anxious experience. Often, such experiences are insufficiently accounted for in a nutrition program, creating a missed opportunity for relevant and meaningful participant engagement. It is crucial that all stakeholders involved in community nutrition recognize the impact of trauma. Program planners must understand the different types of trauma and adversity to effectively plan and deliver programs in this space. Evaluators must understand the link between food and trauma to choose appropriate metrics from which to determine program efficacy. Additionally, program participants may not perceive the connection between stress and trauma, their dietary health, and/or the food norms of their community. Thus, nutrition education curricula should reframe conceptualizations of dietary health to consider stress, toxic stress, and other related topics.

In addition to creating the curriculum, Leah's Pantry developed a robust implementer training program for staff working on SNAP-Ed funding and similar programs. This program begins with an opportunity for the implementers to reflect on the meaning of food in their own lives. There is also basic training provided on the science of trauma and resilience, especially as it relates to food. When implementers have the space to realize the implications of trauma on their communities, they are better positioned to issue a trauma-informed response. By design, this program is open to staff members regardless of whether they plan to implement the curriculum. Indeed, we know that trauma-informed programs are delivered by trauma-informed organizations. Thus, we encourage the participation of people from a range of departments, as well as staff engaged with other projects.

Unlike many community nutrition programs, *Around the Table* avoids reducing food to a tool for achieving long-term physical health or weight management. Instead, it recognizes that long-term health and body weight are more than products of dietary choices. Additionally, it also honors the tender place that food occupies in our individual and collective lives. Connecting dietary health to emotional health and stress management helps youth consider how stress impacts their diet and how dietary choices can mitigate some of their stress and emotional dysregulation.

Recognize the Signs of Trauma in Dietary Behavior and Health Outcomes

Adversity during early childhood and the developing years makes one more vulnerable to unfavorable outcomes. When these experiences accumulate over the lifespan, they can create high levels of toxic stress: Known to increase the risk for obesity, diabetes, and other diet-related diseases. A report by the Robert Wood Johnson Foundation describes contemporary, widely accepted research on the mechanisms by which childhood trauma may increase the risk for obesity (Robert Wood Johnson Foundation, 2017). It observes that changes to biological pathways can promote obesity, in addition to demonstrating behavioral path modifications that do the same. For example, toxic stress in early childhood impacts the way the prefrontal cortex functions, which may alter decision-making. Furthermore, adversity and toxic stress affect an individual's relationship to food. After all, psychosocial factors—especially those present during childhood—shape one's food-related habits and perspectives (Hemmingsson, 2014).

As such, the anxiety of food insecurity, for instance, can trigger a feast–fast cycle. Indeed, the overconsumption of available food is often triggered by one's anticipation of periods when it will be less accessible (i.e., at the end of the month when the money runs out). This is especially true of high-calorie or highly satiating processed food. From a different perspective, cheap but low-quality food is often a feasible way for low-income families to celebrate or demonstrate affection. Harmony Cox (2018), a former public health practitioner, elaborates on this phenomenon:

> In the reality of feeding a struggling family, the food pyramid is irrelevant. Keeping us fed was a source of pride, junk food was a source of joy, and so our diets endured. I don't remember parents who didn't love me. If anything, they loved me too much, and their love language came deep-fried. It may have hurt me in the long run, but that's never been a sign that something wasn't borne from love.

In other words, when we consider the socioeconomic contexts in which counterproductive food choices occur, they are frequently shown to be rational behaviors within those circumstances. From this contextual perspective, we also understand the development of disease as an outcome of toxic stress and adversity. Indeed, Cox herself discussed being overweight despite learning and practicing healthier eating habits as an adult.

Accordingly, *Around the Table* encourages participants to consider how stress impacts food choices, how food can help with anxiety, and how to manage stress through self-care. Furthermore, we were careful not to demonize foods or stigmatize food choices; weight management is not a topic of this curriculum. Instead, we champion the recognition of trauma's impact on food as an alternative to the traditional disease-prevention messaging prevalent in this field.

The topic of recognition also features in implementer training. During self-reflection, participants often reframe their dietary habits through the lens of stress and trauma. Thus, the program emphasizes self-awareness, self-regulation, and self-care as critical steps toward community care. As implementers reflect on their program participants, they often see traumatic adaptations where they once saw irrational or uneducated behaviors. Spending meaningful time on these first two steps—realization and recognition—lays a solid foundation for trauma-informed responses.

Building Blocks of a Response: Trauma-Informed Principles in Nutrition Programs

Because nutrition education enhances awareness of trauma and adversity, our programs must respond with compassion for these experiences while guiding people toward health and wellness through nutrition. In practice, this means that programs should align trauma-informed principles and practices with curriculum objectives, content, facilitation, and evaluation. Notably, a trauma-informed approach necessitates collaboration with broader efforts that facilitate these objectives, such as mental health services, housing, medical care, education, and social services. This comprehensive approach may increase engagement, reduce participant stress, and support a holistic, healthy, and resilient relationship to food.

The six SAMHSA principles for trauma-informed responses are also appropriate for nutrition education interventions. This section focuses on the latter by considering implications for program design and delivery. It must be noted, however, that commitment to trauma-informed practices at the organizational level is necessary for genuine programmatic success. Of course, implementation may be tailored to the needs of different programs and diverse audiences. Facilitators come to understand these principles through training. Thus, they not only integrate them into *Around the Table*'s curriculum topics and instructor guide, they ensure the principles are reflected in participant engagement at every opportunity (Table 11.2).

Informed by these principles, *Around the Table* is more than a curriculum that centers hands-on cooking. It is facilitated by flexible conversations and interactive activities grounded in trauma-informed principles and healing practices. It is also a resource that serves to help participants develop and practice autonomy, self-awareness, and other strengths needed for a healthy relationship to self, community, and food. They can:

- Share memories and stories about food.
- Explore their personal relationship to food and share their wisdom with others.
- Improve cooking and food resource-management skills.
- Learn about nutrition for good physical and mental health.
- Explore healthy coping and self-nourishment skills.
- Plan, prepare, and eat a meal together.
- Practice mindful eating, grounding, and gratitude.
- Take leadership roles throughout the series.

During the six-week program, participants learn, practice, and then reinforce these skills, culminating in a final reflection and celebration of their experience.

In addition to reframing conceptualizations of nourishment and adding the components listed above, the workshop experience had to accommodate those with a history of trauma. Dr. Bruce Perry's (2014) Neurosequential Model was used to design a structure that was responsive to the neurobiology of stress and trauma. Colloquially known as "Regulate, Relate, and Reason," this model recognizes that we must achieve a regulated nervous system (i.e., not over- or

Table 11.2 SAMHSA Principles in Community Nutrition Programs

Safety and Security	The physical setting is safe and interpersonal interactions promote a sense of emotional safety for participants. Programs incorporate stress reduction, conflict de-escalation, and self-care practices.
	Participants' food security is intentionally factored into the program. Linkages to food security screening or food access are offered. Participants' food insecurity, dietary habits, and health status are destigmatized.
Transparency and Trustworthiness	Staff is well-trained to deliver relevant, reliable, and high-quality education. Content includes audience-appropriate information on factors that affect nutritional health beyond eating habits and exercise, such as adversity or socio-emotional well-being.
Peer Support	Peer support and mutual self-help are key program vehicles, serving to promote participants' health and well-being by establishing safety and hope, building trust, enhancing collaboration, and centering lived experience. Participants are supported to forge connections and share strategies, skills, and resources.
Mutuality and Collaboration	Program staff partner with each other and with participants, recognizing that people are the experts of their own lives. Health and well-being require quality relationships and meaningful power-sharing and decision-making. Concerted efforts are made to level power differences between staff and participants for successful collaboration.
Empowerment, Voice, and Choice	People are recognized as wise, creative, and resourceful. The program incorporates an understanding of how clients' voices and choices have been historically diminished, then seeks to mitigate that impact. Programs support clients' dignity and ability to shape their own lives by emphasizing strengths and self-advocacy.
Cultural, Historical, and Gender	The program intentionally seeks to move past cultural stereotypes and biases (e.g., assumptions based on race, ethnicity, sexual orientation, age, religion, gender identity, geography, etc.). The program is responsive to community needs and experiences and leverages the healing value of cultural traditions and communities of belonging. The program incorporates policies, protocols, and processes that are responsive to the gendered, ethnic, and cultural needs of individuals served, while recognizing and addressing historical trauma.

under-activated) before we can relate to others in positive ways. This process, in turn, enhances a participant's ability to reason. Accordingly, *Around the Table* workshops begin with activities that establish safety, connection, and sensory grounding before other cognitive activities like learning.

Our experience with workshops and curriculum testing reveal that young people often arrive in dysregulated states due to their experiences of the world beyond the safety of the room. Taking time to bring people's bodies and minds inside the class heightens engagement and limits distraction. After we hold space for nervous system regulation with mindful breathing and eating activities, participants are ready for conversations that foster a sense of interpersonal connection. Then, peer-led group cooking solidifies the collective bond. This structure aligns with the principles of mutuality, collaboration, and peer support. Facilitators then present nutrition and culinary information within this safe, enjoyable, and regulated environment. All classes follow a similar structure and include a set of regulation activities that allow participants to apply what they have learned. For example, a popular mindfulness activity is used most weeks, with small changes made to keep participants engaged. This focus on regulation and consistency is beneficial even to facilitators.

The companion training program introduces trauma-informed principles both as they relate to *Around the Table* and to organizations, systems, and other programs. Compassionate facilitation is a critical component of the agenda. The training also provides specific classroom engagement strategies designed to create a safe, transparent, and trusting environment. Furthermore, the training reflects the interrelated components that comprise the broader program ecosystem from the participants' and implementers' perspectives. The latter's training topics include introductory modules on multi-system collaboration, organizational development, evaluation, communication, and trauma-informed food security initiatives.

Resisting Re-traumatization

Trauma-informed principles serve as guidelines to help organizations and practitioners avoid inadvertently causing anxiety, feelings of disempowerment, or lack of protection—all of which may re-trigger trauma responses. When we are not conscious of our practices, we are more likely to re-traumatize individuals and communities. For example, relying on discrete tactics concerning nutrition curricula (i.e., making a list, comparing unit prices, portion control) may unintentionally increase shame by failing to accommodate a more holistic perspective. Consider a teenager whose experience of household instability has created anxiety regarding access to food. She may eat a lot of pizza at a school event due to the understandable fear of not having enough. In this way, she maintains a "feast or famine" mindset despite knowing that overeating may contribute to poor health. If we are not gentle and thoughtful in our discussions about portion control, we may trigger adverse emotions. Simultaneously, facilitators must take care not to convey an overly controlling demeanor in food and diet messaging, which may perpetuate disordered eating, e.g., orthorexia, anorexia, and bulimia.

Of course, nutrition and cooking classes are part of an overarching system of social services and medical care. Thus, highly burdened healthcare systems, service providers, and educators may have created stressful or even harmful experiences for our participants (Figley, 1986). As program providers, failure to acknowledge the larger context of peoples' experiences around food and within institutions undermines our ability to support nutritional health. Furthermore, this failure perpetuates anxiety and shame, thereby compounding trauma despite our best intentions. Programs grounded in trauma-informed principles avail avenues to counteract the genuine risk of humiliation and disempowerment that program participants face.

In a similar show of caution, *Around the Table*'s training program requires that facilitators consider their own biases, reflect on organizational practices, and engage in empathy-mapping activities to capture participants' lived experiences and perspectives. The curriculum also follows a structure that supports enjoyable, consistent, and predictable experiences. Certainly, anxiety reduction is a tenet of the curricular philosophy, as evidenced by the following example. During a workshop, a participant raised in foster care recounted having an anxiety attack in the produce aisle of a supermarket earlier that day. The incident was prompted by her inability to open a plastic bag used for produce. Because the class structure welcomes participation and provides opportunities for regulation, she had a safe space to process the anxiety complicating her quest for a healthier diet. Significantly, what could have been a buried, solitary experience was met with compassionate understanding, along with group suggestions about how to open the unhandy bags more easily.

Nourishment Can Foster Resilience and Healing

While a trauma-informed approach requires deep understanding and compassion for challenges, it also invites us to consider the conditions that enable resilience. Just as adverse experiences can harm the body and psyche, positive ones can protect, heal, and promote well-being. The research on protective factors shows that loving, strong caregiving can reduce the likelihood of childhood trauma in the face of toxic stress and adversity. Moreover, healing practices can reduce the impact of both issues among children, their caregivers, and other adults with histories of trauma.

Good nutrition aids resilience by providing protection and healing. A nourishing diet can improve stress response, emotional well-being, and cognitive functioning. Nutrition education rarely includes this message, yet concerns about stress and emotional well-being are pervasive. Indeed, the connection between healthy diet and emotional health is a potential motivating factor for participants. Still, it takes more than health messaging to inspire healthier eating. What one consumes has much to do with their relationship to food. For those who have experienced or are experiencing adversity, having the opportunity to build a positive relationship with food may be especially important.

The evaluation requirements of many nutrition education programs equate program success to changed eating habits. This results in missed opportunities to engage participants on a deeper level and nurture protective and healing qualities. There are obvious connections between protective factors / healing practices and nutrition. For example, the association between sleep and nutritional intake is well established but often excluded from nutrition education. Similarly, the quality of family relationships is a key factor in good nutrition. Embedding this knowledge into programs is a relatively simple way to enhance experiences and strengthen nutritional and health outcomes. For example, by addressing parenting or community connections around food, nutrition education can incorporate protective factors and healing practices. Following the collaboration principle, partnering with programs and organizations that align with parenting, self-care, healthy relationships, nature, or mental health services can enhance the impact of nutrition education.

Around the Table makes several protective factors salient. We prioritized much of the Search Institute's (1997) Developmental Assets framework, which "integrates insights from [the] fields of prevention, resilience and youth development to identify critical relationships, opportunities, and personal strengths young people need to thrive." Some of the internal and external assets we aim to cultivate in participants' lives are listed below:

- The support of people who love, care, accept, and appreciate them.
- Feeling valued and valuable.
- Clear rules, consistent consequences for breaking the rules, and encouragement to do their best.
- Opportunities (beyond school) to learn and develop new skills and interests with other youth and adults.
- Appreciation of the enduring significance of learning and belief in personal abilities.
- Skills to effectively interact with others, make difficult decisions, and cope with new circumstances.
- Belief in their self-worth, and a sense of autonomy.

Ultimately, *Around the Table* rests upon a theory of change which stipulates that developing these assets is essential to building food and nutrition literacy. Thus, curricular activities support asset development while integrating nutrition and healing practices such as mindfulness, relationship building, mental health, and self-awareness. For instance, there are opportunities to expand the conversation beyond healthy eating and discuss the ways in which food affects mood and energy or personal goals and strengths, and even to incorporate interpersonal connection around mealtime.

The implementer training program also encourages educators to frame their work more broadly. By introducing the protective factors framework, implementers map how their program interacts with others that address protective factors in their community. They also consider how they can impact collaborative initiatives and improve the consistency of nutrition messages across sectors, such as early childhood education or healthcare.

A Trauma-Informed Model for Nutritional Health

Beyond adopting trauma-informed principles and a holistic, relational model of nourishment, Leah's Pantry considered fundamentals of human behavior and psychology while developing *Around the Table*. Therapist and dietitian Ellyn Satter (2007) has done similar work, creating a model of the hierarchy of food needs based on Maslow's hierarchy of needs. Our model of healthy nourishment demonstrates a similar rationale to Satter's model. Notably, however, Satter focuses on individual work while we consider positive relationships to food and the dietary role of resilience in community contexts.

According to most experts, trauma is caused by circumstances in which emotional and physical needs were not met along with the lack of social support to recover. It is, therefore, crucial to restore safety, security, love, and belonging while building higher-level skills for health, self-care, and care for others. Applying this to nourishment means that reliable, desirable, and dignified food resources and support are fundamental. Thus, community nutrition education should occur in conjunction with efforts to bolster food security. Furthermore, emotionally rich personal and interpersonal experiences are markers of effective programs. Programs can build on these experiences to introduce cognitive and instrumental aspects of food found on our model's top level.

Beyond informing the curricular development process, this model served as a guide to evaluation outcomes. From this perspective, we added several categories of indicators to our *Around the Table* evaluation tool, e.g., self-perceptions around eating and attitudes about healthy eating. We found that youth participants developed significant self-awareness around how quickly they eat and the effect of food on their mental state and stress level. We also measured specific changes in competency related to food and cooking skills, an indicator that is (perhaps surprisingly) absent from the SNAP-Ed program.

Participant interviews allowed for quantitative data collection, highlighting a consistent theme of confidence stemming from cooking competency. This demonstrated that culinary literacy may support young people's ability to envision themselves as capable adults. Furthermore, qualitative data collection reinforced the efficacy of the curriculum's mindfulness activities. Reflecting on her most memorable lesson, one student stated: "being mindful about the foods we eat, using the five senses to try foods, which is something we did at the beginning of each class." Finally, the interviews provided insight into one of the model's principal factors—nourishing others. Participants felt empowered to use the skills they learned and felt a responsibility to champion health in their families and social groups. Students reported that they immediately texted information learned to siblings and family members, encouraged healthier snacks, and adopted greater roles in family food preparation (Table 11.3).

Table 11.3   A Model of Nourishment

Physical and Mental Health Good nutrition for a healthy body and mind; protection against stress.	*Self-Regulation* Mindful and self-aware eating; joyful movement.	*Nourishing Others* Cooking for, and feeding family and community.	*Justice and Equity* Awareness of the socioeconomic dynamics of the food system; advocacy opportunities.
Identity and Self-Expression Sharing food memories, telling stories, and honoring heritage.	*Positive Experiences* Enjoyment, gratitude, and sensory experiences with food and the body.	*Supportive Relationships* Foster relationships by cooking and eating together.	*Autonomy and Competency* Cooking skills, food literacy, growing food.
Safety and Security: Reliable, desirable, and dignified food resources and support.			

Conclusion

We hope this approach can serve as a helpful resource to guide a variety of community nutrition interventions in the federal SNAP-Ed program and beyond. Since its release, the *Around the Table* curriculum has already undergone various adaptations to accommodate different settings: Including high school classrooms and virtual environments—the latter being a necessity during the current COVID-19 pandemic. Ultimately, we welcome the evolution of our trauma-informed model of nourishment and specific curricula and programs that align with this framework. We also believe this model is a useful tool for adapting existing programs. In many cases, program implementers need only make simple adjustments to class structures, facilitation strategies, message reframing, and content to enhance the impact of existing curricula or programs.

Note

1. There is much debate about what constitutes unhealthy dietary habits. For the purpose of this chapter, we define it as an overall diet whose nutritional content is significantly below that required for healthy development and disease prevention.

References

Baum, F., & Fisher, M. (2014). Why behavioural health promotion endures despite its failure to reduce health inequities. *Sociology of Health and Illness, 36*(2), 213–225. https://doi.org/10.1111/1467-9566.12112

Coleman-Jensen, A., Rabbitt, M. P., & Gregory, C. A. (2020, September 6). Definitions of food security. *USDA Economic Research Service.* Retrieved from https://www.ers.usda.gov/topics/food-nutrition-assistance/food-security-in-the-us/definitions-of-food-security.aspx

Cox, H. (2018, May 7). My life as a public health crisis. *Memoir, Narratively.* Retrieved from https://narratively.com/my-life-as-a-public-health-crisis/

Felitti, V., Jakstis, K., Pepper, V., & Ray, A. (2010, Spring). Obesity: Problem, solution, or both? *Permanente Journal, 14*(1), 24–30. https://doi.org/10.7812/TPP/09-107

Figley, C. R. (Ed.). (1986). *Trauma and its wake.* Bristol, PA: Brunner/Mazel.

Hemmingsson, E. (2014). A new model of the role of psychological and emotional distress in promoting obesity: Conceptual review with implications for treatment and prevention. *Obesity Reviews: An Official Journal of the International Association for the Study of Obesity, 15*(9), 769–779. https://doi.org/10.1111/obr.12197

Lender, D. (2020, May/June). Hot chips. *Psychotherapy Networker.* Retrieved from https://www.psychotherapynetworker.org/magazine/article/2460/hot-chips

Perry, B. D. (2014). Understanding traumatized and maltreated children: The core concepts [info sheet]. *SLPS.org.* Retrieved from https://www.slps.org/site/handlers/filedownload.ashx?moduleinstanceid=53801&dataid=47987&FileName=The%20Brain%20AA%202020%20Info%20Sheet.pdf

Robert Wood Johnson Foundation. (2017). Stress in early life and childhood obesity risk. *Healthy Eating Research*. Retrieved from https://www.acesconnection.com/g/aces -and-nourishment/fileSendAction/fcType/5/fcOid/480105569145119157/fodoid /480105569145119156/her_stress_obesity_5-30.pdf

SAMHSA. (2014, October). *SAMHSA's concept of trauma and guidance for a trauma-informed approach*. SAMHSA. Retrieved from https://store.samhsa.gov/product /SAMHSA-s-Concept-of-Trauma-and-Guidance-for-a-Trauma-Informed -Approach/SMA14-4884

Satter, E. (2007). Hierarchy of food needs. *Journal of Nutrition Education and Behavior, 39*(5 Suppl), S187–S188. https://doi.org/10.1016/j.jneb.2007.01.003

Search Institute. (1997). *The developmental assets framework*. Search Institute. Retrieved from https://www.search-institute.org/our-research/development-assets/ developmental-assets-framework/

Stoewen, D. L. (2017). Dimensions of wellness: Change your habits, change your life. *Canadian Veterinary Journal, 58*(8), 861–862.

The Mayo Clinic. (2018, February 18). *Eating disorders*. Mayo Clinic. Retrieved from https://www.mayoclinic.org/diseases-conditions/eating-disorders/symptoms -causes/syc-20353603

Chapter 12

Trauma-Informed System Change in Child Welfare

Cambria Rose Walsh and Melissa Bernstein

Public child welfare is a group of services that are driven by the goals of ensuring the well-being and safety of children and working to help children achieve permanency. As part of their role, Child Welfare System workers investigate reports of child abuse and neglect and provide a multitude of services to support children and families. During the 2018 fiscal year, Child Welfare agencies received approximately 4.3 million total referrals alleging abuse and neglect which involved approximately 7.8 million children. Approximately 2.4 million of those referrals led to a response from child welfare (U.S. Department of Health and Human Services, 2020).

Child Welfare System workers make critical decisions at times of crisis to support many of the nation's most vulnerable children. Children and youth in foster care are more likely to have been exposed to multiple forms of traumatic experiences, such as abuse, neglect, violence, exploitation, and grief (Dorsey et al., 2012). On top of this, separation from family, friends, and community create additional stress. Within the last decade, researchers and practitioners have come to understand the high prevalence of child trauma, and the devastating short- and long-term impacts on individuals, families, and communities. This body of work, highlighting the biological, physiological, psychological, and social consequences of childhood trauma, has sparked a movement to transform child-serving systems into systems that can effectively and efficiently respond to, and serve, those exposed to trauma.

DOI: 10.4324/9781003046295-15

This concept of recognizing and addressing the impact of trauma at an organization level is often termed Trauma-Informed Care (TIC). Generally, TIC consists of organizational initiatives focused on workforce development (e.g., trauma training, secondary traumatic stress), the organizational environment (e.g., changes to organizational policies and practices, system collaboration, partnering with children, youth, and families), and service delivery (e.g., screening, assessment, evidence-based practices) (Hanson & Lang, 2016, SAMHSA, 2014). The Child Welfare System has answered the call to create trauma-informed systems through recent state and federal funding initiatives. The Administration for Children and Families (ACF), which oversees federal child welfare policy, has prioritized funding to support trauma-informed system development in Child Welfare Systems (Sheldon et al., 2013). From 2011 to 2013, ACF awarded approximately 20 state and local agencies and other organizations discretionary grants to address childhood trauma. The focus of these grants was screening and referring children to treatment, implementing or expanding trauma-focused, evidence-based treatments, and increasing collaboration between the child welfare and behavioral health systems. Additionally, the National Child Traumatic Stress Network (NCTSN), which was established by Congress in 2000, includes multiple committees designed to address specific topic areas related to the field of child trauma. In particular, The Child Welfare Committee of the NCTSN was created to support the development of products, interventions, and services for children involved in the Child Welfare System.

The literature on TIC also provides guidance on advancing trauma-informed change practices in Child Welfare. TIC efforts in the Child Welfare System range from individual initiatives focused on one domain of TIC, such as screening or partnering with children, youth, and families (e.g., Crandal et al., 2017, Sullivan et al., 2016) to multipronged statewide approaches which attempt to intervene in multiple trauma-informed domains (Bartlett et al., 2016; Jankowski et al., 2019; Kerns et al., 2016; Lang et al., 2016). The most commonly evaluated elements of trauma-informed change in Child Welfare Systems include training outcomes (e.g., perceived knowledge, capacity, skills) and service use outcomes (e.g., child PTSD symptoms, child behavioral health needs, caregiver stress), followed by trauma-focused services and evidence-based treatments (Bunting et al., 2019).

A recent comprehensive systematic review of organization-wide implementation initiatives provides evidence for the efficacy of implementing organizational TIC approaches in Child Welfare Systems. In other words, many Child Welfare Systems have been successful in establishing key elements of TIC into their organizations and have seen immediate and sustained increases in staff knowledge, confidence, and/or skills (Bunting et al., 2019). Notably, there is more work to be done in ensuring that implementing TIC leads to positive changes for children and families. The authors outline preliminary evidence for improvements in service outcomes such as reduced caregiver stress and improved placement stability, yet these results were often associated with weaker study designs and limited generalizability.

While the field of TIC and its application in Child Welfare Systems has certainly grown over the last decade, a divide continues to exist between commitment and practice. In our experience, this divide is not due to a lack of motivation by leadership or lack of desire from organizations to be trauma-informed. There are limitations in the field itself that hinders the uptake and advancement of TIC. TIC is not an intervention per se, but an approach or framework that is left up to organizations to implement in a way that suits their needs and their system. This makes it difficult for leaders to find guidance on where to begin and how to determine their scope of work. Initiatives around TIC have also focused largely on training and training outcomes, without clear guidance on implementation and sustainment (e.g., how to do it and make it last). There are also challenges unique to the Child Welfare System that may serve as barriers to TIC advancement. Below we highlight some of these challenges and offer suggestions, followed by two examples of trauma-informed change initiatives we hope will serve as a guide for those looking to advance TIC organizationally.

Challenges to Implementing TIC in Child Welfare Systems

The Child Welfare System is complex and there are several challenges that commonly arise when working to create trauma-informed system change. The complexity of the system is itself a challenge. There is no one-size-fits-all for Child Welfare Systems since each state, and in some cases individual counties or jurisdictions are run very differently. Therefore, TIC initiatives within the Child Welfare System need to be flexible and adaptable to the individual needs of each system. As TIC is composed of many different pieces, each Child Welfare System will be at a different place on their journey. Needs and organizational assessments are a helpful first step for leaders looking for guidance on choosing a meaning-ful starting point. Champine and colleagues provide a comprehensive review of measures for a system-wide, trauma-informed approach (Champine et al., 2019).

Despite the many differences in Child Welfare Systems structure and processes, the transitory nature of its workforce is one common denominator. The levels of turnover in Child Welfare Systems are notably high. The average turnover rate is 30% with some jurisdictions being considerably higher and others lower (National Child Welfare Workforce Institute, 2011). Since a part of being trauma-informed is reliant on individual practice, this turnover can have an adverse effect on the time spent providing training and technical assistance and the attempts at larger system change. One strategy to prevent the loss of trauma-informed skills within an organization is to include individuals from all levels of the workforce. Particularly important is the inclusion of leadership, which tends to be more stable, and has the power to bring people together with a shared value and trauma-informed vision. Mid-level managers are also essential in helping to guide implementation efforts, and the inclusion of frontline workers helps ensure trauma-informed practices fit with local needs.

Another hallmark of the work of Child Welfare is the large numbers of families in which intergenerational trauma exists. Intergenerational trauma is trauma that affects one family across two or more generations and can be passed on through family norms, beliefs, habits, etc. (Walsh et al., CWTTT, 2020). There is also a high prevalence of parental trauma history in families that are active to the Child Welfare System, whether or not such trauma is considered intergenerational. Therefore, being trauma-informed requires attending not just to the child's trauma, but the parent and caregiver's trauma as well. Partnering and supporting parents who may be responsible for the abuse and neglect while at the same time investigating them and holding them accountable can be a challenge. Trauma-Informed Child Welfare systems understand the importance of not only addressing parent trauma histories, but involving parents at the policy, system, program, and service levels to ensure that case management is trauma-informed. At the service level, best practice entails sharing power by creating partnerships in which parents have an equal voice in decision-making, and whenever possible authority over their own case plan. At the system, program and policy levels including parents with lived expertise helps to reduce power differentials and ensure parent perspectives and experiences genuinely influence the system and its associated programs and policies.

An additional challenge to creating Trauma-Informed Child Welfare Systems lies in the fact that most families involved in the Child Welfare System are involved in multiple complex systems (e.g., educational, legal, mental health). Part of being a Trauma-Informed Child Welfare System is collaborating with and across child-serving systems. Children and families who have experienced trauma are vulnerable to re-traumatization when the systems that serve them are uncoordinated and, at times, at odds with one another. At the state level, guidelines on multi-system trauma-informed approaches have recently been developed (e.g., Brennen et al., 2019). However, these approaches often require considerable time, effort, and resources. At the local level, Child Welfare Systems can work to create a shared language between systems through cross-sector trainings, joint meetings, or developing data-sharing agreements across agencies.

Finally, the Child Welfare System is one that is often reactive, whether it be to new legislation, policies, or legal action. At any given time, there are multiple new initiatives, new policies to abide by, changes in funding, and changes in leadership that require time and attention. Competing with these needs to push forth trauma-informed policies and practices can be challenging. It is therefore suggested that developing a trauma-informed lens by which to review these new and changing requirements rather than viewing TIC as a separate requirement is the key to success. At an organizational level, for example, leaders can ensure that TIC appears as a core principle in agency policies, practices, and service information. In addition, they can ensure that individuals with lived experience have leadership roles in reviewing and creating these organizational policies, and that agency budgets reflect a commitment to TIC.

Two Examples of Trauma-Informed System Change in Child Welfare

To assist Child Welfare Systems in their journeys to overcome these challenges and to become more trauma-informed, two examples of trauma-informed system change that were developed out of Rady Children's Hospital are detailed below. The first is focused on a training series that focuses on knowledge and skill development across the workforce, the second on implementation of trauma-informed change at an organizational level to assist Child Welfare Systems in making targeted trauma-informed changes to their system.

The Center for Trauma-Informed Policies, Programs, and Practices (TIPs Center)

The Center for Child Welfare Trauma-Informed Policies, Programs, and Practices (TIPs Center) was funded through a grant from SAMHSA in the fall of 2016 as a part of the National Child Traumatic Stress Network (NCTSN). The TIPs Center's focus was to provide support for trauma-informed knowledge and skills to permeate into child welfare organizational cultures, at all levels and among all roles, resulting in positive sustainable changes in the systems, policies, and practices which lead to better outcomes for children and families served by these systems. The central focus of the TIPs Center was creating the 3rd edition of the Child Welfare Trauma Training Toolkit (Walsh et al., CWTTT, 2020). The 3rd edition of the CWTTT was released in April 2020. This version provided a refinement of the Essential Elements that were used in the earlier versions of the curricula. See an updated list of the Essential Elements below:

A Trauma-Informed Child Welfare System is one that:

1. Continuously Expands Workforce Knowledge and Skills about Trauma and its Effects.
2. Addresses Primary and Secondary Traumatic Stress of the Workforce.

3. Partners with Children, Youth, and Families.
4. Partners with Agencies and Systems that Interact with Children, Youth, and Families.
5. Maximizes Physical and Psychological Safety of Children, Youth, and Families.
6. Routinely Screens for Trauma-Related Needs of Children and Youth.
7. Delivers and Connects Children and Youth to Services and Supports that Promote Well-Being, Healing, and Resilience.
8. Understands Parent and Caregiver Trauma and Delivers and Links to Services and Supports that Promote Family Well-Being, Healing, and Resilience.

The goal of the CWTTT training is to infuse the knowledge of trauma into the day-to-day work that is done in the Child Welfare System. This includes developing specific practice strategies that can be used within interactions that happen with clients, whether it be during home visits, removals, at child and family teams, or in making placement decisions.

The overall premise of trauma-informed child welfare is that it is meant to be an overlay to other initiatives, programs, and overall practice, not to be a stand-alone effort. This idea is presented throughout the training and is meant to help the Child Welfare System think more proactively (how do I integrate knowledge about trauma into new initiatives and protocols) versus falling back into the tendency to be reactive.

As a way of addressing the need for buy-in at all levels and to emphasize the building of a trauma-informed culture, the CWTTT 3rd edition was updated to specifically include the entire child welfare workforce. The two foundational trainings were designed for everyone in the Child Welfare System including support staff, caseworkers, supervisors, and leaders. This was in response to feedback that the past edition of the training mainly focused on caseworkers and that in order to truly impact on culture change, everyone working in the system needed to have a basic understanding of trauma and trauma-informed systems. This includes front desk staff, visitation supervisors, case aides, security guards, policy staff, child and family team facilitators, as well as those in supervisory and leadership roles.

The first foundational training is a Trauma 101 training which provides information on types of trauma, the impact of trauma on children and families, resilience, and how trauma intersects with the Child and Family Service Review goals of Safety, Permanency, and Well-Being. This training was meant to address the first element of a Trauma-Informed Child Welfare System— that such a system *Continuously Expands Workforce Knowledge and Skills about Trauma and Its Effects.* The second foundational training is focused on reviewing the seven remaining Essential Elements to provide a broad overview to the entire workforce of

Trauma-Informed Child Welfare. These two foundational trainings are built on by two more in-depth skills trainings based on the Essential Elements. One is designed specifically for caseworkers and the other is a parallel training for supervisors to support the caseworkers. Also, new in this 3rd edition is an ongoing consultation series for supervisors to aid in transfer in learning. The Supervisor Consultation Series was designed as a way to help reinforce the strategies taught in the training and to assist supervisors as they provide support to caseworkers specifically around Element Five (Maximizing Physical and Psychological Safety of Children, Youth, and Families) and Element Two (Addressing Primary and Secondary Traumatic Stress of the Workforce). It includes checklists for supervisors to assist them as they support caseworkers during supervision as well as tip sheets for caseworkers to help them apply the knowledge that they learned in training and in supervision. This consultation is in line with the knowledge that we have from implementation science that a single training event does not translate to practice change. There needs to be opportunities for continued learning and support in applying the learning to make true change occur.

The curriculum was also updated to strengthen the sections on Essential Element two, Addressing Secondary and Primary Traumatic Stress of the Workforce, which are factors that have some impact on the transitory nature of the child welfare workforce. The training sections on this topic were moved earlier in the training to be sure to acknowledge and address the impact of trauma on the workforce before moving to addressing how it impacts the clients they serve. In addition, there is material about secondary and primary traumatic stress in the foundational trainings to ensure that all levels of the workforce are given a background as well as strategies for how to address the impacts of working in a trauma-exposed workplace.

Addressing the historical traumatic stress and the interconnections between race and culture and trauma, was another area that was reviewed and addressed in the updated edition of the CWTTT. There is an acknowledgment that while it is not a training about culture, you cannot be trauma-informed if you are not culturally sensitive. To this end culture is addressed throughout the training. Another change from earlier versions is a larger focus on resilience and what the child welfare workforce can do to build and enhance resilience.

There is also more of a focus on intergenerational trauma and on understanding parent trauma and its impact on parents as well on parenting as reflected in the training on Element Eight (Understanding Parent and Caregiver Trauma and Delivers and Linking to Services and Supports that Promote Family Well-Being, Healing, and Resilience). Additional information on how to support resource parent and parent collaboration was added into the CWTTT 3rd edition. Throughout the training series there is more of a focus on partnering with children, youth, and families, both in individual cases, but also when making organizational decisions as we honor their lived expertise and important voices.

One of the other areas that is stressed within the CWTTT 3rd edition is Essential Element Four—Partnering with Agencies and Systems that Interact with Children, Youth, and Families. The focus is on the need to work with other systems as many of the families in the Child Welfare System are involved in multiple systems. There is acknowledgment of the barriers that exist when trying to engage in cross-system partnership and discussion of how to address these. Since leadership is meant to be involved in the foundational training there is some space to highlight the concerns that may need to be addressed organizationally. In the caseworker/supervisor training the focus turns more to how individual workers can address the barriers when making changes to the larger bureaucracies is out of their control.

Acknowledging the complexity of the system and the need to consider local context is a critical area for trauma-informed work to take hold and be sustained. To this end, several supplements to the training curricula were created. These include an Implementation Guide for organizations who are considering implementing the Child Welfare Trauma Training Toolkit[1] and a Tips for Facilitators document that provides information on how to deliver the trainings. In addition, there is an administrator's guide on trauma-informed child welfare that is in the process of being developed as of this printing. All of these supplements provide information on the core information that is in the training, and guidance on how to make local adaptations. In the CWTTT Implementation Guide, there is specific information on meeting with Child Welfare System leadership to gather information on that particular system and how to use that information to make local adaptation to the trainings.

The Advancing California's Trauma-Informed Systems (ACTS) Project

Ideally the goals, values, and mission of an organization create the lens in which that organization operates. However, as described above, Child Welfare Systems often face challenges in transforming their vision of trauma-informed support and healing into everyday practice. Still lacking is a clear framework for creating trauma-informed system change. Our goal with the Advancing California's Trauma-Informed Systems Project, or ACTS, was to create an evidence-informed framework that provides child welfare leaders with a systematic way to implement, sustain, and infuse trauma-informed change into their organization.

The ACTS project is a partnership with the California Department of Social Services, Office of Child Abuse Prevention,[2] and Rady Children's Hospital, San Diego. Our framework for implementing TIC consists of three phases over a course of nine months (see Figure 12.1).

Before we begin our partnerships, we work with child welfare leaders to assess their readiness for change (e.g., motivation, general capacities, innovation-specific capacities) to take on a trauma-informed change initiative (Scaccia et al., 2015). Another prerequisite for participation is leadership engagement. We have found the most successful Child Welfare Systems are those where leadership are dedicated to the project and involved in the change process. Leaders that let themselves be seen, are vulnerable to engage in TIC work, and create that space for their staff take a huge step in not only advancing TIC but sustaining it.

Once participation is determined, child welfare leadership complete a self-assessment, where they chose an area of the TIC Menu to focus implementation efforts (see Figure 12.2).

As the field is relatively new, the literature does not provide clear guidance on where organizations should start their trauma-informed journey. For this project, child welfare leaders chose their TIC focus based on organizational commitments, ongoing initiatives, motivation, and resources (e.g., time, available staff, funding). Often a System Improvement Plan will guide which area of TIC is chosen. To date, 66% of our participants chose to address Secondary Traumatic Stress (STS) as a way to advance TIC in their Child Welfare System. Other areas of interest have included trauma training and awareness, organizational policies and procedures, and partnering with children, youth, and families.

To enhance the adoption, implementation, and sustainment of the project, each Child Welfare System creates an implementation plan which documents

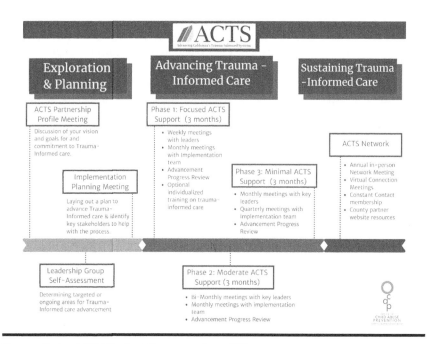

Figure 12.1   ACTS Project Framework and Phases.

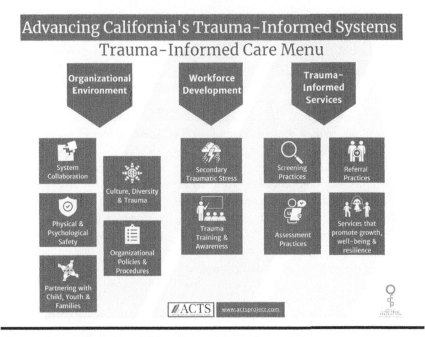

Figure 12.2   Advancing California's Trauma-Informed Systems.

steps needed to achieve their goal (e.g., objectives, tasks, leads, resources, time frame, outcome measurement). For example, one of our Child Welfare Systems chose the area of STS and created the following implementation goal: "Executive leadership and managers will have an understanding of STS and the knowledge, capacity, and skill to assist staff in exploring the emotional experience of their work." Additionally, champions, defined as dedicated individuals who have the ability to influence and elicit change in the organization, are assigned to help move the plan forward. Typically, Child Welfare Systems have chosen two to three staff members from the manager and supervisory level to serve as champions. An implementation team is put together to offer feedback and input on the direction of the TIC initiative. Successful implementation teams are typically made up of individuals from varying levels of the organization including the leadership, supervisory, managerial, and line staff level, as well as stakeholders or other system partners. Having assigned staff with assigned time to focus on TIC has been the most consistent feedback we received from participating Child Welfare Systems around implementation success.

We strongly believe that Child Welfare Systems engaging in TIC should commit to measuring the change they hope to see. There is much to learn about how Child Welfare Systems best implement TIC and there is a dearth of outcome data around the impact of TIC on child and family outcomes. Many of our participants have relied on data they are already collecting to examine long-term outcomes such as turnover, sick leave, and placement changes. Short-term outcomes, including supervisor and staff attitudes, skills, and knowledge are typically measured through electronic surveys. In the case of STS, free available measures such as the Secondary Traumatic Stress Inventory—Organizational Assessment have been used (Sprang et al., 2017).

As of fall 2020, the ACTS project has partnered with nine Child Welfare Systems across California that vary in size, geographical location, resources, and experience with TIC. Our approach to trauma-informed organizational change is one of many, and not necessarily right for all organizations. However, success has been garnered in an approach that relies on focused, small, incremental change guided by implementation science and practice.

Discussion

In the projects described above, both set out to advance TIC in a CW setting. Keeping in mind the considerations for system change in child welfare we sought to create trauma-informed organizational change that would not only be meaningful but sustained over time. Across both projects the reliance on and inclusion of executive leadership proved essential in creating trauma-informed change. While involving leadership in change is not new, oftentimes trauma-informed initiatives start with, or exclusively focus on, supervisors and line staff. It is commonly believed that these staff members are most in need of trauma-informed knowledge and skills since they are most directly in contact with children, youth, and families exposed to trauma. However, when creating change at an organizational level it is leadership who must first be brought on board. In both of the projects described above, the vulnerability and modeling that leaders showed when talking about their own response to working with and around trauma gave others in the organization permission to reflect on their responses to trauma and the way it shows up in their work. Another variable for success across both projects was the value placed on exploration and planning. For the purpose of this chapter these multifaceted implementation stages are simply defined as the ability for child welfare leadership to take a pause and consider the needs of their organization, and create a plan for how trauma-informed change should be implemented.

Perhaps because of the unique cultural and global context in which these projects took place (e.g., during the global pandemic of COVID-19), or because of a shift in societal acceptance of bringing feelings into the workplace, it is undeniable that child welfare leaders are ready and willing to address Secondary Traumatic Stress in the workplace. Both of the aforementioned projects were met with a great desire and willingness among child welfare professionals to learn about, discuss, and address STS. STS was not only a foundational piece of the CWTTT and a predominant focus of the toolkit revisions, but training on STS was moved earlier in the training and lengthened based on feedback from participants. STS was also a large focus in the revision of the Child Welfare Trauma Training Toolkit including information on both individual and organizational strategies. The ACTS project has found training, coaching, and consultation in reflective supervision and practice for child welfare supervisors and managers to be a key mechanism of change in shifting organizational culture toward one that is observant, accepting, and responsive to the unique emotional needs of the workforce.

Finally, one cannot be trauma-informed if they are not culturally and racially informed. The intersection of these lenses is inextricable. At times, both projects attempted to integrate cultural awareness into all aspects of training and technical assistance; however, the reality was that more time was needed to address culture—an umbrella term not unlike TIC that encapsulates a wide array of important topics. For some organizations individual training can be a first step in addressing culture and equity and can be particularly effective when participants are given opportunities for self-critique and reflection. Beyond training, identifying and fixing power imbalances within the organization, and developing mutually beneficial advocacy partnerships with communities who are advocating for defined populations are just some ways in working toward cultural humility (Tervalon & Murray-Garcia, 1998).

Overall, Child Welfare Systems have come a long way in the past several years in realizing the widespread impact of trauma and recognizing its impact on clients, families, staff, and others involved in the Child Welfare System. There has been an increase in responses at the local and national level by implementing TIC initiatives within organizations and across states. The literature on TIC in child welfare is growing and points to promising outcomes for organizations and the children and families served. Yet there is still more to learn and to be done. Child Welfare leaders are in need of guidelines, standards, and case examples to help transform their vision of TIC into practical organizational change. The projects described above are just two examples of TIC initiatives in Child Welfare Systems and it is hoped that the lessons learned from them will serve as a foundation as new efforts and initiatives are designed to bolster trauma-informed policies, programs, and practices in child welfare.

Notes

1. All the curricula and supplemental materials are available to download for free on the National Child Traumatic Stress Network's Learning Center.

2. **The project described is funded through a contract with the California Department of Social Services (CDSS), Office of Child Abuse Prevention. The contents of this report are solely the responsibility of the authors and do not necessarily represent the official views of the CDSS.*

References

Bartlett, J. D., Barto, B., Griffin, J. L., Fraser, J. G., Hodgdon, H., & Bodian, R. (2016). Trauma-informed care in the Massachusetts child trauma project. *Child Maltreatment*, *21*(2), 101–112.

Bernstein, M., Killen-Harvey, A., Secrist, M., Hazen, A., & Crandal, B. (2021). *Implementing trauma-informed supervision in child welfare to address secondary traumatic stress* [Unpublished manuscript]. Chadwick Center, Rady Children's Hospital.

Brennen, J., Guarino, K., Axelrod, J., & Gonsoulin, S. (2019). *Building a multi-system trauma-informed collaborative: A guide for adopting a cross-system, trauma-informed approach among child-serving agencies and their partners*. Chicago, IL: Chapin Hall at the University of Chicago & Washington, DC: American Institutes for Research.

Brown, B. (2018). *Dare to lead*. New York: Penguin Random House LLC.

Bunting, L., Montgomery, L., Mooney, S., MacDonald, M., Coulter, S., Hayes, D., & Davidson, G. (2019). Trauma informed child welfare systems-A rapid evidence review. *International Journal of Environmental Research and Public Health*, *16*(13), 2365.

Champine, R. B., Lang, J. M., Nelson, A. M., Hanson, R. F., & Tebes, J. K. (2019). Systems measures of a trauma-informed approach: A systematic review. *American Journal of Community Psychology*, *64*(3), 418–437.

Crandal, B. R., Hazen, A. L., & Reutz, J. R. (2017). Identifying trauma-related and mental health needs: The implementation of screening in California's child welfare systems. *Advances in Social Work*, *18*(1), 335–348.

Dorsey, S., Burns, B. J., Southerland, D. G., Cox, J. R., Wagner, H. R., & Farmer, E. M. Z. (2012). Prior trauma exposure for youth in treatment foster care. *Journal of Child and Family Studies*, *21*(5), 816–824. Retrieved from https://www.ncbi.nlm.nih.gov/pmc/articles/PMC3667554/

Hanson, R. F., & Lang, J. (2016). A critical look at trauma-informed care among agencies and systems serving maltreated youth and their families. *Child Maltreatment*, *21*(2), 95–100.

Jankowski, M. K., Schifferdecker, K. E., Butcher, R. L., Foster-Johnson, L., & Barnett, E. R. (2019). Effectiveness of a trauma-informed care initiative in a state child welfare system: A randomized study. *Child Maltreatment*, *24*(1), 86–97.

Kerns, S. E., Pullmann, M. D., Negrete, A., Uomoto, J. A., Berliner, L., Shogren, D., … Putnam, B. (2016). Development and implementation of a child welfare workforce strategy to build a trauma-informed system of support for foster care. *Child Maltreatment*, *21*(2), 135–146.

Lang, J. M., Campbell, K., Shanley, P., Crusto, C. A., & Connell, C. M. (2016). Building capacity for trauma-informed care in the child welfare system. *Child Maltreatment*, *21*(2), 113–124.

National Child Welfare Workforce Institute. (2011). Workforce demographic trends. Retrieved from http://ncwwi.org/files/Workforce_Demographic_Trends_May2011.pdf

Scaccia, J. P., Cook, B. S., Lamont, A., Wandersman, A., Castellow, J., Katz, J., & Beidas, R. S. (2015). A practical implementation science heuristic for organizational readiness: R = MC². *Journal of Community Psychology, 43*(4), 484–501.

Sheldon, G. H., Tavenner, M., & Hyde, P. S. (2013). Tri-agency letter on trauma. Retrieved from http://www.medicaid.gov/Federal-Policy-Guidance/Downloads/SMD-13-07-11.pdf

Sprang, G., Ross, L., Miller, B. C., Blackshear, K., & Ascienzo, S. (2017). Psychometric properties of the secondary traumatic stress–informed organizational assessment. *Traumatology, 23*(2), 165–171.

Substance Abuse and Mental Health Services Administration. (2014). *SAMHSA's concept of trauma and guidance for a trauma-informed approach.* HHS Publication No. (SMA) 14-4884. Rockville, MD: Substance Abuse and Mental Health Services Administration.

Sullivan, K. M., Murray, K. J., & Ake, G. S. (2016). Trauma-informed care for children in the child welfare system: An initial evaluation of a trauma-informed parenting workshop. *Child Maltreatment, 21*(2), 147–155.

Tervalon, M., & Murray-García, J. (1998). Cultural humility versus cultural competence: A critical distinction in defining physician training outcomes in multicultural education. *Journal of Health Care for the Poor and Underserved, 9*(2), 117–125.

U.S. Department of Health & Human Services, Administration for Children and Families, Administration on Children, Youth and Families, Children's Bureau. (2020). *Child maltreatment 2018.* Retrieved from https://www.acf.hhs.gov/cb/research-data-technology /statistics-research/child-maltreatment

Walsh, C., Pauter, S., & Hendricks, A. (2020). *Child welfare trauma training toolkit (CWTTT)* (3rd ed.). Los Angeles, CA and Durham, NC: National Center for Child Traumatic Stress.

Index

Page numbers in bold denote tables, those in *italic* denote figures.

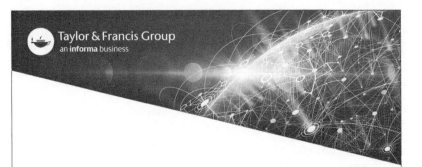